INSIDE
BELMARSH

INSIDE BELMARSH

Banged Up in Britain's Toughest Prison

JONATHAN LEVI & EMMA FRENCH

First published in the UK in 2025 by Blink Publishing
An imprint of Bonnier Books UK
5th Floor, HYLO, 105 Bunhill Row,
London, EC1Y 8LZ

A CIP catalogue record for this book is available from the British Library.

Paperback ISBN: 9781789468885

Also available as an ebook and an audiobook

1 3 5 7 9 10 8 6 4 2

Design and Typeset by Envy Design Ltd
Printed and bound in Great Britain by Clays Ltd, Elcograf S.p.A.

The authorised representative in the EEA is
Bonnier Books UK (Ireland) Limited.
Registered office address: Floor 3, Block 3, Miesian Plaza,
Dublin 2, D02 Y754, Ireland
compliance@bonnierbooks.ie

www.bonnierbooks.co.uk

'I was quite sorry to leave Belmarsh.'
(Jonathan Aitken)

Contents

Prologue

There would be plenty of time for questions later.

At this moment, though, an attack was going on that was serious enough to land a man in Belmarsh's infamous segregation unit, or The Seg, as the prisoners call it.

'The regime on the unit is brutal. I was sent there because I stabbed another offender with a pen on the vulnerable prisoner unit. The man had killed his own baby and at court got away with a manslaughter charge. I am in no position to judge, but his attitude was appalling. Firstly, he got a ridiculously short, fixed sentence. He was walking around the unit saying he was no nonce and acting up like a gangster. He said something to me which I took offence to, and I hit him. I had the pen in my hand, and I just stabbed him in his face with the pen.'

It's the prisoner's word against anyone else in terms of what happened next, but his account of it is striking either way.

'So I was taken to the segregation unit. I was actually attacked by staff within this unit. It was the DST (Dedicated Search Team), or "men in black" as offenders call them because all their uniform is black. Yes, DST came to my cell to search it. I was set up. They asked me to squat with my pants down, this is normal as it allows them to use a mirror to inspect your buttocks to ensure you have nothing cheeked. As I did this squat, they pushed me forward on purpose. Then they all attacked me in the cell. They hit the alarm bell and claimed I attacked them. Of course, within the cell there was no CCTV. I was bent up and assaulted. They claimed my injuries and bruising was the result of me resisting being restrained, which was ridiculous given I did nothing wrong. This was their excuse to assault me and get away with it.'

Some Major Contributors

We have used 'some' major contributors for a reason. HMP Belmarsh is different to any other prison. It reminded us of Broadmoor in its level of secrecy and cautious access to information. The majority of even those who were happy to be listed below requested pseudonyms.

There are many more voices in this book. Voices of both staff and prisoners who have passed through Belmarsh, or spent a number of years there, who requested an extreme degree of anonymity. As always, we respected the degree of privacy requested by any individual, and that respect has allowed us to include many more astonishing stories and insights than we otherwise could have done.

Jonathan Aitken, a former Conservative Party politician imprisoned for perjury, granted us the privilege of an evening in his company just before Christmas 2024, and allowed us to hear his extraordinary story, from Belmarsh prisoner to prison chaplain. Tall and imposing, he still exudes authority, though age has softened his presence. The dashing politician of the 1980s, almost James Bond-like, with his bespoke suits and swept-back hair, has transformed into a twinkling, thoughtful and spiritual man, who retains a razor-sharp intellect.

Jeremy Dein KC is widely recognised as one of the country's most respected defence barristers. He has conducted numerous homicide trials, primarily at the Old Bailey. A former Director of Education for the Criminal Bar Association, he now practises from 25 Bedford Row Chambers, where he was also Joint Head. Jonathan first met Jeremy while making the documentary *Tulisa: The Price of Fame* for the BBC, during which Jeremy acted as Tulisa's defence counsel during her 'Fake Sheikh' trial. When interviewing him for this book, we met him ahead of a busy day in court, where he was representing a woman charged with murder. Impeccably turned out, cerebral and with kind, intelligent eyes, Jeremy is the sort of advocate you would want in your corner at your lowest moment.

Known as 'Nik' for the purposes of this book, he is a former officer at HMP Belmarsh. When we met he cut a striking figure. Broadly built and exuding a calm confidence, he was smartly dressed in a bright green knitted shirt as he recounted his tenure in the infamous high-security prison. After experiencing a brutal assault and years of exposure to extreme violence and trauma, Nik decided it was time to leave. His candid reflections pull back the curtain on a world few get to see.

'**Mike**' is the name we're using for a charismatic, attractive ex-Belmarsh inmate who tells the most extraordinary stories. The day that we met him in a central London club, his burly frame was swathed in a green designer jacket. He had box-fresh white Nike trainers, a silver and diamond-encrusted watch, ripped jeans and tattoos all over his knuckles. Mike makes a lot of eye contact and has presence, charm and humour, which apparently has been quite effective in seducing prison staff over the years. To him, Belmarsh was a 'horrible place'.

Matthew spent 19 years working within the prison service, not just in Belmarsh but in HMP Maidstone and HMP Isis too. He gave us a compassionate, engaging and considered insight into these secretive environments. He finds humour a great way to break down barriers and his calm, thoughtful demeanour appears to have served him well in some highly challenging environments and situations.

Colin was in and out of prison for 40 years. He told us that he 'adapted to trauma by being in highly predatory environments and around a lot of bad people'. His is an incredible redemption story, though, with both he and his wife completely turning their lives around and living happily by the seaside with two teenagers. Jonathan Aitken described him to us as 'a very thoughtful, clever Belmarsh prisoner', and he is one of the Belmarsh prisoners that he has remained friends with.

Vanessa Frake-Harris MBE is a retired prison governor. She worked in the prison service for 27 years, starting as an officer at Holloway in 1986 and going on to become Head of Operations and Security at Wormwood Scrubs in 2002. Her experiences range from spending time with serial killer Rose West to throwing Libertines frontman Pete Doherty into segregation, and she received her MBE in 2012 for her wonderful work in the prison sector. Measured, articulate, open and charming, she shared her expert insights on the current state of the prison service with us.

'Caroline' spent five years working at HMP Belmarsh and HMP Isis. For personal reasons, she has now left the prison sector. After our conversation with her, we could not help feeling what a loss to the profession she was. Pragmatic, discreet, ethical and intelligent, we sensed that she could have gone all the way to governor. She appears to have taken the most challenging situations in her stride, and to have won the trust of fellow officers and many prisoners alike.

Jo Taylor is a witty, down-to-earth woman, and as a straight-talking, 'firm but fair' former officer at both HMP New Hall and Wakefield, she's seen it all, having spent

15 years in the service. She has fantastic hair, as you'd expect from someone who left a career in the prison service to specialise in bespoke scalp micropigmentation treatments. Possibly the most entertaining contributor from our last book, *Inside Wakefield Prison*, we were keen to hear her memories of some of the prisoners who have moved from Belmarsh to Wakefield.

Phil Ashford is co-founder and director of an organisation called Enterprise Exchange. A positive, grounded and ethical man, he gave us an engaging, humane account of the vital work that he does in prisons with some of the most vulnerable people in society. He was alert to the challenges facing prisons, but for him, that is even more reason to keep up the good work.

Few storytellers possess the power and precision of **Jeff Pope**. The creative force behind landmark series like *Philomena*, *The Reckoning*, *A Confession* and many other acclaimed works, Jeff has built a reputation for transforming real-life events into gripping and unforgettable television drama. With numerous awards and widespread critical acclaim to his name, his writing and producing continue to set the gold standard in British television and film. Jonathan had the good fortune to work as the factual producer for Jeff on *Hatton Garden* for ITV. Jeff's particular relevance to this book lies in his creation of the outstanding BBC drama *Four Lives*, which explored the case of Stephen Port, an infamous prisoner at Belmarsh.

Select Glossary of Prison Slang and Jargon

Prisons the world over have always developed their own coded language, and Belmarsh is no exception. Below is a selection of common slang, jargon and acronyms heard within its walls.

Prison Life and Movement

Nick: Slang for prison.

Box: Solitary confinement, often used as punishment or for safety.

Being on the book: Refers to an inmate moving around the prison under authorised escort or supervision.

Weighed off: To be sentenced.

All day or natural life: A life sentence; 'natural life' often refers to a whole-life order with no chance of release.

Porridge: An old-fashioned slang term for serving time in prison. Sometimes also called 'stir'.

A six-and-eight: Someone who has chosen to 'go straight' or live a law-abiding life after release.

ROTL (Release on Temporary Licence): A programme allowing certain prisoners to leave prison for a short time under strict conditions – used for resettlement, employment or compassionate reasons.

Prison Jobs and Roles

Listener: A prisoner trained by the Samaritans to offer confidential, peer-to-peer emotional support to fellow inmates, often during times of distress or crisis.

PO (Principal Officer): A senior member of prison staff, responsible for overseeing daily operations and supervising officers.

SO (Senior Officer): Another managerial rank within prison staff, often acting as a shift supervisor or team leader.

DST (Dedicated Search Team): A specialist team within the prison responsible for conducting targeted searches for contraband and maintaining security.

Contraband and Concealment

Mash: A mobile phone, highly sought after and strictly prohibited within prison.

Snout: Cigarettes or tobacco, often used as a form of currency within prison.

Spice: A man-made drug that mimics cannabis but is

much stronger and more unpredictable. Often smoked, it's popular in prisons because it's cheap and harder to detect, but it can cause serious health problems and unpredictable behaviour.

Cheeked: To store or conceal contraband between the buttocks.

Prison Wallet or Prison Purse: Slang for concealing items, typically drugs, phones or weapons, in the anal or vaginal cavity.

To keep it down: Keeping something hidden, usually contraband.

BOSS Chair: Acronym for Body Orifice Security Scanner – a non-intrusive chair used in Belmarsh to detect metal objects hidden within a prisoner's body.

Violence, Offences and Disciplinary Terms

String up: To attempt or commit suicide by hanging – typically using improvised materials like bed sheets or clothing.

Shank: A makeshift knife or stabbing weapon, commonly crafted from everyday objects.

Bend you up: To physically overpower or assault someone, often implying restraint or dominance.

Kettling: Also known as 'prison napalm', it's the intentional use of boiling water, often with added sugar, to inflict severe burns.

Potting: An assault in which a prisoner throws excrement or bodily fluids at staff or another inmate.

Dirty Protest: A form of extreme protest where a prisoner smears or throws urine or faeces in their cell.

Being Spun: Having your cell searched, often without notice, for prohibited items.

Offender Categories and Behaviour

Lifer: A prisoner serving a life sentence.

Nonce: A derogatory term for a paedophile. Other slang terms include *bacon*, *bacon head* or *animal*. These offenders are often segregated for their own protection.

Ride with: To perform favours – often sexual – in exchange for protection, drugs or other contraband.

Secure Environments

HSU (High Security Unit): A highly controlled area for the most dangerous or high-risk prisoners.

CSC (Close Supervision Centre): A specialised unit for inmates deemed extremely disruptive or violent, often involving near-constant observation. **CSCs are small, specialist units located within six of the high-security prisons,** including Belmarsh, and the staff we spoke to tended to use the term 'CSC'.

Ex-prisoners, on the other hand, often used the term CSU (Care and Separation Unit) for their solitary confinement or segregation. Prisoners can be moved to CSUs for their own protection if they are at risk from other prisoners.

SELECT GLOSSARY OF PRISON SLANG AND JARGON

Sweat Boxes: Small, claustrophobic holding cells inside vans used to transport prisoners between courts or facilities.

This glossary offers a glimpse into the distinct language of prison life. It's a language shaped by necessity, secrecy and survival instinct.

Chapter I

Introduction to Belmarsh: Britain's Toughest Prison

'In general life you could walk down the road, and you won't know who you're interacting with, what they're about or anything, but in this type of environment, you know the worst traits of people and what they're capable of.'

(MATTHEW)

HMP Belmarsh. Arguably the most infamous prison in the UK. How did a facility that has been open for less than 35 years gain such a fearsome reputation?

Built as the first adult male prison in London since Wormwood Scrubs – which finished construction way back in 1891 – Belmarsh was revolutionary from the start, not just in design but in function. However, its notoriety stems from many other unique features, as well as its inmates.

One notable example of this is that Belmarsh is the only prison in England and Wales with such a purpose-built prison within a prison, otherwise known as the

High-Security Unit (HSU), surrounded by five-metre high concrete walls and monitored by dozens of cameras, designed to house some of the most dangerous criminals in the country. While Belmarsh can hold up to 910 men, just 48 can be confined within the HSU at any given time.

The prison also contains a segregation unit, which we describe in more detail in Chapter 9, and two notorious cells known as 'The Boxes'. These are bleak, windowless isolation rooms with no beds, sinks or toilets. Over the years, the HSU has held a chilling mix of IRA bombers, KGB spies, al-Qaeda terrorists and even Charles Bronson, whose violent reputation earned him his own private spur.

Yet, despite its Category A prisoners, Belmarsh also functions as a standard prison. Around one in five inmates is a convicted murderer, yet many others serve time for lesser offences. How do staff balance handling petty criminals alongside serial rapists, terrorists and gang leaders? And what happens when such high-risk individuals are forced to coexist?

This book explores some of the most notorious inmates to have passed through Belmarsh's gates, including Abu Hamza al-Masri, Hashem Abedi, Michael Adebowale, Great Train Robber Ronnie Biggs, Wayne Couzens, Usman Khan, Jordan McSweeney and John Worboys. Many infamous prisoners remain there today, such as David Copeland, Daniel Khalife, Stephen Port and Khairi Saadallah.

As one former Belmarsh inmate put it:

'Over the years, you can be sure that with all the

high-profile cases heard at the Central Criminal Court or Woolwich Crown Court, the offenders were detained at HMP Belmarsh, some of whom I have personally met: Mark Dixie (The Sally Anne Bowman case), Steve Wright (The Suffolk Strangler), Stuart Hazell (The Tia Sharp murder in Croydon), Barry George (The Jill Dando case), John Worboys (The Black Cab Rapist) – who is now known as John Radford. He changed his name. Wayne Couzens (The Sarah Everard case), Steven Barker (The Baby P case), John Duffy, the 1980s railway killer, Kenny Noye, Ian Huntley (The Soham Murders), and Lea Rusha, Roger Coutts, Stuart Royle, Ermir Hysenaj, and Jetmir Bucpapa, who all pulled the largest cash robbery in UK history – the Securitas robbery in Tonbridge, Kent, in February 2006.'

His list didn't end there, either.

'Terrorists, the London bombers, The Hatton Garden Job crew, Reader, Jones and the others. Many high-profile cases over the years have had the pleasure of experiencing the harsh regime at HMP Belmarsh.'

Belmarsh has held an extraordinarily diverse range of prisoners, many of whom were not convicted of violent crimes. You'll hear from Jonathan Aitken, who shared his experiences inside and told us stories that are shocking, moving and at times, darkly humorous. Of course, Jeffrey Archer and Julian Assange have also spent time within its walls.

With a level of security and surveillance second to none, no prisoner has ever successfully escaped from

Belmarsh. Through accounts of daily routines, brutal fights, gang warfare, drug smuggling and moments of unexpected redemption, this book uncovers the truth about life inside 'Hellmarsh'.

CHAPTER 2

History and Unique Character of HMP Belmarsh

'Belmarsh has a reputation like Wakefield or
Broadmoor. But it's not just high security.
It's also general population, mostly local people
in for drug offences or burglary.'
(PHIL ASHFORD)

H MP Belmarsh is located on Western Way, Thames-mead, in South-East London, SE28 OEB. It's an odd part of London, inaccessible from almost everywhere. The construction of HMP Belmarsh began in the late 1980s as part of a government initiative to address growing concerns over prison overcrowding and the need for a modern high-security facility. Built on part of the former Royal Arsenal site in Woolwich, the prison was strategically positioned near Woolwich Crown Court to enable the movement of inmates between court proceedings and detention.

When Belmarsh became operational on 2 April 1991, it was designated as a Category A prison, meaning it would hold prisoners who posed the highest security risk. We enter into more detail about prison categorisations later in this book, and also about the fascinating High-Security Unit (HSU), a separate and highly controlled section within the prison specifically designed for inmates requiring the most rigorous levels of supervision.

Since 1991, Belmarsh has been a totally key high-secure institution within the prison system. It's the number one facility for holding men accused or convicted of terrorism-related offences, as well as those awaiting extradition for serious crimes.

A report on an unannounced inspection of HMP Belmarsh by HM Chief Inspector of Prisons, from June 2024, gave a useful snapshot of the demographics of who is in there. There were 717 prisoners held at the time of inspection, which was fairly near capacity. At the end of June 2024, the operational capacity – the maximum population the prison can hold – was 773. Out of those, 98 prisoners were Category A. In total, 2,422 new prisoners are received each year, which is around 200 per month. Of those, 199 are foreign national prisoners, and 59 per cent of prisoners are from black and minority ethnic backgrounds. Around 60 per cent of prisoners are unsentenced, in other words, more than half the prisoners in there are on remand.

Although dating back to 2018, the introduction to a report on an unannounced inspection of Belmarsh puts its unique character and complexity in a brilliantly succinct and timeless manner:

'HMP Belmarsh in South-East London is one of only three high-security core local prisons in England and Wales. Probably the most high-profile prison in the UK, it held an extremely complex mix of men. There were young adults, and low-risk men similar to those held in other local prisons, but also over 100 with an indeterminate sentence, and those in custody for the most serious offences. The high-security unit (HSU), in effect a prison within a prison, held some of the highest-risk prisoners in the country, adding a further layer of complexity. In addition, there were a large number of foreign national prisoners, others who needed to be protected because of their offence, and a small number requiring specific management arrangements because of their public and media profile. Meeting the demands and priorities of these various groups remained a hugely complicated task.'

All of these characteristics appear to remain the same today.

In addition to housing convicted criminals, though, importantly, Belmarsh is also used for the remand of prisoners awaiting trial or sentencing. This is very significant in terms of the prisoner 'mix'.

As one former officer at Belmarsh put it to us:

'Belmarsh is a local prison. Belmarsh is a mix of both Wakefield and Broadmoor. We meet all the most interesting people and spit them out again. Belmarsh is very unique. Each house has different functions, such as over-fifties, first night, drug rehabilitation. There are 30 per cent shared cells, doubles and singles.'

7

The prison complex consists of multiple wings, each with its own designated function. The High-Security Unit remains the most restricted part of the prison, containing single-occupancy cells with the highest levels of monitoring.

An interesting extra bit of (ancient) Belmarsh history was uncovered in 2009, during construction work on the prison grounds, when an archaeological excavation revealed a prehistoric wooden trackway dating back approximately 6,000 years. This discovery provided valuable insights into the early human settlement of the Thames Valley and demonstrated the historical significance of the land upon which the prison now stands.

Given what we found out about the astonishingly secure and choreographed movement in and out of Belmarsh today, it's striking and strange to think of ancient transportation on wooden trackways fading into history until it was replaced by today's high-tech vans.

One of our prisoner contributors, who has a very intimate and long-term knowledge of Belmarsh, added a nugget about an unpleasant and lasting side effect of the decision to situate Belmarsh where it is.

'HMP Belmarsh was built in the 1980s. The prison is built on a marsh. Hence the name Belmarsh. As a result of this, even today the prison during the hot weather has an issue with flies and gnats, which plague the prison.'

According to former inmate Mike, there is other wildlife there too: 'A peregrine falcon hunts at Belmarsh; it kills pigeons.'

Describing Belmarsh, Nik, an ex-officer, painted a picture of stark contrasts, calling it 'quite a newly built prison. It lacks the decay of older Victorian jails. It's quiet and it's quite new, which means there's not a distinct smell to it. It feels like you're walking in a hospital.'

He added that the building is certainly daunting due to its high security.

Matthew, who spent many years there as an officer, agreed when sharing his memories of his first few days at Belmarsh:

'Prison is a really weird environment. It's incredibly sterile. It runs to a rigid regime: everyone gets up at a certain time; everyone goes to work at a certain time; everyone eats at a certain time; everyone cleans at a certain time.'

Like Nik, certain smells and little details have stayed with Matthew.

'No matter where you were in the house blocks, you knew what the routine was, you could smell the same smells, you could smell whether they were using the right detergent to clean the floors or whatever meal was on one house block would be the same on all the others. The staff were always immaculately dressed. They wore shirts and ties.'

Matthew's varied experience allows him to draw interesting parallels with lower-category prisons:

'It's little things like when I was in Maidstone, every prisoner knew the staff's first name. They'll go, "Hi, Matt. How are you?" And I'd say, "I'm good, thanks, John," or Chris, or whoever it was. In Belmarsh, It was always mister and surname. There was never any informality. Eventually there was some informality because you got to know people and they got to know your names and were able to talk to you, but the initial first thing off the bat wasn't "guv", it was "Mr Palmer" and that type of thing. So it was a very regimented environment and that's because people needed rules and everything was just like a well-oiled machine. Everyone knew what needed to happen and where it needed to be.'

Matthew had heard some stories about what Belmarsh was like before his time, too.

'Long before I started, there was the stick and whistle parade where the chief would come along and say, "Show us your sticks and whistles," and make sure all uniform was up to date. None of that happens any more. That was something that died out, but if you were in charge of a house block, like I was, you'd always make sure that people were dressed accordingly if they looked right, because if suddenly, someone started looking a bit dishevelled, your first port of call would be, "Is there something going on?" Then they suddenly change.'

We would learn that it was typical of Matthew's contribution as a former officer to combine descriptions of prison routine with a vigilance regarding the wellbeing of the prisoners and staff, with any changes in routine, however tiny, being potentially revealing of a larger issue. He gave us more detail on historical demographics too.

'At that time in Belmarsh a lot of the people were ex-service people or from an official background, so there was a personal level of care where everyone wanted to be well presented. Part of the induction process back then instilled that you needed to look presentable and smart, so it was always done from the start. I don't think it's as strict now; it's a bit more relaxed.'

Having been in and out of prison over a period of 40 years, Colin was able to share many other historic points of comparison with us, as 'it changed dramatically in that time. The police and the criminal justice system changed a lot, too.'

We delved into his history, which was so emotive that he struggled to share it at first, but he was on safer ground when talking about more factual recollections:

'When I first went inside, one of the first prisons I was in was Wandsworth. That's the "original Belmarsh" in some ways. They used to hang people in Wandsworth.'

Indeed. Although the last executions took place in 1961, they didn't dismantle the gallows until 1994! We pressed Colin to carry on.

'Wandsworth still had the old-school prison design. They called Wandsworth "the Big Stick" back then, and it was brutal. They were still using bread and water as punishment.'

From Colin's point of view, having been incarcerated in both prisons, not much has changed.

'Belmarsh was just a modern version of that. There's one wing in Belmarsh now called "The Hell Wing", but it's all part of the system. Prisons have changed over time, but at the end of the day, Belmarsh is now like any other prison. It could be Albany, it could be Parkhurst. It's all the same.'

Though most former prisoners we spoke to were negative about Belmarsh, Colin and Jonathan Aitken took a far more measured, reflective and humane view. By way of example, Colin's perspective is that 'the civil service in this country is really good. The ethics in this country, to me, are profound. When was the last time you had to bribe an official? Right? I think people miss that. They miss it altogether.'

He felt a formality in his interactions with prison staff but also a humanity: 'Many of my interactions with police and prison officers were almost medical. It was like dealing with psychiatric nurses. And I knew a lot of these officers from the army. A lot of ex-forces go into that line of work. Sure, you always get bad teams in any sector, but the criminal justice system in this country really, really struggles to take people on and not kill them. So, I knew this was happening.'

Unique because it is both a high-security prison and a local remand prison, Nik described this as 'the quirk of Belmarsh':

'It creates an unusual atmosphere,' Nik noted. 'You've got everyone from first-time offenders to hardened criminals, and you're managing them all together.'

Noise is another constant. Just as Matthew was trained to be alert to changes in routine or behaviour, so was Nik, telling us, 'There's a constant hum, shouting and banging. If it ever goes quiet, you know something's wrong.'

Caroline also commented on the unusual blend of prisoners in the prison as a marker of its distinctive character.

'Belmarsh is so mixed because it's remand but also Category A horrendous criminals. So, you get those horrendous criminals mixing with a homeless guy who smashed a window to get a bed to sleep in.'

A former prisoner further explained how Belmarsh's categorisation did not always match its inmate population.

'While HMP Belmarsh is a high-security prison, it is not exclusively a prison where just high-security prisoners are held, indeed it is a local prison which serves the courts within London. Therefore, sentences and security status can often be mixed. For example, you can often see drink-drivers serving six months being picked up from the courts and taken to HMP Belmarsh with an offender of the highest security with a sentence of natural life. However, within the reception area, the lower-category (lower-security) offenders will be segregated from the higher-security offenders, but on the wings they will all be located on the same wings unless they are exceptional high-risk, in which case they will be held on the CSU (Closed Secure Unit). This is in fact a prison within a prison. I have actually been located on this unit.'

As you can see, Belmarsh does seem to have housed a particularly odd mixture of criminals, with many of the most horrifying killers of recent times, including Stephen Port, Steven Barker and Wayne Couzens, but also Ronnie Biggs, Jonathan Aitken, Jeffrey Archer and Julian Assange.

As an aside, we are very proud of the access that we do get, but we must confess that we didn't get Jeffrey Archer. Archer is an author, former politician and ex-Belmarsh inmate. He was a Conservative MP and later a peer in the House of Lords, but he was convicted of perjury and perverting the course of justice in 2001, resulting in a four-year prison sentence. Archer was initially sent to HMP Belmarsh for the first three weeks of his sentence. He was subsequently transferred to HMP Wayland and then an open prison, HMP North Sea Camp, before his release in 2003. During his time in prison, he kept a diary detailing his experiences, later published as *A Prison Diary*, offering insight into the conditions within the UK's prison system. Though we tried to reach Archer for an interview for this book, he declined. Perhaps this was connected to the reflection that Jonathan Aitken made about him, that he 'hated Belmarsh. Yes, he called it Hellmarsh, didn't he? And I didn't find Belmarsh bad at all, really. I was quite sorry to leave it because I'd got into the routine, and Standford Hill was much more difficult in some ways. Jeffrey is not a humble man. I wasn't either, but I sure became one.'

Though Belmarsh was designed to be a state-of-the-art facility when it was constructed, incorporating modern security features and surveillance systems to ensure maximum control over its population, the reality for most is clearly quite different. In one ex-inmate's account, in fact, the cells sound old-fashioned, if anything:

'HMP Belmarsh is quite small compared to other

prisons. It is shaped similar to the letter L, and around the outside of this L, you have small holding cells which hold the high-security Category As. The doors are identical to prison cell doors with a small flap which acts as an observation panel. Directly in front of these cells is two large cages about 10ft x 10ft square. These hold the Category B lower-security offenders. These cage-type holding rooms can be very busy during the mornings and evenings. I say cage-type because that is what they are, metal cages. Within them is a TV mounted in a see-through box and some benches running up either side.'

Another very distinctive quirk of Belmarsh is the hum of activity as movement takes place in and out of the prison. We describe this in much greater detail in due course, but one contributor gave an overview that brought it to life for us.

'Each morning and evening, the reception area of the prison is very busy, Serco prison vans collecting Category B offenders to take them to court and in the evenings returning them. There is also the HMP Belmarsh Category A prison vans collecting offenders and ferrying them to the Central Criminal Court (Old Bailey) from HMP Belmarsh and returning them in the evenings. So let me explain how this works. Serco vans have many inner holding cells within their vehicles. One van may have to pick up offenders from HMP Belmarsh, HMP Brixton, HMP Wandsworth and so on, all the London prisons – they are allocated various areas to collect. Each offender will be collected from their prison and loaded into separate cells on the van, and each van depending on size can hold different amounts of offenders. For example, a lorry could have 12 cells within the van, whereas a smaller van may only have enough single cells to hold six offenders. These Serco vehicles will collect and then deliver to the courts. This can be a very long day for the offender, especially if they are the last to be dropped off. Category A offenders will be escorted by prison staff in prison vans, and these vans have roughly no more than three cells within them. Remember, each Category A offender must be escorted by four prison officers and a senior officer, so if two Category A offenders were to be placed in the same van there would need to be rear seating for ten prison officers.'

This level of staff resource, however, given years of underfunding, cannot be sustained across the prison estate. When we met Phil Ashford, Director of Enterprise Exchange, he discussed the significant impact of austerity measures on the prison system following the Conservative government's election, and why it meant initiatives like his mattered.

'The criminal justice system isn't working. Reoffending rates are high, and prisons often lack rehabilitation, especially post-2010 austerity cuts. Evidence shows that people who leave prison with a job are less likely to reoffend.'

As he explained, 'Suddenly, there was less rehabilitation and more of a "just lock them up" approach. They didn't have the staff to do anything else. I've really noticed how young, and few the new staff are. I've seen 19-year-old girls – not that they can't do it – looking after a whole wing. It's worried me a lot.'

Despite these issues, Phil acknowledged that Belmarsh, as a Category A prison, was better staffed and more organised than many other facilities.

'Belmarsh has a reputation like Wakefield or Broadmoor. But it's not just high security. It's also general population, mostly local people in for drug offences or burglary.'

Its high-profile nature and the need for experienced personnel meant it operated more effectively than lower-category prisons that had suffered more severely from budget cuts. However, he made it clear that Belmarsh housed a wide range of prisoners. While some were high-profile terrorists, he only worked with Category C inmates. These were prisoners who were nearing release.

'I was briefed by the governor and staff and realised it's a typical population. It's probably better run because it has more funding, it's easier to get space and there are fewer lockdowns.'

He contrasted it with the neighbouring institution, where he had a much less favourable impression.

'I also worked at HMP Isis across the road. It's more of a gang prison. Lads had to attend in shifts to avoid rivals. Total chaos. Belmarsh has issues too, but it feels better run. Staff I've worked with there have been great, really welcoming. For a prison, it's quite cheerful. I've never felt intimidated. The key is who you work with inside.'

As we can see, despite its fearsome reputation,

Belmarsh's structure, funding and experienced staff contribute to a relatively stable atmosphere, unlike HMP Isis.

CHAPTER 3

HMP Isis

'London gangs bring lots of violence. Isis is
horrendous. Very tense. You might be pleasantly
surprised by Belmarsh after that.'
(ANONYMOUS)

In 2010, a separate young offender institution (YOI), HMP Isis, was established within the Belmarsh complex in Thamesmead. The complex also includes HMP Thameside, a Category B local resettlement prison. London's only private prison, it opened in 2012, is operated by Serco and has capacity for over 1,200 convicted and remand male prisoners.

Designed to house young male offenders aged 18 to 25, HMP Isis operates with a focus on rehabilitation and education, providing structured learning and skills development opportunities to prepare inmates for reintegration into society. It takes its name from an ancient name for the River Thames.

HMP Isis consists of a mix of single and double cells housed within two residential blocks. In addition, it features an entry building and a central activities centre, which includes a learning academy, a segregation unit and a physical education academy. However, the facility does not have in-patient healthcare services.

In May 2009, the Ministry of Justice awarded a £110 million contract to Interserve for the design and construction of the new prison on underutilised land within the perimeter wall of Belmarsh. Although built to Category B security standards, Isis functions as a Category C YOI. The project was completed in April 2010, and the prison became operational shortly afterwards, in late July of that year.

Matthew spent nearly two decades working in three different prisons, providing him with valuable insight into their contrasts:

'I was in the prison service for about 19 years from start to finish until I left in 2020. I am still a civil servant but doing something completely different now. I started in Maidstone prison, which was really old. It was a Category B prison and it was the prison where all the longer-term notorious prisoners liked to go. Because it was a very peaceful prison, and had the likes of Reggie Kray in there. I stayed there for about nine years.'

Isis proved to be a stark contrast to the 'peaceful' atmosphere of Maidstone. Matthew indicated that Isis and Belmarsh share the same perimeter wall 'but there's another wall in between to separate the two prisons. Isis is a young offenders' prison and interestingly it was the first public sector open prison in 25 years when it opened. I stayed there for a couple of years and then I went into Belmarsh'.

Matthew, a seasoned former prison officer, described the particular challenges of working at Isis, noting the immaturity of many of the troubled youngsters and their struggle with basic responsibilities.

'Simple things like they couldn't get out of bed in the morning. It was dealing with teenagers, and they just couldn't get out of bed. You'd spend most of your time trying to wake people up, or people would be play fighting constantly because that's what young adult males tend to do or generally pushing the boundaries.'

It was not just their youth driving the problems, though. There was another scourge which preys on vulnerable and underprivileged men. Gangs, as Matthew had seen:

'That was really the time at Isis when gang culture was at its peak, especially how in London areas you had many different types of gangs, and that was the same in Isis prison. Unfortunately, you would have a lot of peer-on-peer violence, purely because of the postcode they lived in.'

It didn't even have to be personal beef. Fights could break out among complete strangers based on the gang turf they were associated with. Matthew said, 'A lot of the time they didn't know each other, it was just violence, and that transcended eventually into Belmarsh, where older gang members came in but it was a different culture. Maidstone you could be less stringent with the rules because people knew the rules and lived by them.'

As he summarised, 'Isis had to have firm rules because they were kids, and they didn't bother with rules, and Belmarsh was setting the rules for them to live for the rest of their sentence really.'

We wanted to get a better understanding of whether there was any movement between Isis and Belmarsh, but it does not really work like that, as Matthew explained:

'Generally, it works on an allocation process . . . Belmarsh is a high-security prison, Isis is a lower-category prison. So, for them to transfer next door to Belmarsh they would have to have done something incredibly naughty: potentially killing another offender or taking a member of staff hostage. Most young offenders would either move on to lower-category prisons or other young offender institutions. Unfortunately, what I did see was some young offenders that I worked with that were released, that then came back into Belmarsh as Category A prisoners because their criminality continued.'

Nik, another former officer, recalled his first experience as a prison officer at HMP Isis while awaiting security clearance. He described the high levels of violence among young gang-affiliated inmates and how it was 'just unmatched to Belmarsh. In the three weeks I spent at Isis, I had more fights than I had in Belmarsh for a year,' Nik said. 'Five times a day,' just constant violence.

Other former officers corroborated this view.

Back in 2012, concerns were raised over the prevalence of gang culture within HMP Isis, with Governor Grahame Hawkins acknowledging that this was a significant issue, and it does not appear to have gone away. That said, in an inspection report soon before that, Isis was praised for some things, including low drug use and robust support systems to prevent or mitigate self-harm.

A decade later, a 2022 inspection of HMP/YOI Isis still revealed significant concerns regarding the treatment and rehabilitation of its young adult male population. The prison, accommodating approximately 595 inmates aged 18 to 27, faces challenges due to a high turnover of around 80 new prisoners monthly, many with gang affiliations.

Inspectors noted that efforts to prevent gang-related conflicts led to the segregation of inmates into cohorts, inadvertently resulting in extended periods of confinement. Many prisoners were confined to their cells for up to 21.5 hours daily, limiting access to education, work and training opportunities. The quality of teaching was inconsistent, and staff shortages further hindered rehabilitation efforts.

Public protection measures were found lacking, with support in the community often arranged too close to release dates. Notably, restrictions for prisoners posing risks to children were not always in place. Resettlement support, including assistance with finance and debt management, was insufficient. Despite the segregation strategy, violence remained prevalent, and there was no comprehensive plan to address it.

While the governor demonstrated a commitment to improvement, the prison requires a concerted effort to enhance safety, rehabilitation and sentence progression. Addressing these issues is crucial to ensure that young offenders receive the support necessary for successful reintegration into society.

If one depressing trajectory for the youth in Isis was their destiny, then at some point they would endure the unique ordeal of entering Belmarsh for the first time.

CHAPTER 4

Entering Hell

*'Belmarsh very much encapsulates and reflects the
daunting concept of being imprisoned.'*
(JEREMY DEIN KC)

Jonathan Aitken's mesmerising account of his entry into
Belmarsh and his first night comes later in this book,
but another ex-Belmarsh prisoner's detailed recollections
of how it feels 'on arrival' had us totally gripped:

'The reception area at HMP Belmarsh is very small
compared to other prisons, and it can be very busy when
staff are processing offenders out and in. [For Category
A offenders] Inmates will be collected by prison staff at
6:00am and taken to the reception area. There they are
placed in one of the Category A holding cells; the offender
will then be strip-searched and placed on to the body
scanner, and the offender is then given a set of prison
issues clothes.'

Certainly, at the time that this contributor's recollections
date to, the clothes prisoners were given had what sounds
like a very distractive style, which as he went on to explain

is partly to ensure that they would be very conspicuous if they somehow managed to get out in public.

'The clothes include underwear – these are called sterile clothes. The offender is also given a boiler suit to put on, with green and yellow patches with HMP PRISONS written across the back of the suit. This is to ensure if one was to escape then they would be clearly visible wearing such clothes in public. The offender is then placed in another Category A holding cell, this being called a sterile cell. The offender is left within the cell until such time as the escort staff are ready.'

This 'reception' sounds beyond brutal. The early start, the strip search, the standard issue clothing, the purposeful delays and waiting all sounds so dehumanising. What comes next when the staff are ready is a full-on interrogation.

'Upon the staff being in place, the offender is then taken to the small desk and checked out. Questions will be asked to check if you are who you say you are, for example, "What was your address when you came to prison?" "What is your mother's maiden name?" "Do you know what court you are going to today?" "What is your date of birth?" "Where were you born?" Of course, staff know who you are, but this is an example of the security measures and policies they follow.'

Belmarsh staff don't just reply on verbal responses, though. They need biosignatures and physical restraints too.

'After the questioning the offender will be asked to

place his finger on a flat screen, which will identify the offender. The offender will then be searched again and placed in front of a wand metal detector. The offender will then be placed in handcuffs. Then another set of handcuffs are used to handcuff the offender to a prison officer. The reception SO (supervising officer) will then check the handcuffs to ensure they are not too loose.'

This all seems like pretty standard procedure, but we were intrigued by the detail that followed regarding the escape pack and security intelligence.

'The reception SO will hand the escort staff the offender's escape pack. A sealed envelope only to be opened if an escape does happen. These packs hold intelligence on the offender, such as family addresses, likely places the offender would go to. There is another file handed to the escort staff, called an SIR file: "Security Intelligence Received". This holds an A4 up-to-date photo of the offender with various bits of relevant history, for example faking illnesses, manipulation, is he a danger to females?, no lone contact with females, should the offender's window blind be closed while in transit, weapons, offending history, previous manipulation tactics used, violence – the list of intelligence is extensive. Under subject access request to personal data, I have indeed obtained a copy of my own SIR file and it is extensive and long. This will be read by all the escort staff.'

Jeremy Dein has an intimate knowledge of Belmarsh from a wholly different perspective, that of a prominent KC.

'I have visited Belmarsh prison on many occasions. It is

a daunting place. When you arrive there, you see the walls. It's intimidating; it's intriguing to know what is going on, behind this sense of relief that you're not in – on that side of the wall. It's incredibly complex to get through the visiting area, to get in to see your client. And then you're in this bizarre environment, where, you know, your client is guarded and controlled.'

Always a reflective man, these visits guided Jeremy towards more philosophical and societal observations.

'I've always found the concept of incarceration both an unattractive and a fascinating one, albeit a necessary feature of our society. Belmarsh very much encapsulates and reflects the daunting concept of being imprisoned. So that's what I would have to say about Belmarsh. It's also somewhere that's very difficult to get to. Thoughts about it are always negative: traffic, queuing, difficult staff, being searched, being asked to go back through the search centre because you've got a tiny bit of foil stuck to your foot or something. It's a complex place, but obviously nowhere nearly as intimidating as if you're banged up there, that's for sure.'

Our contributor, Phil, felt the same going into Belmarsh and contrasted it with other prisons.

'I've held keys in some prisons. Belmarsh is different. Getting in is a hassle. Your name has to be on the gate. Often, it isn't. That's common. At Belmarsh, you get fingerprinted, photo taken, security is tighter. It's like an airport. Metal detectors and all that. With the film crew, they'd almost just walk through, but you must be so careful. You can't take in USBs or anything electrical. If you're caught, it's serious. Even my workbooks had to have the binders removed. I bring them in loose-leaf.'

Phil's experience summed up one paradox of Belmarsh perfectly: bureaucratic, tough, and yet undeniably fascinating. That sense of tension, of being simultaneously inside and outside the prison, carries directly into the next chapter as we explore what it means to move in and out of the fortress-like walls.

CHAPTER 5

Movement In and Out
of Belmarsh

'The cell is tiny and your knees touch the thick
steel wall in front of you. The handcuffs are left on
the offender throughout the journey.'
(ANONYMOUS FORMER INMATE)

Having seen what the reception area in hell was like, we were eager to learn more about the carefully choreographed comings and goings from Belmarsh. It was such an emotionally charged thought imagining the wild journey from the paparazzi flashing their cameras outside the Old Bailey to the high-security confines of Thamesmead.

One former inmate who has made exactly this journey recalled it in the following terms:

'Upon the checks and further security measures being put in place, the van will be parked directly outside the door of the reception area. The security measures are so tight, that even though the walk to the van involves no more than a six-foot walk, the offender has to walk outside, so a dog handler will be called to supervise the short walk. Call sign, ZULU ONE. The rules are strict: when you are told to walk, you walk and cannot stop, and if you even try to stop, they will all just jump on you, a term called "bend you up".'

Every detail of the transfer process is meticulously planned to eliminate any risk of escape or trouble. This security extends beyond personnel, incorporating physical barriers to prevent any external intervention.

The former inmate expanded on some of the further security measures for us.

'The outside area inside HMP Belmarsh has anti-helicopter wire running overhead. These are thick steel cables which make it impossible for a helicopter to land. Upon entering the van, staff will be waiting inside the van with the cell door open. The cells are known as "sweat boxes" because they are so small and cramped. The offender will be placed inside the cell standing up, the officer whom the offender is cuffed to will put his arm inside the cell door, the door is part shut with a chain put on the door to enable the officer to take off the handcuffs attached to his or her wrist. The door is then closed – it has an electronic lock and a key lock. The electronic lock is controlled by the two staff locked in the front cab of the van.'

Once inside, the miserable captive is totally cut off from the outside world. Every movement and journey stage monitored, to ensure that security is never compromised.

'Upon the staff being located in the van, even the side

door is controlled by the cab crew who are locked in the cab separate from the escort staff in the rear of the van. Within the rear of the van, the senior officer on the escort will then use his link radio to inform the police they are leaving. This radio is a direct link to the police network and is updated every ten minutes with the location of the van being tracked. Within the van cell there is a hatch in the roof. This is controlled by the cab crew in case of an emergency or van accident. I am not aware if these have ever been used. Even if you stand up and push on it, an alarm will sound. The cell is tiny, and your knees touch the thick steel wall in front of you. The handcuffs are left on the offender throughout the journey.'

Forget about a quick screech off the kerb. Every exit is checked and double-checked, eliminating any chance of interference.

'The van will then enter the main gate, known as the airlock. This is an enclosed space; the van will enter and the huge steel gates will slide open and close behind you, leaving you in a small secure area. The gate officers will enter the van and board the van. They will come to the cell and shine a torch in on the offender's face and ask the offender another set of questions. "Who are you?" "Do you know where you are going today?" "What was your father's first name?" They will then check the van, search the van, even the officers' bags. The officers will exit the van and be subject to body searches. They will have to hand in their prison keys and be subject to being metal-detected themselves. Their lunch boxes opened.

The papers related to the offender checked, the court warrant checked. The prison escort van checked underneath. This process can take at least 20 minutes.'

The ex-prisoner's account concluded by describing what happens after the officers are locked in the van. Once everything has been scrutinised, once every security measure has been satisfied, the final stage of the journey begins where 'the doors will be banged and checked they are all secure. Because of the bulletproof thick tinted glass in the small porthole-type windows and lack of any outside light, it is very dark within the van. No lights are turned on, even at night, just little dim lights. The senior officer on the escort will again check in with the police and the other set of gates will open and the vehicle will depart HMP Belmarsh.'

Once the van moves beyond the final gate, the prisoner is finally in transit, locked in a tiny, dark compartment with no sense of time or place. Except that they are headed to or from Belmarsh.

CHAPTER 6

Woolwich Crown Court and the Old Bailey

'I had a Victorian experience of trial. It was at the Old Bailey. I was in the same court that the Krays got sentenced in.'

(MIKE)

Whereas the Central Criminal Court of England and Wales, more commonly known as the Old Bailey, is situated in the City of London and serves as the principal venue for major criminal trials across the country, Woolwich Crown Court, located adjacent to HMP Belmarsh, is a high-security court specifically designed to hear serious criminal cases, often involving terrorism or organised crime, becoming operational in 1993.

While the Old Bailey handles some of the most high-profile and complex cases in the UK, Woolwich Crown Court often hears trials directly linked to inmates held at HMP Belmarsh, given the logistical and security advantages of their proximity.

On one occasion in early 2025, Emma made an

impromptu solo visit to Woolwich Crown Court, to get the measure of what a typical day looked like.

Emma arrived at Court 2 in time for a live session of a case linked to a drug line. They talked about an active phone being seized in SE18, with the police having taken the phone from its owner, oddly, at Thorpe Park. In the public gallery, Emma was the only one present. Elevated behind glass, the two rows of folding seats offered a clear view of the courtroom below. The courtroom itself was old-fashioned, with wooden panelling and sky-blue fabric seats. The blue carpet, along with the general 1990s aesthetic, hinted that the building had opened in 1994.

Moving around the other courts, Emma discovered a buzz of activity in Court 1, which was a completely different story. The witness box had a blue curtain that could be drawn around it for privacy, and the coat of arms 'Dieu et mon Droit' was proudly displayed above the judge's chair. In this case, six family members and friends of the accused were in the public gallery, sitting in the front row. Emma took a seat behind them, alone. The solicitor had failed to show up. 'He'll be about an hour,' someone whispered. 'He was only notified yesterday.' It created chaos.

The others in the gallery eyed Emma, sitting alone and trying to blend into the background, with suspicion, so she explained that she was a writer. 'You're here for fun?' one of the young girls scoffed, clearly sceptical.

Instead of the expected case, a sentencing was called. There was an annoying issue with the sound system at the start of the hearing, but things settled when the jury requested a note they had brought for the judge, which they read out again. It was a stalking case, and the jury had reached a unanimous decision on four out of five counts. The foreman was asked to deliver the verdicts again after the jury had initially entered without their note.

The counts were read as follows:

Count 1: Stalking – guilty

Count 2: Pass

Count 3: Common assault – not guilty

Count 4: Damaging property – not guilty

Count 5: Damaging property – guilty

Leaving the court, Emma noticed that security was lighter on the way out than when entering. On arrival, the process was similar to an airport – bag search, scan and body scan. They were particularly interested in the number of coins Emma had on her. There was a small cafe on site, but that was about all there was to the place.

It was a very strange atmosphere and somewhat at odds with our expectations. Prisoners and staff have corroborated and elaborated on all our impressions of the Old Bailey and Woolwich Crown Court. So we were curious, of course, to talk to contributors about the Old Bailey too, which by all accounts has a very different vibe, but though geographically distanced, still has an important connection with Belmarsh. One former prisoner was happy to offer his impressions of the Old Bailey.

'I think it is important to give you an insight into the inside of the Central Criminal Court because part of the underground holding area is run by HMP Belmarsh.

The Category A holding part of the court is staffed by HMP Belmarsh officers only and no other court staff are allowed entry to the mini prison. No Serco staff, no court staff.'

We found this glimpse behind the Old Bailey's facade, into this rather secretive world, very interesting. We picked up on the degree of control that Belmarsh likes to exert a lot while writing this book, and it is clear they are also in charge here: not the court staff, and certainly not any external staff. The former prisoner continued:

'Upon entering the Central Criminal Court by the side entrance, the court will be alerted prior and the doors will open. The van enters a tunnel which dips down under the court, and upon the van entering no one will leave the van until the gates are closed. The parking area is so small that there is a commercial steel turntable to turn the van around. There is even a secure parking area for the Belmarsh vehicles. Lower-category offenders will have to check in with Serco staff at their reception area. However, upon being handcuffed to the Belmarsh officer, the Category A offender will simply be walked straight through the underground court reception to the Belmarsh-staffed holding area.'

Structurally, and perhaps to wield even more control, Belmarsh seems very partial to units within units, where the degree of security is even more ferocious. The same former inmate told us more about the 'long walk down long underground walkways to the Belmarsh holding area. Upon entering the mini prison (holding area), you are met by Belmarsh prison officers. They unlock the steel-barred gate and let you in. You are then held in an airlock and then you enter the holding area through another steel-barred gate. Within this area there are legal visiting rooms, holding cells, toilets and a staff area, and there can often be up to 20 staff there. Any legal visits by solicitors or barristers are very strict, and they are all subject to vigorous checks. Everything is searched; there are even external lockers prior to entering the unit for them to place their mobile phones in.'

Levels of security we haven't really seen since Broadmoor Hospital are being described here. From the underground network of tunnels and checkpoints to the airlocks to the constant surveillance and scrutiny, everything is about control and threat mitigation. We were taken aback that even legal visits are subject to the same strict measures.

For the staff, these security measures seem to involve an awful lot of waiting around. The former inmate who was filling us in on all this inside information explained that, 'the escort vans are left with the cab crew sitting in them all day, and HMP Belmarsh staff also have their own radio communications within the court. The holding area, the communications, all exclusively to HMP Belmarsh officers and staff only. Upon being processed into the holding area, the security measures are again implicated. The offender will be told to strip and all the escort clothes are sealed in a bag with a plastic seal placed on the bag to secure the clothes. These seals are tamper-proof and numbered, and the number is logged with the bag being placed in a secure locker. The offender's court clothes which came separate to the court are then unsealed from the bag and searched again. The offender is then taken out of the cell and placed in another holding cell. Even the doors to these cells are high-security, Home Office-approved doors. They are in fact the same doors which are used within HMP Belmarsh. None of the other cell doors within the Central Criminal Court which holds offenders outside the Belmarsh holding area are the same.'

The physical searches are intensive and intrusive.

'When being searched, even the mouth, hair, nose and ears are inspected. This is how tight the security is at HMP Belmarsh and the Central Criminal Court. Prior to entering the court dock, even this is searched by Belmarsh staff prior to entering the court. For the escort to the court along the underground tunnels, the offender is still handcuffed with a separate set of handcuffs being used to enable the offender to be handcuffed to the prison officer. All the handcuffs are removed prior to entering the courtroom. Upon returning to the holding area, and then the return journey to HMP Belmarsh, the procedure is repeated. The whole experience can be intimidating. I was on trial over months, as a result of this and with the constant use of handcuffs my wrists were bruised. The whole experience, collecting the offender at 6:00am and leaving you waiting until 7:30am before even processing you, then the long day, then on return after processing.'

In the gruelling and relentless process being described here, nothing is left to chance and everything is about control. Power dynamics are carefully established, with a stripped offender cuffed, isolated and vulnerable. The bruising of his wrists and the enervating hours spent waiting can only have contributed to his intense stress, which he recalls so vividly years later.

Whichever court you were in, you were there to go on trial, a unique and highly emotive situation for all involved.

Our contributor Mike, an ex-offender, told us that he 'had a Victorian experience of trial . . . at the Old Bailey. I was in the same court that the Krays got sentenced in.'

Asking Jeremy Dein the same question, he agreed that 'there are parts of the Old Bailey that seem Victorian: the old courts. They're very small, they have extremely old furniture and they're not conducive to modern-day trials. And when you're in them, you do feel like you're going back in time. Those are the old courts.'

This is by no means the whole story, though – the Old Bailey is very much a blend of the old and the new, as Jeremy explained.

'However, there's a whole section of new courts which is very different. So, I can't say that overall, I perceive it as a Victorian experience. But then, I've been going there for so long. To me, it's a very modern, very well-functioning court. Moreover, it's got a fantastic sort of family atmosphere. If you're known, the staff, the judges are very nice, and everyone trusts each other and has respect for each other.'

This reflection on the contrast between historic and modern spaces within the Old Bailey set the scene for a deeper look into how behaviour within those spaces is managed during trials. Intriguingly, one ex-prisoner described what he perceived to be a manipulative technique deployed by one prisoner to try to garner sympathy during his trial. He requested a nurse to sit in the dock with him.

'Belmarsh challenged this and staff hounded him over it, but he had a good legal team. This request was likely for show, to create a "poor me" image for the jury. He didn't need a nurse to sit with him, but it was a genius move on his part. It was his idea, and he got his wish.'

We can't be certain if this was a bit of theatre or a genuine vulnerability, in what was a complex case.

We wanted to put a question to Jeremy that another one of our contributors, Matthew, had put to us when discussing how prisoners carried themselves in the dock in front of victims' families.

'That's one of the more difficult things: seeing victims of crime or the families daily and listening to some of the things that happened to them. I don't know whether their own counsel tell the prisoners to do this, but then, the prisoners sit there very plain-faced and no response, no emotional reaction, despite the things they're hearing and that sticks with you. I don't know how people don't react to some information, especially when other people are distressed by the information that's being heard.'

Jeremy was able to corroborate this from his expert legal perspective.

'On the concept of telling defendants to be impassive

and emotionless in trial – that is right. In fact, I always make that clear to the defendant because the jury look at them periodically and their body language is very important. They're charged with serious offences and it's important that the jury don't infer anything correct or incorrect. You know, jurors are humans, and they could read into the way someone sits, the way someone smiles, whom they talk to, how they talk, something negative that could be a false lead to convictions. Therefore, I'm very clear with everybody that I represent that they should be emotionless and passive and allow the jury to decide the case on the evidence and the evidence alone.'

Following this consideration of courtroom presentation and perception, we turned to the broader personal and professional experience of working as a KC at a globally renowned institution like the Old Bailey.

'On the question of being a KC at the Old Bailey, obviously that is a very enjoyable experience. After all, it's probably the most famous court centre in the world, and being a Queen's Counsel, or King's Counsel, you know, you appreciate you've done well in your career and that you're accessing the most serious level of cases. And there's an element of historical feeling about it as well. So, I can't comment on how other people feel in terms of their roles, but certainly it's been a very fulfilling experience for me.'

Building on this sense of prestige and tradition, Jeremy went on to describe the rare privilege and emotional impact of sitting as a judge there.

'I've sat as a judge at the Old Bailey. That was an incredible experience. Obviously, walking through the door through a courtroom, especially one of the old courtrooms, has this overwhelming sense of history, and it's surreal. As a kid from the East End to be sitting as a judge at the Old Bailey and to have that sense of power . . . it's very important to keep feet on the ground and to treat people with respect, but clearly an exciting experience. Furthermore, appearing at the Old Bailey as a defender, making closing speeches in historic courtrooms, in a historic building – or even the new building – where many very serious trials have happened, is an incredibly exhilarating experience; the power of persuasion, the art of persuasion are all extremely valuable and, you know, unique commodities.'

Jeremy was able to offer fascinating insights from the 'other side of the curtain' so to speak. Matthew was also fascinating on the emotional impact of trials from a staff perspective:

'I've done a lot of trials with a lot of different people over the time I was there and it's always the families that get to you. It's the evidence you are listening to. Generally, with Category A prisoners they've committed a murder or horrendous crimes. You would be sitting there looking at the families and their reactions. That was always difficult because you must come across as professional and you must come across as non-judgemental more than anything despite what's being reported in the media and what's happening. You always got this sense that the family are looking at you thinking, "How can you be sitting there next to this person?", or "How can you be keeping this person safe, knowing what they've done?" That's a difficult thing, that you always have to portray a stoic outlook, where you don't give anything away, even though you might be thinking, my goodness, what? This crime that this person has allegedly done, it's horrendous,' Matthew told us, the emotion clear in his voice.

Matthew expanded on this, though, and the often distressing reality of learning at trial all the details that were too disturbing to be released to the general public by the media.

'You would hear the specifics about their crimes that the media were unable to report. You'd have to process that information and take that on board. And there were a few bits and pieces where you would then move those people out and bring them back and this would happen for however long a trial would go on for.'

Jeremy Dein spoke similarly about this aspect of being at trial and how, 'In terms of serious trials, most information is in the public domain. Obviously, there are sensitive issues, and they remain in the courtroom. Dependent upon age, whether it's a sexual offence, circumstances. But the principle of open justice is very much obeyed in this country, and lawyers and judges adhere to it. And at the Old Bailey, that's certainly the case.'

It was a fascinating insight into the trial process and what both offenders, staff and insiders experience before sentencing. Whatever the similarities and differences between the Old Bailey and Woolwich Crown Court, one key outcome of any trial leading to prosecution is information that feeds into what category of prison the defendant is headed to.

CHAPTER 7

Prison Categories

*'The Cat C system has higher levels of violence than
Cat A. One Cat C prison, HMP Highpoint, was nicknamed
"Knifepoint". In Highpoint they are sharpening their own
handmade weapons all the time. I have seen guys having a
medieval sword fight. They would also soak orange blankets
and run into your cell and cover you with them. You can't
move when they do that.'*

(MIKE)

England operates a structured prison system, with its
maximum-security prisons housing the most dangerous offenders. They form part of a wider categorisation
system, explained in this chapter, that determines where
prisoners are held based on their risk levels. The system
always has to strike a balance between ensuring public
safety and reclassification as the prisoner's risk assessment
changes. Not easy!

There are eight maximum-security (Category A) prisons
for adult males in England. There are none in Wales and
one in Northern Ireland, Maghaberry prison. Scotland
has a different system. In addition to HMP Belmarsh,

they are HMP Frankland, HMP Full Sutton, HMP Long Lartin, HMP Wakefield, HMP Manchester, HMP Whitemoor and HMP Woodhill. Many of the prisoners mentioned in this book, such as Wayne Couzens, John Worboys, Ian Huntley and Steven Barker, have been transferred between these prisons during their sentences. Category A prisoners are routinely moved from time to time for security reasons.

All eight of these high-security prisons operate under His Majesty's Prison Service. HMPS manages prisons in England and Wales and also serves as the National Offender Management Service for these regions. The Northern Ireland Prison Service and the Scottish Prison Service oversee their respective regions. Additionally, the three Crown Dependencies – the Isle of Man and the Bailiwicks of Jersey and Guernsey (the Channel Islands) – maintain independent prison services.

Male adult prisoners are classified into one of four security categories. Women and young offenders have separate designations.

The categorisation of male prisoners is determined by several factors, including the nature of their crime, sentence length, risk of escape and potential for violence. The latter involves assessing both internal and external threats – how much of a risk they pose to the stability of a prison and the likelihood of them harming the public if they were to escape. Every male prisoner over the age of 18 is assigned a security categorisation shortly after entering the prison system.

Security levels range from Category A to Category D, with Category A being the highest. HMP Belmarsh is undoubtedly one of the most prominent prisons in this category. Category D, the lowest level, applies to open prisons, while Categories A, B and C are classified as closed prisons.

So, for male prisons in England and Wales:

Category A are high-security prisons, housing men who pose the highest threat to national security, the police and/or the public if they were to escape. Among the offences that can land men in a Category A are plenty that you would expect: murder or attempted murder, rape or attempted rape, sexual assault, manslaughter, wounding with intent, kidnapping and terrorism offences. However, men have also been banged up for offences under the Official Secrets Act, possessing or supplying explosives, armed robbery and importing or supplying Class A controlled substances.

Unsurprisingly, an awful lot of scrutiny is put on the risk of prisoners in Category A escaping. As part of this, Category A prisoners get split into Standard Risk, High Risk and Exceptional Risk on the basis of their likelihood of escaping. There is also a Provisional Category A condition. That's for men who are waiting to be tried on the most serious of offences and therefore cannot be held in Category B conditions like most men on remand.

Let's remember, Belmarsh has never had a prisoner escape.

One former officer, fascinatingly, described some of the different personality traits exhibited in different categories of prison, saying, 'With Category A you see lots of complaints and litigation. Staff make complaints and try to make money.'

After a while, the prisoners can pick up on this too. 'Where they are in the system and have been in Category A for longer – the prisoners learn how to work the system; they are litigious.'

With plenty of time on their hands, the more manipulative prisoners try to game the system for their advantage.

Category B prisons serve as either local or training prisons. Training prisons accommodate long-term and high-security prisoners, while local prisons hold individuals coming directly from court in the surrounding area, whether they are on remand or have been sentenced. While Category B prisoners do not require maximum security, preventing their escape remains a big priority.

Category C prisons function as training and resettlement institutions and house the majority of male prisoners nationally. These facilities focus on rehabilitation and equipping inmates with skills to improve their chances of reintegrating into society upon release. While these prisoners are not yet deemed suitable for open conditions, they are also not considered to pose a high escape risk.

As many have told us with experience of Category C, they are absolutely not a soft option. Our contributor Mike asked us a very direct question:

'Why is Cat C worse than Cat A?'

He meant more violent, and in his time in Category C prisons he had witnessed everything from sword fights to punch-ups.

Matthew, however, offered a slightly contradictory view to Mike, as might be expected, from a staff perspective:

'The lower down the security category that you go in prisons, the more relaxed it is for prisoners. There are not so many rules and regulations, because they're trusted more as the security conditions lower. In a Category C prison, you're not as stringent in your rules as you would be in a Category A prison. Belmarsh is the prison that sets the standard for the rest of your sentence. So, when you immediately come in from custody, a lot of people really struggle with rules and regulations because they have never had that in their lives. It's very much like dealing with children because they rebelled against rules; they didn't like rules. A lot of people really found it difficult to apply the rules and so it got the name as Hellmarsh. There was a lot of stuff in there that wasn't very harsh or difficult, but if you've never lived within rules or never had to set rules or, never had to do a simple thing, like get out of bed and go to work . . . People would struggle with things like that.'

Matthew's view is partially informed by what sounds like a relatively gentle experience of Cat C working at Maidstone, which he acknowledged had a very different feel to Isis and was 'a throwback in time. Prison goes through evolutions of crime and how criminals react to criminality. When I was in Maidstone in the early 2000s, you had a different type of criminal: armed robbers, not many drug-related offences. People did their time, got on with it, complied with the rules and lived law-abiding lives within custody. It was very different when I went into Isis, the young offenders' prison.'

Prisoner categorisation can change over time too, particularly if an individual is no longer deemed a risk. A clear example would be a prisoner who has significantly reduced mobility or has aged considerably since their initial categorisation. Naturally, such factors lessen their threat level; however, other considerations also play a role. Prisoners undergo continual assessment, with regular sessions involving psychologists and probation officers, and their responses to these sessions are taken into account. People are capable of change, and if every Category A prisoner remained in that classification indefinitely, the system would quickly become overwhelmed.

Matthew was very clear and articulate throughout our conversation with him, and his description of recategorisation was no different, saying that 'every single prisoner is categorised and reviewed over a period of time and that's to do with their level of offending. Partly that's to do with their offending behaviour, the nature of their offences, other factors, and another element will be that there's a level of intelligence regarding the crime that they've committed that dictates that they're there for that period of time.'

Despite the tabloid headlines, as Matthew describes it, there is a solid process in place that reviews very carefully case by case and at regular time intervals.

'Further information means that can be reviewed, and the risk factor might be deemed lower, and then people can be moved around, including moving out from HSU, if the review cycle shows they have addressed what they needed to or security intelligence. That's how people progress through the system: by looking at risk factors and moving them around. Upon conviction or upon a sentencing review, there might be further information to say that that risk factor is no longer as high because of these reasons.'

Even though England's prison categorisation process is rigorous and judgement-based, errors can and do occur. Given this, it is only fair and reasonable that categorisations are subject to continual review by prison staff – not only when an individual is first sentenced but throughout their time in custody. If a prisoner's risk level is assessed to have increased or decreased, staff can initiate a transfer to a more appropriate category of prison. This means that a prisoner does not necessarily remain in the same category for the duration of their sentence, as Matt explained:

'People can be moved around and that's how people progress through the system in general. They'll generally look at their risk factors and move them around and that's not just for higher-security reasons, that's all prison. You might have someone who started off in the HSU but as the review cycle has gone on and they've addressed whatever they've needed to address, and security intelligence is not as severe or as likely, then they can move around. At some point in some prisons, you'll come across prisoners who were in high-security prisons or even the HSU that eventually will probably be Category B or even Category C prisoners after, probably, a considerable number of years.'

Category D prisons, by contrast, are open prisons with minimal security, as it is considered reasonable to assume that inmates will not abuse the privilege and attempt to escape. Prisoners in Category D establishments are allowed out on licence for most of the day to pursue education or work. Entry into a Category D prison requires a thorough risk assessment to ensure the individual is suitable for open conditions. These prisons are commonly referred to as 'D Cat'. The licence permitting prisoners to work or study in the community is known as ROTL: Release on Temporary Licence. Typically, around a quarter of the way through their sentence, eligible prisoners may also take a bit of home leave once they have passed their FLED: Full Licence Eligibility Date.

As we have seen, in a Category A like Belmarsh or Wakefield, additional measures are in place to enhance security, particularly for problematic or unpredictable individuals deemed too dangerous to be housed with the general prison population.

Many prisoners assigned to these units would be classified as having 'personality disorders' – a condition where individuals are deemed to be 'wired differently' and display unusual behaviours, though not necessarily linked to any specific mental illness.

Mike had described to us his first-hand exposure to individuals in Belmarsh with severe personality disorders. We should note that, though it's true that there have been deaths in Belmarsh, 'all the time' is an exaggeration.

'People die in Belmarsh all the time.'

Mike also remarked on the vulnerable mental state of many of the inmates:

'There are people with severe special needs. When I was there, there was someone in there with a mental age of seven who was in there for shoplifting. He walked into the shower with his clothes on. The Tate attempted murderer raped a blind guy in the shower. There are psychopaths in Belmarsh.'

It's distressing to think of these vulnerable individuals in such a challenging environment, but we take Mike's comment about the rape with a pinch of salt, like many of his stories. Mike was referring to Jonty Bravery. On 4 August 2019, Bravery, then 17 years old, pushed a six-year-old French boy from a viewing platform on the tenth floor at the Tate Modern in London. The incident occurred around midday when the boy, visiting the gallery with his family, was standing at a window overlooking the city. Bravery, who had been seen acting weirdly that day, approached the child and suddenly pushed him through a metal barrier. The child fell approximately 100 feet to the ground below and was left with life-threatening injuries, including multiple fractures and a bleed on the brain. The boy was later transported to hospital in critical condition but thankfully survived the fall. It is a tragic story, particularly when we know that Bravery had been under close review from social workers due to a history of mental disorders throughout his life.

Bravery was detained at the scene by bystanders until police arrived. During his arrest, Bravery made statements suggesting he had planned the attack, claiming he had chosen the victim randomly and had intended to cause harm. He later told investigators that he had wanted to 'kill a child' to impress others and was said to have 'smiled' immediately after the attack.

Bravery's is also an interesting journey through the prison system, offering some insights into categorisations and sentence extensions. In January 2020 he was in Broadmoor Hospital on remand when he attacked two staff, punching a female nursing assistant in the head and face after she informed him she was going to clean his room. When another staff member intervened, Bravery bit his finger. He received an additional 14-week sentence after pleading guilty to two counts of common assault. Appearing via video link from Belmarsh prison, where he had been moved by then, Bravery was sentenced at Westminster Magistrates' Court. At the time of the new attacks on the staff, Bravery was already awaiting sentencing at the Old Bailey, where he later pleaded guilty to attempted murder over the 2019 attack at the London art gallery.

When we first heard about this case, and after our time spent researching inside Broadmoor, we both agreed that he seemed to be a prime candidate for Broadmoor and it turned out to be the case, at least initially. However, in July 2020, when Bravery pleaded guilty to the charge of attempted murder, the court acknowledged his mental health issues but also emphasised the seriousness of the crime, particularly given the victim's vulnerability and the nature of the attack. In sentencing, the judge noted that Bravery's actions were 'entirely unjustified' and that he had intended to kill the child, even if he had not succeeded. He was sentenced to life imprisonment, with a minimum term of 15 years, meaning he would not be eligible for parole until at least 2035. Although Bravery was only 17 when he tried to kill the boy, rather than being sent to Broadmoor as a patient, he was sent to Belmarsh, where he is treated as a high-risk individual. An ex-inmate has since chillingly recounted to us that Bravery told him he was 'sorry that the boy didn't die'.

More typically, younger offenders go into young offender institutions, such as Isis, which house prisoners aged between 18 and 21. Youth Custody is reserved for individuals under 18 who are either on remand or serving a sentence imposed by the courts. As we have seen, many of our contributors describe the young offender institution attached to Belmarsh – HMP Isis – as even harsher than Belmarsh itself. It is certainly not a lenient option for either the young offenders or the staff working there, but it does raise wider questions around the treatment of young and vulnerable individuals in the system.

With that said, prisoners are continually monitored and assessed throughout their sentence, and recategorisation can take place at any time for both sentenced and remand prisoners if an event occurs or new information emerges that significantly affects their risk assessment. Outside of exceptional circumstances, prisoners serving sentences of more than four years undergo an assessment annually until they reach the final two years of their sentence, at which point assessments are conducted every six months.

All Category A prisoners must be reviewed in collaboration with the Prison Service Head Office to ensure appropriate security measures are upheld. In contrast, Category D prisoners do not require recategorisation unless their risk level has changed. Naturally, many prisoners are dissatisfied with their categorisation or recategorisation, and they have the right to appeal.

Prison categorisation affects every aspect of an inmate's experience, from their daily routine to the level of security surrounding their movements. One former prisoner explained how categorisation plays a crucial role in determining how individuals are transported to and from prison:

'At Belmarsh, your categorisation also very much impacts on how you are moved in and out of the prison. Category A offenders can be given different levels of security. They are: standard escape risk, high risk and exceptional high risk. This only comes into force upon leaving the walls of HMP Belmarsh. Such risk factors can depend on a wide range of intelligence received. For example, an offender who is on trial for a multi-million-pound fraud (not violent or a danger to the public), can still be high risk due to their financial backing. They have millions in the bank or are connected to people with money. Therefore, they have the means to employ people to facilitate an escape. However, the offender can be deemed such a risk to the public due to their index offences that escape must be made impossible, therefore they too can be deemed as high risk. In short, one has money, the other is a monster.'

He gave us a very useful breakdown of how different risk categories have different procedures.

'Standard escape risk when departing HMP Belmarsh will just follow procedures and check in with the police and travel alone to the Central Criminal Court. High risk upon leaving will be met by two armed police cars which will travel with the van and just turn on the blues at traffic lights to enable the prison van to never be stationary. Exceptional high risk when departing HMP Belmarsh will have a helicopter and armed police escort to the court and will travel at speed on blue lights all the way.'

There was something very cinematic about the image he created, evoking scenes from high-stakes crime dramas. These prisoners' movements require extensive coordination to prevent any possibility of escape. It also affected how these individuals are typically housed within the prison, with our source adding, 'These offenders are normally located within HMP Belmarsh CSU or HCSU (High Closed Secure Unit). So, upon leaving HMP Belmarsh, the travelling arrangements can be different (depending on risk).'

We relished this level of detail from a former prisoner, but we wanted confirmation from an experienced prison staff member who had been directly involved in these operations. Matthew, who had worked in high-security prisoner transport, was more than happy to offer his perspective, telling us he 'was part of the Category A team and part of that was for the really high-profile prisoners' and confirming what we'd been told by the former prisoner, in that 'Category A prisoners are moved differently to lower-category prisoners. Lower-category prisoners are moved by Serco and GEOAmey: the normal external contractors. High-risk and Category A prisoners are moved by prison staff. So, they would be moved in secure vehicles to various court proceedings for however long that would be. I was one of the custodial managers in charge of that.'

We've heard a few accounts of HSU already, but as such a dramatic and unique feature of Belmarsh, with so many of the world's most famous prisoners passing through, it deserves a deeper exploration.

CHAPTER 8

HSU: The Prison within a Prison

'You could tell the minute you walked into the high security that it did exactly what it said on the tin.'

(MATTHEW)

The High-Security Unit (HSU) and the CSC are distinct, and distinctive, areas within Belmarsh, with the HSU housing high-risk prisoners and the CSC, or 'Segregation Unit', handling segregated prisoners.

One former inhabitant helped to describe it to us, stating that 'High Security holds Category A and high-risk offenders. In short, the conditions must be so that it is impossible to escape. For triple Category A prisoners, they would be held on the HSU (High-Security Unit) at HMP Belmarsh. This is the only HSU in the UK.' The ex-prisoner had actually been located here confirming that it is 'a prison within a prison. It has its own reception area and also has a tunnel which leads direct to Woolwich Crown Court. Therefore, one can walk from the prison directly into the courtroom.'

This so-called 'prison within a prison' is an incredible revelation, as is the mention of a tunnel linking Belmarsh to Woolwich Crown Court. We had heard about it before – one of the most striking features of Belmarsh is its bombproof underground tunnel, designed to transport the most dangerous offenders to court in a highly secure way. The tunnel takes you under the prison through a series of automatic gates. Matthew told us a bit more about the tunnel, which runs directly from the CSC to Woolwich Crown Court:

'It enables terrorists and exceptional high-risk offenders to be taken to a court appearance making it impossible for any escape plans to be carried out. I have never used or seen the tunnel, but it is well known publicly that such a tunnel is used often.'

Matthew's rich experience and excellent memory enabled him to give us a meticulous account of the features of the HSU, which is surrounded by its own five-metre high concrete wall.

'The unit is generally only there for the higher risk category prisoners. There's a degree of sectioning for high-risk prisoners and the ones that are deemed not appropriate to mix with the general population. That could be for several reasons: it might be because of their ability to influence the people in the prison or just the nature of their offending. There are a number of Category A prisoners that live on general house blocks anyway. You would only segregate those ones whose crimes dictated they were segregated or because they were deemed as the highest risk to British society, by police, crime or security intelligence.'

Corroborating what we know from others, Matthew explained that it's run as a separate environment, with a custodial manager in charge. If he needed to go and move people, 'certain escorts required people of certain ranks to be in charge. We would move people that needed to be moved for various reasons, but the HSU is an extremely secure environment that is even more restricted than normal regimes.'

The appearance of the HSU added to this appearance of control and security, with physical constraints every-where, 'whether that's the exercise yards or the prison spurs: the spurs were a lot smaller and they didn't have as many locations for people to be on. The level of physical security was extremely high and tight compared to the house blocks. The house blocks were highly secure, but HSU was another level. You could tell the minute you walked into the high security that it did exactly what it said on the tin. It was secured so those within the unit could do everything within those walls. They were only let out for specific reasons and if they had to go, it would be a carefully orchestrated thing. They were deliberately segregated from the rest of the population. Even the staff that went over there were highly trained and had to have a number of factors before they were allowed to work over there; you had to have a minimum level of service because of the types of personalities that work in that environment and because some people have been in those types of prisons for a number of years.'

As part of the clever overall design, the spurs can be locked down easily, which prevents large numbers of prisoners gathering together and causing trouble.

According to one ex-inhabitant, even the food is recalibrated for security purposes:

'Meals are delivered by staff from the kitchens and the food is picked at random within the kitchen from other wing meals to ensure that no previous notice is given to offenders who work in the kitchens that the meals are to be forwarded to the HSU. This is to prevent notes, messages or other items being smuggled into the food containers.'

Movement as well as food must be planned with extreme precision. In terms of moving people from the HSU to Category A, Matthew described a carefully orchestrated movement allocation that ran 'like clockwork; it's a well-oiled machine. You know when they're coming. They wouldn't go into the main reception because the HSU has its own reception, and they would be moved around from there. It was a completely siloed experience. Normal prisoners went to reception, and those doomed for the HSU would go a different way into the prison and they would not mix with other prisoners.'

Matthew added that moving a prisoner to avoid them being threatened by another prisoner was carefully managed at Belmarsh. Over his years working in prison, he saw a raised awareness of conflict, gang culture and those trying to gain influence. He also saw prisoners themselves speaking more openly about whom they were in conflict with, imminent threats, and 'you would move those under conflict by themselves. If there was a serious threat to people's lives, then they wouldn't be associated out on the house block at the same time as other people, to try and keep them as safe as possible.' Movement was choreographed with technology.

'They would always be moved around, with movement organised via radio communications. You'd let people know that stuff was moving and you always had to be aware because sometimes this person might be under threat for a reason, but you might not know who that person is threatened by. So, you're constantly aware of when you're out and around with individuals who are under threat that they could be targeted at any time. So, your level of intense scrutiny has to be high.'

This careful choreography of movement aimed at preventing violence highlights the constant vigilance required to manage threats within Belmarsh. However, when a prisoner's behaviour becomes unmanageable, they may be moved to the Segregation Unit, home to some of the most dangerous and high-risk individuals in the system.

CHAPTER 9

CSC: The Segregation Unit

'CSC units are made for the most manipulative and violent prisoners.'

(CAROLINE)

C SC stands for Close Supervision Centre, but it is commonly known as 'The Seg' in Belmarsh by both screws and inmates. Caroline's recollection was that in her time, there were two CSC prisoners in the Seg and two CSC cells appointed, which, most of the time, were full.

She told us that 'CSC units are made for the most manipulative and violent prisoners. Those who have tried to kill staff or other prisoners. CSC prisoners do not socialise with any other prisoners. Generally, they have a lot of perks.' As a prison officer, 'they will try to charm you. All they have got is time. Some prisoners are like the "big I am". I had a guy in the Seg like that. The only proper psychopath I think I ever met. He wanted to hurt people, not just kill them. He was CSC.'

Her experiences highlighted the need for extreme

67

caution and vigilance when dealing with CSC-designated inmates. It was something felt by the other prisoners too, as we discovered when talking to an ex-prisoner who recalled it well, and the impression it made:

'The CSU is a prison within another prison. It is completely isolated from the main jail in every way. Most offenders when entering HMP Belmarsh will be processed through the main reception, however the CSU, actually has its own reception on the unit. When you leave the airlock (main gate), the van would turn to the left for the main reception area. However, for the CSU the van turns right up an internal road to the far end of the prison. There you are met with a huge 20ft-plus wall and gate. When the gate is opened, an alarm sounds. The wall has a roller on the top, which makes it impossible to grip a rope, and there are touch censors and many CCTV cameras. After going through the first gate and this being closed, you are met with another gate and high fence with razor wire, bundles of it on the top of the fence. You are then driven through the second gate and then you enter the reception area. The reception area has its own body scanner, Boss Chair and scanner pole. A tall pole which offenders have to walk around.'

Even the staff are bespoke to this unit as another way for the Seg to establish that it means business. The ex-prisoner described the reception staff as 'doubled, all big lads. I cannot say for certain, but I am convinced these staff are chosen for this position based on their height and build. They are intimidating and do not engage in any conversation with you apart from the standard questions and communications relating to their duties.'

He recalled the segregation unit as being very clean, describing the units themselves – no more than 15 of them on the unit as being 'similar to those on the main wings, however the windows are smaller and slightly different. They have steel air vents whereas the windows on the wings open slightly; both windows on the CSU and the wings also have a steel cage on the outside wall over the window'. Not a place for the camera shy because you are constantly on film in the CSC, as the former inmate continued:

'There is a small association area, cameras everywhere, and you are watched 24 hours a day. Some cells even have cameras in the cell, with the toilet area being the only blind spot. I could not handle my time on this unit. At night-time I had to take all my clothes off and give them to staff; these were placed in a box and taken, and I was given prison-issue PJs to wear. My cell had a night light which was left on all night to enable them to see me. During the day, if you were an escape risk, or had previous, for escape endeavours, you were forced to wear patches, blue and bright yellow clothes. Your every move on this unit is written down and recorded in what they call the "yellow book", in other words, the exceptional high-risk book.'

The surveillance extends further than the 'yellow book' as well. While in the segregation unit on a daily basis you are visited by three people: the governor on his rounds, the chaplaincy on their rounds, and healthcare on their rounds. At separate times these people will come and check on you and ask if you are OK. Normally six prison officers will open your door, and the governor will simply ask, 'Are you OK?' and move on to the cell next door. There is a strict protocol for how these individuals are approached though, as we were told:

'You are not allowed to approach the entrance of the door when it is opened, and you are told to stand at the rear of the cell. However, in cases when staff have assaulted an offender, and the offender has visible bruising which staff do not want these visitors to see, they will place you on a non-communication status. They will just walk past your cell and not allow any person to speak with you. They do this all the time and deep down, the governors are aware of this practice but will simply ignore it. When I was in the segregation unit they did this to me. I never had any contact for three days until my bruising faded. It was my word against theirs. It is what it is and happens to this day in most prisons.'

In segregation you have to be ready for anything, and they are. One ex-prisoner assured me that 'there is nothing that segregation staff cannot deal with', in part likely because 'they are heavily staffed; when you are opened, there is a minimum of four staff'.

As always, protocol is determined with risk mitigation in mind:

'Depending on your status, for example if you are known for attacking staff, then you can be on an eight-man unlock. You are told the rules, keep walking, do not suddenly stop, do not even turn around and look at the officer behind you, keep your head down and just follow the orders. If you breach any of these then staff will with no warning just bend you up. This policy is set throughout most segregation units but HMP Belmarsh staff are brutal and have a lot of attitude. Bullies in my opinion. All massive lumps – they are also at Belmarsh, which I have not seen at other segregation units – wear protective clothing such as arm and shoulder protection pads, gloves and vests. They are always "kitted up" as we say.'

More than just the staff themselves, there are many special kinds of cells in the unit too, as explained by one ex-inmate below:

'Dry cell: A cell which is sealed, your toilet contents are checked, you are on CCTV 24 hours a day. These cells are used for offenders who conceal contraband within their backside. You will not be released from the dry cell until you have passed the contraband and your body scan is clear. The cells are a policy for all segregation units.

Padded cells: These are designed to stop self-harming. Anti-ligature vests are often placed on offenders. A body belt-type vest. Your arms strapped up, you are stripped prior of all your clothing and placed in these vest-type contraptions. I have seen one of these being used. They are derogatory.

Violence reduction cells: These are cells with a steel hatch on the door – they are used to feed the offender as staff cannot open them up due to their violent behaviour, and again, these cells are in all segregation units throughout the high-security estate.'

71

Even the bureaucracy differs from the paperwork on the wider prison estate, but it is possible to earn privileges.

'Within the Belmarsh segregation unit everything is done via application. Your rights in segregation conditions are as follows:

'A daily phone call for ten minutes.

'A daily shower for no longer than ten minutes.

'Daily exercise for a minimum of 20 minutes.'

These rights must be earned and, as an ex-inmate explained, you are given a slip the previous day, you simply tick which you require and then put it under your door for staff to collect. If you do not complete this application, then you will not receive any of these rights. This prisoner makes accusations against Belmarsh staff that we must stress are not substantiated by our own staff interactions.

He claims, however, that it is 'common for staff to lie and claim they received no slip and therefore you get nothing'. This kind of story is at odds with some of the misconceptions that are often aired in the media about Belmarsh and the lack of control of prison officers. It was something our ex-prisoner was keen to discuss, telling us that:

'When I see these ex-offenders going on television claiming they run HMP Belmarsh, that they have attacked many inmates and staff, I know for fact this is not true. Yes, they may have assaulted a member of staff, and yes, they may have attacked an inmate, but they are dealt with harshly and often beaten by the segregation staff at HMP Belmarsh, so they will not repeat this. HMP Belmarsh segregation unit is a high-security unit and part of the high-security estate. They are in full control of the segregation unit and the whole prison.'

Nowhere is this dominance more directly expressed than in the Seg, where keeping the inmates in line is a matter of life and death.

CHAPTER 10

Prison Life

'HMP Belmarsh is a brutal place, and every movement
around the jail is inside along long internal walkways.
Every move you make is monitored. It is run by staff who
set examples to instil fear into you. They have a saying:
treat them as you expect to be treated. If you keep your
head down, you will be left alone, but if you are rude then
they will target you. The Ministry of Justice will of course
never admit their prison is run on intimidation with a hard
line, but it is. To be fair to them, as much as I personally
am not a fan of Belmarsh, given the serious nature of some
of the offenders' offences, I guess it has to be run in a firm
and brutal fashion to keep good order and discipline.'

(FORMER INMATE)

We've explored the specific daily routine and rituals in the segregation unit, but what was the rhythm of a typical day in Belmarsh, if there even was such a thing?

When we asked Matthew about daily life, he started by describing how the day begins:

'The staff would go round of a morning and open the cell doors to let everyone out for their morning time out of their cell before they went off to work. Because the house block is split off into spurs, each would have their labour allocation board. So, you'd have a person's name and where they were reporting off to that morning. After the offenders have gone out, made their phone calls, had a shower etc., the landing staff would coordinate the movement off the wing so they would say, "Movement to labour," and you'd tick off and search the people that went off. To the house block, the remaining ones that were unemployed returned to their cells. Then the wing cleaners would come out and clean the wing.'

This led to a couple of hours 'where all those that were gainfully employed would be in workshops, education behavioural courses, visits'. This was the opportunity for staff to organise all the endless cleaning and catering.

'The wing operatives: the cleaners, the orderlies and stuff would be cleaning the house block and then the wing orderlies go and collect the lunchtime meal. You'd start by serving the meal to the ones on the house block; the ones that then would come back from morning movement, they would then collect their meals.'

We wondered to what degree this was a communal activity. Matthew indicated that this was not the norm, and in his view, this was the prisoners' choice.

'Although we had the facility for dining out where they could sit out and eat, most people chose to take their food back to their cells and eat within their cells. That's just comfort a lot of the time. Then it would be lunchtime lock-up, so everyone would be locked up while there was a roll check. Then the staff would have their lunch and then in the afternoon the same procedure again, where it would be unlocked for afternoon activities: work, social visits, other visits, behavioural courses, further cleaning, then back again for evening meal. Then, if it still goes on, it was called "evening association" when I was around.'

This involved the prisoners coming out of their cells for an evening spent on 'showers, phone calls, pool games'.

Matthew had referenced work, and certainly some prisoners are allowed to work at Belmarsh. As one ex-officer said, suggesting that this was one of the plus points of work: 'If they work, they can be out all day.'

When we asked him about the prisoners' jobs, Nik said that 'the best job was cleaning'. This was because 'they were out of their cells more than anyone else. They'd be let out first thing in the morning, locked up for lunch, then out again straight after'.

'Prisoners with skills could use them to their advantage,' Nik explained further. 'If they were good at something, they could get better jobs or favours. Those prisoners were usually safer because they were useful.'

Nik also draws out an interesting point about manipulation by prisoners here that we will revisit later in the book.

Another of our ex-prisoners, Mike, simply 'didn't want to be bothered' in his daily life.

'I was a high-risk prisoner so I couldn't share a cell,' but 'if you're on remand, you've got to share a cell.'

One contributor recalled that John Worboys, the 'Black

Cab Rapist', worked within the workshop constructing files, 'basically lever arch blank files to be later used within the medical industry'.

He indicated that when they were doing time there, 'jobs were limited. Education or the choice of one workshop'. VPs were given the task of pulling blank medical folders together, but he acknowledged that may have changed now. There was a broader offering for the general population.

'Main offenders have a wide choice at Belmarsh, from bricklaying to hobbies to making furniture.'

Mike observed that in his experience, some of the best prison jobs went to the worst people.

'The honour killing. The guy who put his daughter in a suitcase. He made tea for the prison officers at Belmarsh. Some multiple murderers, horrible human beings, get privileges like that.'

He's talking about the case of Mahmod Mahmod, who orchestrated the murder of his own daughter with accomplices including her uncle.

Two cousins of the victim, Mohammed Saleh Ali and Omar Hussain, and a third man, Mohamad Hama, were sentenced to life imprisonment in 2010 for the murder of Banaz Mahmod, a 20-year-old Iraqi Kurd from South London. Banaz was strangled in January 2006, and, as Mike references, her body was buried in a suitcase in an area of Birmingham.

Banaz's father, Mahmod Mahmod, and her uncle, Ari Mahmod, had been convicted in 2007 for orchestrating the murder, sentencing them to life imprisonment with minimum terms of 23 and 20 years. Judge Brian Barker described the killing as a 'barbaric and callous crime', stating that Banaz's father and uncle had decided she must die to restore 'family honour'. He condemned Ali and Hussain as 'hard and callous men' who willingly participated in an 'agonising death' and the shockingly disrespectful disposal of her body, which had lingered in Mike's memory.

Banaz was considered to have dishonoured her family by leaving an abusive marriage and beginning a relationship with Rahmat Sulemani. Before her death, she had informed police that her life was in danger and identified Hussain and Ali as those likely to kill her. After overhearing a phone call from her uncle plotting her murder, she reported her fears to the police. On New Year's Eve 2006, Banaz escaped an initial murder attempt by smashing a window. She recorded her fears on video in hospital, which was later used as evidence. However, an officer dismissed her claims as fantasy and even considered charging her with criminal damage. Following the murder, an Independent Police Complaints Commission report in 2008 found that Banaz had been failed by the police.

During his trial, covert recordings made while Hama was on remand at Belmarsh prison revealed chilling details of the crime. In these recordings, Hama recounted the brutal assault on Banaz, expressing a lack of remorse and even laughing about the violence inflicted upon her. He described how Banaz was subjected to degrading sexual acts and physical violence before being strangled to death. Hama's callousness during these taped conversations indicated a hideous mindset in which women were property and honour-based sadism and murder were legitimate. Committing this level of violence was commonplace among the prisoners at Belmarsh. Mike recalled another depraved murderer having a degree of responsibility in Belmarsh, too.

'The Colindale killer has a funny eye. He had a job giving out milk. He killed a woman on an allotment because he wanted to run the allotment.'

Mike is referring to Rahim Mohammadi. In February 2017, Lea Adri-Soejoko was found dead at the London allotments she was the secretary for. An 80-year-old widow, she had been beaten and then strangled with a lawnmower cable. On day one of the trial, the prosecution stated that the killer must also have been a tenant at Colindale allotments because they had a key to the padlock of the shed Mrs Adri-Soejoko was found in.

Mohammadi, a committee member of the allotments, had clashed with her in a meeting of the allotment's association months before, calling her a 'bloody old witch'; it was evident at this meeting that he, as Mike said, wanted to take over the running of the allotments. On the day of her murder, he beat her in another altercation and then, fearing she would report the assault, and he would lose his allotment plot, he murdered her. He denied murder but the jury unanimously disagreed with him, and he has served at least part of his 19-year sentence in Belmarsh.

A job giving out milk doesn't sound like vital work. Jonathan Aitken expressed some scepticism to us about the validity of prison jobs, while also describing his own experiences.

'Prison work was a joke: getting paid 80p for a day's work, putting washers on to something . . . it was pointless. By the time I got to Standford Hill, I became a wing cleaner and all sorts of things. I got quite savvy about prison jobs. But there's no real work, it's all just "make work".'

In a presaging of his future calling as a prison chaplain, Jonathan became involved in more informal work too, which he described in his trademark humorous and humane fashion.

'People kept coming up to me asking for help. They'd hand me their papers to read or ask me to write messages to their girlfriends.

'Some of these messages were very explicit! "Would you mind telling her that I'm longing to fuck her a different way?" You know, endless.'

What really struck Jonathan was their vulnerability, though:

'Many were completely messed up. One guy, I found out, should have been released already, but nobody had told him. "Your release date passed four days ago. Go and take this," I said. "Are you kidding?" he replied. "No, I'm not." All the time, I felt like I was on the funny farm, yet at the same time, people confided in me. "Do you think my wife will ever let me back?" or "How will I ever lift up my head again?" I was a middle-class bloke, and there was a lot of agony-aunt-ing. But I did feel I was being of some use.'

In many other prisons we have researched, the inmates are keen to use the gym and exercise yard, as some break from the monotony as well as for physical fitness. One ex-inmate of several prisons described the exercise yard at Belmarsh to us in the following terms:

'The exercise yards are small and secure, nowhere near the boundary fence. No spur mixes with another spur on exercise. The surrounding fence and wall are huge with razor wire running around the top, CCTV watching your every move. If you stop and bend down to pick something up off the floor you are challenged there and then this is a regular occurrence at HMP Belmarsh.'

This partly indicates a vigilance about contraband and anything that might have made its way over the fence, however unlikely that is. The contributor continued to describe more security methods and even a security mantra.

'This is even after the exercise yard was previously checked and searched by staff prior to the inmates even going out on the yard. I guess a testament to their paranoid security measures. There are posters on the walls throughout the prison warning staff. They state, "Believe nothing, check everything, keep calm and carry on".'

These motivational slogans on the walls sounded like reasonable suggestions to survive Belmarsh.

'The exercise yard is unreal. You cannot see anything but a huge wall, and you feel like you're in a compound.

There are no fences, just a huge wall, maybe 50 feet high, I've never seen anything like it. You are watched constantly from observation points. A steel cage over the top.'

He was able to enrich the description with some other details, too. There is 'a phone on the yard; it is in a small quad with the building going around it; it has exercise tools on it, built in, a stepper made from poles not electric, a garden in the middle, and you can walk around it. OPs will be given exercise while all the other offenders are locked up.'

According to Caroline, 'Some people would turn down exercise.' For the same reason, others avoided the dinner plate.

'Prisoners who felt threatened would not go to the dinner plate. Some prisoners would refuse to lock up and would go into their mate's cell.'

Colin found it hard to articulate anything of note about these mundane features of prison life.

'How did I survive prison? I never carried a knife. I never had a weapon on me at all. I'd seen prison life for what it was. I knew all kinds of people. Some were really good, some were much worse. But I knew that if I ever touched a gun, that was a line I'd never come back from. Somehow, I managed to stay on the right side of that line.'

Colin reiterated to us several times that he survived four decades in and out of prison life by keeping his head down. He recollected it as a life of monotony and claustrophobia and said that it was 'hard to describe prison life because it's so breathless, soulless. You walk in circles during exercise, looking around at the same grey walls. There's nothing to say about it'.

Unlike others who valued an hour outside, Colin didn't like yet another version of being trapped in a space.

'There was an indoor gym, but I never used it. The problem is, if you go to exercise, you're locked out for an hour. So, I just stayed inside.'

In addition to the exercise yard, we always want to know about the prison food. For Colin, it was as bland and grim as the exercise facilities.

'Prison food? It's exactly what you'd expect. You've been around the block, you know. It's standard, the same wherever you go.'

Another former inmate echoed this, stating that it was the same as other prisons in his experience.

'Cold meal at lunch, except Friday and Saturday, Friday fish and chips, Saturday brunch, sausage or bacon, tomatoes, fried bread and a hard-boiled egg. You have about five menu options, you just tick the box, and they scan it and each day you get the meal you chose. You complete the menus at Belmarsh two weeks in advance.'

Jonathan Aitken lacked fond memories of the prison food.

'At Belmarsh, I mean, time just stands still, but food was produced, and it didn't seem too bad. It was a sort of macaroni cheese or something.' The next meal, however, was slightly more disappointing.

'I wasn't hungry, but I knew I needed food, and then the first breakfast was pretty disgusting, a plastic bag, which contained some cornflakes and a small bag of milk. I think a teabag. Maybe an apple or something like that. It's breakfast, but I gratefully ate the apple, so I didn't feel as though I was hungry.'

One former officer told us:

'The food looks OK. I haven't eaten in. They serve two hot meals at weekends, one hot meal Monday to Friday. Rice, curry, burgers. Things like that. At weekends you might have a pasty or jacket potatoes. Breakfast is just a small bag of Rice Krispies.'

Nik, another former officer, was slightly less enthusiastic.

'The food was grim, but sometimes we ate it. Some of the curries were actually OK.'

He explained that all the food in Belmarsh was halal due to cross-contamination concerns.

But Nik also recalled a Jewish prisoner who was kept in segregation, who got special kosher food delivered every couple of weeks, 'a special pack. He was very clean, but he was a proper psychopath, the type that will never see daylight again.'

As we found with HMP Wakefield, they do put on a slightly special menu at Belmarsh for Christmas Day. Options in previous years have included chicken breast, turkey, fish fillets cooked with prawns and chilli butter and for vegetarians, a Quorn roast. Sides and trimming were also out of the ordinary, with pigs in blankets (sausages wrapped in bacon), roast potatoes, carrots, Brussels sprouts, parsnips, sage and onion stuffing and gravy.

The teatime Christmas treats have been a little bit more

basic, including a festive turkey slice, instant noodles or vegan sausage rolls. They do all come, however, with a mince pie and spiced flapjack.

We have been told that in other ways, though, Christmas Day is like any other at Belmarsh. No visitors are allowed, so there is often a bit of a rush on Christmas Eve and Boxing Day. This is down to the practical issue of staff shortages and seems to be common to all UK prisons. It doesn't look too festive either. There are some cards on the walls, but when anything plastic or glass could be converted into a sharp object and weaponised or used for self-harm, baubles are out.

It's possible that self-harm and attacks could spike at Christmas too, with miserable prisoners excluded from the festivities and fewer staff around to guard and watch over them. There is some solace offered in religious services.

The religious facilities at Belmarsh are generally regarded with positivity, working well with all faiths, when referenced by our contributors. The chaplaincy department includes a chapel, which doubles up for Christian and Muslim worship, and a small multi-faith room. This is also used as a classroom. There are four full-time chaplains, two Christian and two Muslim, and some sessional chaplains. The duty chaplain sees all new arrivals at Belmarsh the day after their reception. From what we have heard about their arrival to Belmarsh, they would probably be crying out for some spiritual support at that point.

The dates and times of the religious services are

advertised on each house block and conducted simultaneously in the HSU. Prisoners in the special secure unit
(SSU) get slightly different treatment, though. They are
not offered weekly worship, and they are not seen routinely
by the duty chaplain. Instead, they are seen on application
to the chaplaincy.

Going well beyond services, the chaplaincy team also
offers a whole bunch of classes. The Islamic awareness
session is open to all faiths and is particularly highly
regarded by many prisoners, because it is inclusive and
insightful.

These activities aside, most of the time in Belmarsh
is spent within the cells. We were given a comprehensive
account of their interior, with the details corroborated by
other reports.

'On each side there are rows of cells. On one side the
cells are three-man cells; on the other side all the cells are
single cells. The three-man cells normally hold the lower-
category offenders, namely Category B offenders who are
forced to share, while the single cells hold the Category A
offenders. Within the three-man cells there is one set of
bunk beds and one single bed, a partitioned-off toilet for
privacy, a TV and a phone. The living arrangements are
quite small, with no real space within them. Not fit for
purpose and overcrowded.'

The beds themselves sounded utilitarian and horrible,
the 'beds as with all prison beds consist of steel piping
which is bolted to the floor, and steel struts interwoven
which act as a base. The mattress is made from black fire-

resistant foam, which is sealed within a blue plastic non-removable cover; they are very thin and the pillows are made using the same materials. The single cells are fitted with the same beds but no partitioned toilet. The dividing walls are reinforced concrete and again, painted magnolia. The flooring is hard non-removable lino. The heating as with all prisons is a pipe which runs through all the cells, again not fit for purpose.'

This did not sound like much of a dream bedroom. Nik had painted a similarly grim picture from a prison officer's perspective, too, explaining that the living arrangements in Belmarsh vary based on a prisoner's category and the available space: 'There are single cells, but you also have three-man cells.' Category A prisoners will be on their own, but some inmates are in shared cells. These can be either two-man or three-man cells.'

Despite pointing out that he wouldn't want to share a cell if he was a prisoner, Nik said that 'some people are more than happy to share, especially if they are with mates or gang mates'. He added that 'the shared cells aren't much bigger than a single one, as you get a single bed and one bunk bed.' They are not proportionately bigger, so it's cramped. Imagine three men sharing one toilet in the same room; 'It's not pleasant,' Nik concluded.

Perhaps this is as good a point as any to describe how the toilet experience can get even more unpleasant. One ex-Belmarsh inmate laid it out for us, initially framing it blandly in terms of 'damage to cells'.

'Belmarsh run a policy (as do other prisons) where

if an offender causes damage to a cell then they will be held accountable to pay a financial penalty, namely the full cost of replacement or repair. If the offender has no financial means, then an order will be placed on his prison account to retrieve the outstanding monies, and if family send in money for the offender, the prison will simply take this, [or if they get] prison wages, the prison will take weekly deductions from the prison wage. This has reduced damage significantly within prisons. HMP Belmarsh were the frontrunners in implicating this now national policy.'

However, in his typically graphic style, he swiftly moved on, surmising that we would no doubt have heard of dirty protest, or as offenders call it, 'shit up'. We certainly had, but we were curious to learn more about why it happened, and the consequences.

'Offenders use this as a tool to frustrate staff since the rules of paying for the damage came into force. Firstly, offenders are fully aware that should they "shit up" (excuse the term), then to punish them staff will use health and safety laws.'

We were starting to see a strange power dynamic, that blend of the prison exerting control and prisoner manipulation, even in this basic and usually private bodily function.

'Staff will remove all the offender's property from the cell, even if it is not contaminated, and destroy the property. This can be your stereo, DVD player and all your clothes. However, offenders within the system are fully aware of this and act prior to avoid this.'

As always, awareness and observation can lead prisoners to some very ingenious solutions.

'The normal process in Belmarsh, and any other prison, is to self-pack all your personal property prior and ask for it to be placed in your stored property in reception. You pack up everything. This is a prison policy that any offender can do; it is a right. The offender will then be issued with prison issue clothes to wear. Only after all the offender's property has been removed from their cell will they then shit up.'

Once again reading our minds, he said, 'You may ask why on earth do they do this?' The answer was intriguing.

'Prison cells within the segregation unit are limited. They are needed. The moment an inmate starts a dirty protest, the officers know by law the offender must be moved to a clean cell. The staff cannot simply leave the offender in a dirty cell. Staff must kit up in PPE, white boiler suits and other protected clothing to move the offender. Then the cell has to be biohazard cleaned. The offender will simply shit up the next cell, and so this will continue.'

It's clear that this behaviour can cause very significant disruption.

'The offender on the dirty protest is simply taking out usable cells, often three in one day. When spaces are limited within the segregation unit this can cause staff all sorts of problems. It is a headache for them. Offenders learn quickly and they realise that smashing up a cell also gets them moved to another cell, but they are held accountable for the repair fees. However, a dirty protest creates the same problem for staff but there is no financial cost to the offender.'

It would take a lot of cash to sweeten this pill for us, but the ex-inmate described a silver lining to this for those cleaning it up. 'While it is a headache for staff, staff receive a paid bonus for this. They receive extra pay when dealing with a frequent dirty protest.'

He had heard of prisons having 'serial dirty protest offenders' too.

'Staff were given a monthly allowance of extra pay for this. So those are the reasons a dirty protest can happen within prisons.'

This was something we had to get the staff's take on. Caroline had told us she'd known of dirty protests but had not, we were pleased to hear, been involved in the clean-up.

As for Nik, dirty protests were another grim reality. His account made this clear, as well as corroborating many elements of the ex-inmate's narrative.

'You get special cleaners for that who are trained up. That would be quite good because they got paid a lot of money for it.'

Nik added that, 'From my point of view, as inhumane as it might sound, sometimes we wanted them to be at the dirty protest for as long as they could, because you get extra money for enduring the conditions.'

Although he did say that 'I wouldn't have said it was encouraged. Especially in the segregation, because they need to be willing to get off the dirty protest for you to open the cell.' As the special cells in segregation 'have hutches in the door, to deliver food to them, technically as long as they're not willing to get off the dirty protest, you do not open the cell, so they are not let out at all'.

Returning to less revolting ground, we had heard conflicting accounts about the windows at Belmarsh and were keen to learn more about them. One source had a highly detailed memory of the windows, saying they had 'no real views but high 20ft walls and 20ft reinforced steel fences with barbed razor wire. The windows are small, and there is no glass but reinforced thick plastic with bars running through them. The bars are not rounded but thick 3-inch square steel hollow bars. A unique and clever design'.

The design seemed strange but intentional considering that, 'within these hollow bars are a separate steel rotating bar. This is to make it impossible for any person to cut through the bars using a hacksaw. If you were in a position to get a hacksaw, which I suggest is impossible, then even if you cut through part of the 3-inch square bar then you would hit the rotating steel inner bar, and given it would rotate, the hacksaw blade would never get a grip of the inner rotating bar'.

As the source went on to explain, the cunning window design forms part of a much wider security-dedicated ecosystem:

'The design of HMP Belmarsh has catered for all possible security breaches. None of the house blocks are located near any outer boundary walls. Indeed, if a person was to shout from the outside, the house blocks are so far in the centre of the prison it would be impossible to hear them. The design of the open plan but secure house blocks are all interconnecting by way of connecting landings from each spur through gates and steel platforms.'

As he and others have described it, every detail of the cells is meticulously geared up for security too.

'Belmarsh has left nothing to chance when it comes to security. The televisions are see-through. The backing is clear plastic, you can see all the insides. This makes it impossible to hide anything within your television as staff, when doing their daily cell checks, can simply see all the insides of the television. The light switches are steel, bolted to the wall using rivets, no screw heads; even with this there are still security labels stuck over the edges. The lights are sealed into the ceiling with solid thick reinforced clear plastic, unbreakable. The toilet flush system is in an external space, locked; the flush is simply a steel button in the wall. The sink and taps are sealed into the wall. The plug sockets are in steel boxes and sealed into the wall, and even the plugs used for the kettle and TV are sealed, so no fuse access or screws to take them apart.'

Former staff member Nik stated that it is 'definitely regimented', but added that this regime is 'quite purposeful'. Nik explained that the prisoners' routines and daily life are tightly controlled. Of course, even in a prison operating with such strict security and controls, a major curveball can get thrown in, like a global pandemic. Covid changed the prison regime, although in Nik's view there was a silver lining.

'Initially, it was a mess, but once we structured it, everything ran smoother. There was less violence, less bullying. Even the prisoners liked it because it was calmer.'

Phil Ashford, however, on his visits found that 'It was horrific. I went round to speak with guys interested in our income-in-cell programme, but all the wings were shut off. Everyone was locked up 23–24 hours a day. Oppressive. Must've been horrendous for staff too. No life. Free flow was gone. A quiet, desperate, sad atmosphere. Covid was bad enough for anyone, let alone in prison.'

Having worked his way up the ranks from a front-line officer to a non-operational Grade Seven before leaving in 2020, Matthew ultimately found himself in a role detached from the realities of prison life. The pathways to senior operational roles, such as governor positions, were well structured, with various courses and exams available. However, non-prison-focused career progression was limited. He was also keenly aware of the unique challenges of managing a prison during times of crisis:

'I was glad to get out before Covid. Even when there's just a bug circulating, it's incredibly difficult in a prison environment because there are so many older prisoners. Something like a global pandemic would be exceptionally difficult to manage.'

As one former inmate noted, even the visitor car park is locked down at Belmarsh.

'HMP Belmarsh has a small road which runs along the outside wall, this allows HMP Belmarsh staff to patrol this 24 hours a day using a small white dog van. The huge car park for visitors is watched constantly by CCTV operators for any suspicious activity. The car park is Crown property. Simply sitting in your vehicle in the car park for a long period will attract attention and possible arrest if you have no reason to be in the car park.'

No use trying to pose as a workman or contractor to gain access or smuggle contraband, either.

'Even workmen or contractors that enter the establishment are Home Office-approved contractors. All employees having been security-vetted. Even with these vigorous security measures, upon entering the prison they too are escorted at all times by OSG staff.'

We were keen to understand more about the OSG staff and the extent of their powers.

'OSG staff are there to support the prison officers. The censors' department are run by OSG staff who are supervised by a custody manager (CM). A CM is a prison officer and one grade down from a governor. I will address governors and their positions later. Censors' duties are to censor the incoming and outgoing mail. They also listen to all the telephone calls which are recorded. Censors' staff duties are to translate codes or any unusual behaviour. Upon identifying an issue, they will write up an IR, which stands for information received. This is a short report on the offender's communication, and it is passed to the prison security department. Security will then evaluate the intelligence and decide on what action to take, if any.'

The picture that emerges is one of a highly controlled

and deeply challenging environment, made even more difficult during the Covid-19 pandemic. From the oppressive atmosphere of near-constant lockdown to the intense surveillance and strict security protocols extending beyond the prison walls, containment, isolation and control shape daily life.

CHAPTER II

House Blocks and Vulnerable Prisoners

'There's a separate spur on one of the house blocks,
a bit isolated, where the VPs group together.
They're definitely weirder, but some of them were
just as violent as the others.'

(NIK)

C ombined testimony from all our contributors was able
to provide us with a rich picture of life on the house
blocks, including the notorious house block 4, which
houses the sex offenders, and which has space for up to
171 men. The other three house blocks can accommodate
up to 174 prisoners.

House block 1 is quite a mix. We were surprised that
older prisoners and mixed population were grouped in
with those on a life sentence. House block 2 also has mixed
population as well as those on remand and short sentences.
House block 3 houses remand prisoners, as well as being
where men spend their first night. House block 4 is the
vulnerable prisoners (VPs) spur and mixed population.

That first night is an unforgettable experience for every prisoner, after all the introductory rituals and ordeals are over. On their first night, all incoming prisoners are given a first night kit, which includes basic toiletries like a comb, shower gel and body wash.

Nik explained how 'the high-profile prisoners are kept separate from the general population'. He outlines the challenges for the reception staff who decide where to place each prisoner. He talked us through the process as 'they go to a first night centre, which is in House Block 3' and then it is decided where they should be placed. Nik added that 'if they can't make the decision themselves, the staff will talk to governors to plan how they're going to deal with it.'

We asked one former Belmarsh prisoner to explain the structure of the prison, so we could get a better feel for the rhythm of the place and how the prison complex was structured.

'HMP Belmarsh has only four house blocks and the CSU. The house blocks as they are called are house blocks 1, 2, 3 and 4. Each house block has three spurs. Spur 1, 2 and 3. Each spur is separated and secure from each other. Offenders cannot simply walk from one spur to another as they are separated using steel bars, floor to ceiling, with access being gained using the various steel-barred gates. There are no walls separating the spurs, just bars. There is a small centre space which has visual sighting into all the spurs. The open but secure plan is designed for maximum observations by staff. Staff can stand in the centre and observe the whole house block. A very clever design.'

This did sound very clever indeed, and with, as always, security and control front of mind, but how did each house block's population break down into spurs and cells?

'Each spur holds around 90 offenders. In total around 270 inmates to each house block. Each spur has three landings. However, the design is such that the distance from the 3's landing to the ground-floor landing is not a great distance. Not too high up. Each house block is identical. Each spur is very small and compact; they are not huge, long landings. The width I would estimate is no more than 20ft. This is a rough estimate, but the spurs are very small. The length of each spur is no more than 150ft. This is the landing area and does not include the cell space. There is a very small centre iron stairwell at one end; the far end as you walk on, it only has two sets of small stairs. These are painted brown, with all the walls being magnolia in colour, very bland and depressing. Very commercial.'

He continued by giving us a vivid account of the supervised movement.

'Inside HMP Belmarsh, the whole of any movement area inside the prison is inside. There are no areas outside in which an inmate can walk unless supervised by staff and a dog (Zulu One) escort. It is all long, 8ft-wide internal walkways. There are a lot of sealed barred windows so there is a lot of daylight but no fresh air. As you walk along these long walkways, there are little signs for directions.

HCC (Health Care Centre) this way, the Segregation Unit this way with a little arrow, House Blocks 1–2 this way, House Blocks 3–4 that way, Video Link, reception, workshops and so on. All internal walkways with signs.'

He told us that 'there are two types of moves, free flow and radio clearance moves'. To explain this further, he gave an example:

'During a normal day, those offenders on remand or convicted will have to engage in some purposeful activity, work or education. There are set free flow times. All the residential house blocks except house block 4 spur 3 (VP – sex offenders) will walk freely down these walkways to their place of work. These walkways are not manned by staff because CCTV covers all the movements. It is impossible for any person to go missing as the walkways are very secure and monitored by high-tech CCTV.'

This all sounded seamless, but our contributor was quick to point out that issues could certainly arise during this movement, no matter how carefully orchestrated.

'For a high-security prison this is rare; however, violence is an issue while these moves are taking place. Black gun crime and gangs is a huge issue in London. On these free flow moves, violence occurs due to different gang members passing while going to work. The violence is not serious, mainly punching and assaulting each other. The CCTV controller will alert an alarm bell, which is direct to all officers' radios within the prison. The time response is very quick, and it is often dealt with in minutes.'

It was revealing that this individual is so hardened that

he didn't consider gang members punching and assaulting each other on their way to work to be serious violence!

Caroline started her career at Belmarsh on house block 4 with the sex offenders. As she explained it, VPs are people who have committed crimes that mean they can't associate with the rest of the prison.

She was keen to point out that this classification allowed for a broader cohort than sex offenders; it was more anyone who needed to be kept separate for their own good as well as that of others. An ex-Belmarsh prisoner made the same point and expanded on who the other categories beyond sex offenders could be.

'VPs will be escorted to their place of work after the main moves, whether it be Healthcare, visits or other, they are always moved separately. A radio call to the controller, "Permission to move ten from house block 4 spur 3 to workshop," the call will come back yes or no. VP wings are not all sex offenders, many other types can be held on these units, ex-police officers, supergrasses and people from organised crime with a contract on their head. We simply use the term VP (Vulnerable Prisoner).'

This same ex-prisoner also had recollections of John Worboys, known as the Black Cab Rapist 'who subsequently changed his name to John Radford'.

'When he first came on to house block 4 spur 3 (VP) he was lost, and he looked shaken, frightened. I am very full-on and can be very confident and forward with people. I went straight up to him and said, "Are you the black cab man?" I said, "I do not judge, I'm in no position to judge."'

Indeed, he felt not only a lack of judgement but active sympathy.

'I helped him as I felt sorry for him. He is what I call a straight runner, not a criminal but a sexual deviant. These people have never had a fight or dealt with real criminals. He kept himself to himself, but he later opened up to me. He was constantly asking about DNA, and it later transpired that there was DNA in his case, hence him asking me. John Worboys was a standard escape risk Category A offender. He was wealthy, with properties in Bournemouth, Hertfordshire and London. He was no trouble at HMP Belmarsh and very polite to staff and his peers.'

In Caroline's experience, VPs are calmer than the general prison population, which aligns with this appraisal of Worboys, stating, 'They needed you more than you needed them. Some of them felt entitled, but that's a prisoner thing.'

Yet even so, Caroline declared that she preferred the general population. 'They could be a bit rowdy, but . . .' Though she left the sentence unfinished, what she implied was that the manipulative, sometimes disturbing behaviour of the VPs left her willing to swap the relative peace and quiet of the VP wing for the raucous, larger cohort in the rest of the prison.

There are, though, clear restrictions to being a VP in prison. The prison service operates a scheme called accumulated visits. Under the scheme you can apply to move temporarily to a prison nearer to your family to allow them to visit you more easily, including visits to VPs. One ex-inmate explained more, particularly about the restrictions around visits for VPs.

'VP visits at Belmarsh are set days, Tuesdays and Saturday mornings. However, non-VPs, or mainstream prisoners, can have visits daily. VP visits are Tuesdays and Saturdays, non-VPs every day in the afternoon.'

One contributor, however – Mike – expressed scepticism about the effectiveness of the separation of VPs, and suggested, which cannot be verified, that there was corruption involved:

'There are so many paedophiles and sex offenders mixed in with the general population now. They do it by giving them different paperwork, so it is not so easy to identify them and what they did.'

Prison inspection reports raised some different concerns when they delved into whether different house blocks received different treatment, with one noting that 'perceptions of prisoners on house block 3 about the quality of their relationships with staff were starkly worse across a range of indicators.'

Worryingly, a significantly lower number of Muslim and of black and minority ethnic and foreign national respondents than white respondents said that they had a member of staff they felt they could turn to if they had a problem. While specialist staff were found to engage positively and tried to be visible on house blocks, others stuck narrowly to their demarcated roles and went no further. The report stated that:

'Prisoners felt relationships with staff were largely functional. They had confidence that staff would tackle inappropriate behaviour but that they were not always helpful towards prisoners.'

These apparent disparities in treatment reveal the unevenness of care and oversight within the general population of the prison. Against this backdrop, the Health Care Centre stands out as a distinct and heavily scrutinised environment, where medical and security demands converge.

CHAPTER 12

HCC: The Healthcare Centre

'The healthcare units are full of suicide watches,
inmates with severe mental health disorders, violent
and other serious aggressive issues.'

(FORMER INMATE)

The healthcare unit at Belmarsh is a high-security medical facility providing care for prisoners with physical and mental health needs. It includes inpatient beds, primary care, mental health services, substance misuse treatment and specialist clinics. Its staff composition includes nurses, doctors, psychiatrists and healthcare assistants. As always in Belmarsh, security is stringent, with controlled access and constant monitoring. Mental health care is a key focus, addressing conditions like schizophrenia and PTSD. The unit also manages chronic illnesses, conducts suicide prevention interventions and provides emergency medical response within the prison.

The unit is small and structured to facilitate close observation of inmates, as one contributor recalled:

'Belmarsh HCC has two small wards. These hold about eight offenders, and it is open-plan, eight beds. There are not many offenders who are actually in poor medical health, and it is mainly for mental health issues. The windows are large, made from Perspex, which enable staff to observe inside the ward. Indeed, directly opposite the ward is a staffroom from which the offenders within the ward are observed 24 hours a day. Next to the ward is an association room, some nice chairs and table, a small pool table and lots of books available to read. The cells are located on the other side of this small unit. The OP (Own Protection) area is at the rear of the HCC unit. It is kept clean, a huge space which is gated off with bars and an entrance gate from the rest of healthcare. Staff on the HCC unit are encouraged to engage with the offenders.'

Inmates housed in the healthcare unit have access to a limited exercise area, offering a degree of movement within a controlled space.

'There is a small exercise yard which has outside exercise machines that are fixed to the ground. It even has a small phone booth outside on the yard. While the unit is small, it does have two levels. There are cells upstairs. These look out on to the exercise yard.'

The healthcare unit is also used to house high-profile inmates who require isolation from the general prison population.

'The killer of James Bulger, [Jon] Venables, was located there when I was there. He was two cells down. He was a troublesome and needy offender who self-harmed on a regular basis, shouting and being obstructive with staff. He was not allowed out to mix with other offenders when he was located there. I never actually saw him personally but could hear his obstructive behaviour, and his shouting and demanding character. Everyone knew who he was, even with his new name. He was considered violent to staff and inmates. He is a real problem for staff and very needy and seeks a lot of attention from staff.'

Other notorious inmates have also been housed in the isolation unit within the healthcare facility. The same ex-inmate told us that both Wayne Couzens and Ian Huntley 'were held on the special isolation unit located in the healthcare unit at HMP Belmarsh'.

So, as we have seen, placement in the healthcare unit can occur for various reasons, from medical necessity to protective custody.

One of our contributors claimed to us that he once refused to locate on the VP so the governor placed him on OP status, causing him to enter the Own Protection Unit within the Healthcare unit. Caroline told us that 'old prisoners who can't look after themselves are put in Healthcare too'.

Ex-inmate Colin ran into another famous face when he was in there, the one and only Jonathan Aitken. 'I think I was probably one of the first prisoners he spoke to, and he was the first person I spoke to when I got there. It wasn't the same van from the Old Bailey, but pretty much. He came in and went straight to the hospital wing. He was put there at first because they were worried he might hurt himself, but he immediately put in a request to go to the main wing. I was in the hospital unit because I had just been arrested and sent back to prison. I had self-harmed as a coping mechanism. I had cut down my arm. A five-inch gash, so they put me in the hospital unit.'

Colin had a very troubled background. How he ended up in Belmarsh is a hell of a story in itself. Often struggling with his emotions and pausing to collect his thoughts, he managed to narrate his life experiences.

'I came from a good working-class family: Mum, Dad, two brothers, two sisters. When I was 11, I passed the 11-plus and got into grammar school. My birthday is 25 August 1955, so I was the youngest in my class. English grammar school in 1968 was very Victorian. Masters in black capes. Being the youngest and from a working-class background, I didn't fit in. My parents struggled with five kids, both working full-time, Mum doing two jobs. Within six months, I was getting the cane. My older brothers had turbulent adolescences, but we were good kids.'

Jonathan Aitken had already told us how bright Colin was. Today, you would hope that he would be moved to a more suitable school, but things were very different in the late 1960s.

'By 13, I was uncontrollable. I ended up in care for a couple of years. At 15, I got a job as a bench mechanic but couldn't manage the college part. Then my mum got cancer and died when I was nearly 16. She was 37. My dad died of a heart attack a year later. Five kids, no parents.'

In a tragic but all too comprehensible downward spiral,

Colin turned to substance misuse after these unimaginable bereavements.

'Then came heroin, crime, in and out of prison. A lot of people died. My brother took a hammer to the head; he was paralysed down one side and shut away in hospital for 35 years. We all struggled with addiction. I tried rehab, got clean for a couple of years, relapsed, then went back into rehab. I did well but then relapsed again. At the age of 50, I was with Sandy. She was also a heroin addict. She'd had an awful childhood, she was heavily addicted and was a prostitute. Her daughter had basically raised herself.'

Although Sandy was to begin his path to better times, fate still had more in store for him.

'At 50, I was fucked up. I got pancreatic cancer. I had a Whipple procedure. They are usually unsuccessful, but mine wasn't. Ten days later, I was out of hospital. A couple of months later, I quit heroin. Detoxed. Then Sandy detoxed. Sandy got pregnant. Now we have two kids. We moved to Somerset. Now they're 18, in college. My son's doing an apprenticeship and my daughter's doing A-levels. My wife and I have been on this journey 20 years now.'

It was both unbelievable and heart-warming to hear that Colin's story had a happy ending. He clarified, though, how he ended up in the institution we had met to discuss.

It was particularly welcome to hear a good news story when more recent news tends towards the negative. When we spoke to her, former prison governor Vanessa had told us that violence on staff in prisons was up 19 per cent in the last year. At HMP Parc, where there has been a spike of drug-related prisoner deaths, she said, 'About 30 per cent of the prisoners are on drugs. More prisoners come out of there doing drugs than went in.' She sees this as part of a much wider set of issues:

'Lots of prisoners have not had access to rehabilitation. Do we want to lock up pregnant women and drug addicts for non-violent crimes? Look at the Ministry of Justice safety in custody statistics. They state nearly 10,500 assaults on staff. There's more violence, more drugs, bullying, debtors and dealing. There is more violence because there are young, inexperienced staff who don't know how to deal with all of this. Overcrowding doesn't help.'

This, depressingly, would seem to suggest a deterioration in conditions since Colin's day. Although the road was marked by hardship, his journey remains a powerful reminder that rehabilitation is possible, even after the darkest of times. His story offers hope – not just for prisoners, but for families and futures rebuilt through resilience, recovery and support.

'So, back to Belmarsh. During one of my relapses, just before the cancer, in 1999, I was on the run from prison. I was meant to be serving five years. I ended up in an open prison. I absconded. Back on the street, using again. It was an unbelievably tough time for me and Sandy.' His propensity for absconding was what ultimately led him to Belmarsh.

His return to custody meant he experienced first-hand the healthcare provision at Belmarsh. While Colin appreciated the care he received during his time there, concerns about the overall quality of medical services remain among many inmates. Mike told us that 'the healthcare system at Belmarsh is terrible. You could be looking at a two-year wait for a cracked tooth. I knew of a guy in Belmarsh who died of appendicitis.'

The former part of Mike's statement appears to be substantiated by a 2024 report on an unannounced inspection of Belmarsh. The report found that the quality of some healthcare records did not clearly set out the care journey for prisoners, leaving gaps in essential information. Not all patients with ongoing care needs had a comprehensive care plan in place, which was a significant concern. This lack of proper documentation and planning was not in line with professional standards and posed considerable risks to the health and wellbeing of the prisoners. The report noted that there was a disparity in care, an uneven provision which was unacceptable.

Those in the high-security unit, particularly Category A prisoners, experienced delays and unfair access to medical services compared with other inmates. For example, there was a 17-week delay for Category A prisoners in the unit to access dental treatment, in contrast to the much quicker access available to prisoners in other areas. Additionally, two referrals for Category A prisoners had been cancelled in recent months, further highlighting the disparity in the provision of medical care.

According to one former 'patient', and again aligning with the views of others, rather than a conventional medical ward, the healthcare unit primarily houses inmates experiencing severe mental health crises, including those at risk of self-harm or suicide.

'Prison healthcare units are not what you would imagine; you would think such places are a hospital for the sick, unwell people. The truth is only 10 per cent of the population are made up of ill people. This is throughout the prison system. The healthcare units are full of suicide watches, inmates with severe mental health disorders, violent and other serious aggressive issues.'

While the 'mentally deranged' and violent offenders posed a risk to others, the 'suicide watches', known as 'constant watches', posed a risk to themselves.

The Own Protection (OP) unit within healthcare is a distinct area offering a higher level of security and isolation for inmates requiring protection. As one former visitor explained, in Own Protection, the vibe is different from the rest of the healthcare unit once again:

'The OP unit is on the Healthcare Unit but is separated from the main Healthcare Unit. There is a whole spacious part dedicated to the OP part, and it's very nice. It has a shower room with a bath, a cell with TV, even its own exercise yard where no other offender can see you. In short, you do not come into any contact at all, not visually, nothing. No contact with any other offender. You are free to walk out of your cell to bath or shower; it was quite nice. Your cell is at the end of the unit, the shower and bathroom are next to the cell, and there is a large open-plan area. It was very clean with polished floors. I really liked it there.'

Notably, high-profile offenders often find themselves housed in this unit, where special arrangements are made for their security and interaction with others is strictly limited.

'Huntley and Couzens were held on this unit alone, although Huntley was eventually moved to a mental hospital for assessments, then on to HMP Woodhill. I have spoken to both Couzens and Huntley, and there is no doubt they were on this unit. They knew exactly where it was. Officers would often come and play board games with them and cards. Julian Assange was also held on this unit for years until his release. The unit is designed for high-profile cases in which the offenders are at extreme risk of harm from other inmates.'

Former prison officer Jo 'only saw Huntley once. He was transferred to Frankland not long after I arrived.' His physical appearance and demeanour gave no clue as to what he was capable of. While working as a school caretaker in Soham, Cambridgeshire, in August 2002, he abducted and murdered two ten-year-old school friends, Holly Wells and Jessica Chapman. On 4 August, Huntley, manipulating his role as the caretaker at the local secondary school, Soham Village College, apparently lured the girls into his house by claiming that his girlfriend Maxine Carr, who was the two girls' Year 5 teaching assistant at St Andrews Primary School, was also at home, whereas in fact she was visiting her mother in Grimsby. The girls' bodies were discovered in a ditch in Suffolk on 17 August 2002.

Huntley had a long history of violence and sexual

assault, targeting women and children between 1992 and 2002 without ever being brought to justice. He used the alias Ian Nixon when he successfully applied for the senior caretaker position at the college, and no background checks were conducted on him. Soon after his sentencing, Huntley stated of the decades in prison ahead of him:

'I'll rot in here, I know it. I'll spend the rest of my life in here . . . I'm going to be inside forever and it'll be torture.'

This self-pitying tone is familiar to our contributors who spent time with him, with one of our Wakefield staff contributors, Martin, summarising him in a pithy fashion: 'He's a pathetic individual. I can't say anything nice about him because there was nothing nice.'

Huntley had someone at his door 24 hours a day and was never on normal location. It was expensive. 'The cost of looking after him was astronomical really.' Martin paused to sum up Huntley:

'He was such a wet lettuce leaf.'

Former Wakefield prison officer Jo shared some further recollections of him with us for this book:

'He didn't appear dirty or dishevelled. I remember him wearing glasses and doing some kind of clerical work with books. He was neatly dressed, with no hygiene issues. He wasn't intimidating either. Being on the healthcare wing, he was removed from the general population. Physically? I'd say he was about 5ft 8ins. Not tiny, but not tall either. Not a six-footer. Just average.'

According to one ex-prisoner, Belmarsh has implemented an unusual staffing policy within the healthcare unit, which differs from other prisons, including Jo's experience at Wakefield.

'Belmarsh have adopted a good policy to ease up staffing problems. I have never seen this policy at any other prison and was quite surprised to see them adopting it. The policy was bringing in agency nursing staff to watch the offenders to replace prison officers doing this job. A prison officer's pay is higher than that of an agency nurse as these nurses are not proper medical professionals, they are auxiliary nurses. This saves costs and frees up a trained prison officer to conduct his duties within the prison.'

As described by the prisoner, the role of agency nurses is largely observational, with prison officers responding if there are actually any incidents.

'Some of the suicide watch cells have a steel-barred gate with an outer steel door. The outer steel door would be left open, and the agency staff would simply sit on the other side of the steel-barred gate/door watching the offender's every move and recording on the ACCT documents. The ACCT document is a standard document which is opened up for suicide risk offenders. Should the offender try and harm himself then the duty of the agency nurse was to inform prison officers who deal with the offender.'

We were not initially as convinced as the ex-inmate regarding how 'good' this cost-cutting policy was. It seemed to create some points of vulnerability, which is the last thing that you want when you are dealing with the kind of things that can kick off in Belmarsh, but it does seem to be a system that works if the agency nurses maintain vigilance and escalate to officers when necessary.

Just as staffing decisions require careful balance, so too do policies around prison visits, which play a vital role in maintaining inmates' mental wellbeing and family connections. Properly managed visits can offer stability and motivation for rehabilitation, even in a high-security environment like Belmarsh.

CHAPTER 13

Prison Visits at Belmarsh

*'My mum's experience of visiting me in Belmarsh
was so bad that she had a panic attack.'*

(MIKE)

Caroline never worked in prison visits, but she indicated to us that 'there is a process to go through online. Belmarsh has a separate visit section.'

She's right. There is quite a process.

Before visiting HMP Belmarsh, all visitors must be on the prisoner's approved visitor list. Visits must be scheduled in advance, either by phone or email. If booking via email, you have to include the prisoner's name and date of birth in the subject line, and provide the following details for each visitor: full name, full address, date of birth and relationship to the prisoner, along with the preferred date of visit and two alternative dates. You should receive a reply within 24 hours. When booking by email, visits must be scheduled a minimum of 48 hours in advance and up to two weeks ahead. If you do not receive an email confirmation, your visit is not booked. Each visit can accommodate a maximum of three visitors aged ten and over, plus three under-tens.

Visiting times at HMP Belmarsh are:

Tuesday to Thursday: 9:15am–11.15am and 2:15pm–4:15pm

Friday: 9:15am–11.15am

Saturday: 9:30am–11:30am and 2:15pm–4.15pm

Sunday: 2:15pm–4:15pm

Visitors are advised to arrive at least 45 minutes to one hour before their scheduled time to allow for registration and security checks.

All visitors aged 16 and over must bring valid photo ID and proof of address dated within the last three months. Acceptable ID includes a British passport (current or expired within one year, with a recognisable photo), a UK or non-UK photo driving licence (current or expired within one year, with photo and address), EC identity card, Home Office card, immigration photo ID letter, Freedom Pass or discount Oyster card, student or employer's ID card (with name and photo), medical card or a tenancy agreement or rent book dated within the past three to six months. Acceptable proof of address includes a utility bill or bank statement no more than three months old.

Belmarsh uses a biometric system. On your first visit, your fingerprints and facial photograph are taken for future identification. However, you must still bring your ID and proof of address each time.

The slightly bland official information on visiting

Belmarsh is understandable, to put anxious visitors, possibly even coming in with children, at ease. The reality is very different. Even this ID phase is stressful.

This is in part because everyone has to be treated as a potential security risk. When Mike's mum was visiting him inside, she just wanted to see her son. She wasn't attempting to bring any prohibited items in. Even so, she felt profoundly anxious and uncomfortable throughout the process, even having a panic attack during one visit.

'You don't get anything through on visits in Belmarsh. My mum's prison visiting experience of Belmarsh was the worst of any of the prisons she has visited me in. You go through three levels of dogs. You get searched twice, then you get searched again on the way out. They search you stringently even on the way out.'

Visitors are expected to wear smart, family-friendly clothing. Entry may be refused if you wear attire that breaches security guidelines. Prohibited items include hooded clothing, ripped jeans, hats, scarves, bandanas or gloves (unless for religious purposes), football shirts or clothes featuring national crests, stiletto heels, low-cut or see-through clothing, shorts, short skirts or dresses above the knee, excessive jewellery or watches.

Belmarsh has a Visitors' Centre run by Spurgeons, a national charity. Kindly volunteers provide support and advice, particularly helpful for first-time or anxious visitors. The centre offers a registration point for visits, a tea bar outside the prison for refreshments (cash only), guidance on travel, financial assistance and emotional support. Lockers (£1 deposit) are available for storing belongings, and visitors are permitted to bring £15 in cash into the visits hall to purchase refreshments.

Legal representatives can book face-to-face visits via phone or email, providing the prisoner's name, date of birth and preferred visit times. Valid ID is also required upon arrival.

HMP Belmarsh is accessible via public transport (but not very!), with the nearest stations being Woolwich Arsenal and Plumstead. From Woolwich Arsenal, visitors can take bus routes 244 or 380 directly to the prison. From Plumstead station, it's approximately a mile's walk to the facility. For those driving, limited parking is available. It's advisable to arrive early to navigate security procedures and potential traffic.

One ex-prisoner filled us in on how it feels from the other side, as well as the different procedures for visiting a high-risk prisoner:

'The visits are held in the high-risk visit room. Visitors are vetted by the police and it can take months for the visitor to be cleared. Staff will sit in the small visit room with you and make notes of your conversation. When I say sitting in the room, not from a distance but feet away. All phone calls are live monitored. You cannot simply pick up the phone and make a call. Staff have to be made aware prior for the phone to be activated.'

Jonathan Aitken was very eloquent on the power of visits, saying that most prisoners live for visits, as 'a bridge between the inmate and his family, a link with friends, and a window to the outside world.' The Prison Service recognises how crucial prison visits are for the prisoners' wellbeing, so they try to be fair and generous with them, offering extra visits for good behaviour.

As we will see, for the most appalling prisoners, the converse is true. Wayne Couzens was very quiet inside but, in his case, the crime was simply too horrifying.

While entitled to a personal or family visit around once every ten days, Jonathan Aitken was pleasantly surprised to have seven visitors in his first fortnight.

His first was the most renowned prison visitor of the 20th century, Lord Longford. As Jonathan recounts it, the senior officer let Longford, who was 94 years old by then, in to meet him because when he was a young officer at Strangeways, 'He used to come all the way up to Manchester to visit the worst of the worst and the lowest of the low.' That officer went on to make a point that echoed the compassion displayed by some of the more recent Belmarsh staff we have spoken to:

'If you've been in this job for as long as I have, you know that even the untouchables – perhaps especially the untouchables – need to feel the warmth of human kindness. And that's what Lord Longford's been doing for the last 40 years or so to my knowledge, so he's the last man on earth I'm going to turn away.'

While waiting for Lord Longford, Jonathan was 'waiting in an aircraft-hangar sized room for several minutes, watching some 250 other visitors enjoying their visits'.

As well as Lord Longford, Jonathan had family visit

him, like most other people we spoke to. Three of his children, Alexandra, Victoria and William, were driven there by his brother-in-law, Patrick McGrath. We had already noted during our meeting the strange coincidence that McGrath, a renowned novelist, had strong associations with Broadmoor Hospital, where his father, Dr Pat McGrath, was Medical Superintendent during his childhood. We had written of the McGraths in *Inside Broadmoor*.

He also had some other unusual visitors. One of the first, he explained, was not his children, 'but a very famous priest'.

It was Reverend Nicky Gumbel, founder of the Alpha Course. When Nicky was delivering Alpha talks and videos, he liked to dress casually, in jeans and an open-necked shirt. Jonathan tells an amusing story of how, because of a 'curious Belmarsh rule, all ordained ministers entering the prison were required to dress like Victorian vicars'. He was very amused to see Nicky in clothing so out of his normal attire, and as they greeted each other, Jonathan exclaimed, 'Wearing a dog collar! Now I really believe in miracles.'

He had heard that chaplaincy visits could sometimes be granted on compassionate grounds, but the Chaplain of Belmarsh had 'all the world and his wife' trying to get in to meet Jonathan Aitken and was forced to adopt some form of crowd control. That said, he did meet Longford, Gumbel and Canon Robert Wright.

The latter, in addition to being Rector of St Margaret's, Westminster and Canon of Westminster Abbey, was also

Chaplain to the Speaker of the House of Commons. It was this connection that got him his meeting with Jonathan Aitken, because he was sent to Belmarsh on the orders of the Speaker of the House of Commons, Betty Boothroyd.

Though Jonathan Aitken's visitors may have been particularly prominent spiritual figures, access to chaplaincy can be a vital part of prisoner care and mental health provision for all prisoners.

CHAPTER 14

Prisoner Care, Rehabilitation and Mental Health

'Prison isn't a holiday camp. There's that Daily Mail
idea that they've got PlayStations and it's all easy.
When people visit, they see it's not like that at all.'
(PHIL ASHFORD)

As we have seen, the realities of prison life are often obscured by public misconceptions, particularly in media portrayals that suggest prison offers comfort or luxury, though these seem to be becoming increasingly rare. Accounts from those working within the system paint a very different picture, of massive systemic and institutional challenges, and the need for mental health support and meaningful rehabilitation.

At the very sharp end of prisoner care, there are those inmates who are in such a poor mental or emotional state that they want to hurt themselves or even take their own life. This is also a stressful and traumatic situation for officers. Caroline had some insight on self-harm and suicide watch from a former staff perspective.

'One of the worst things was people tying ligatures to harm themselves. I've had to stand by cells before.'

We wondered if there was much self-harm in Belmarsh. She paused to think and then stated, 'I don't know if it's a lot.'

We had several thought-provoking discussions about suicide watch at Wakefield and wanted to see if Belmarsh differed. Caroline noted that 'Yes, there is suicide watch.' She continued that one reason for someone to be put on suicide watch was their trial being very high-profile, and she mentioned Wayne Couzens in this context.

In the April 2022 *Independent Review of Progress for HMP Belmarsh*, HM Chief Inspector of Prisons Charlie Taylor noted improvements in the prison's suicide and self-harm prevention measures. Specifically, constant supervision arrangements for prisoners at risk of self-harm had improved, with staff being attentive and engaging with those under supervision.

However, the review also highlighted that while Assessment, Care in Custody, and Teamwork case manage-ment was more effectively used to support prisoners in crisis, its implementation remained inconsistent, with reviews often lacking multidisciplinary input.

Very sadly, suicides have occurred even so. An inquest into the death of Liridon Saliuka, 29, concluded that multiple failings and discriminatory ill treatment significantly contributed to his suicide while on remand in Belmarsh. Despite his complex health needs following a serious car accident, Liridon's disabilities were repeatedly dismissed, and vital support was inconsistently provided.

The jury found that failures to recognise his disability, make reasonable adjustments and properly coordinate his care, especially regarding his mattress and cell move, negatively impacted his mental health. His family's concerns were ignored and staff failed to check on him for hours before he was found unresponsive in his cell. The jury deemed his death a suicide following substantial institutional failings, and his sister criticised the prison system for its repeated inability to prevent such avoidable tragedies.

Saliuka's death is just one of 15 deaths in Belmarsh in the last decade, five of which were reported to be suicides. Inquests were also held in at least two other Belmarsh suicide cases.

In 2016, an inquest into the suicide of Richard Walsh at Southwark Coroner's Court concluded that he should have been detained in a psychiatric hospital rather than Belmarsh. The jury determined that Richard's death was the result of suicide 'with neglect constituted by the gross failure to provide basic medical care'.

Walsh was 43 when he died. He was found hanging in his cell on 19 July 2015. He had been diagnosed with depression and had a known history of suicide attempts. He had also previously been detained under the Mental Health Act. At the time of his death, he was held in near-complete isolation, confined to his cell for over 23 hours a day, with no access to outdoor exercise or interaction with other prisoners.

The jury concluded that he should have been treated in hospital, stating: 'It is more likely than not that if Mr Walsh had been detained in a hospital instead of Belmarsh he would not have killed himself.' Failings were identified in the care he received after his arrest. The mental health practitioner and two psychiatrists who assessed him at the police station failed to obtain relevant information from the custody record or officer, particularly regarding his delusional behaviour and fixation on a female officer, to look into contacting his family, or to detain him under the Mental Health Act.

A Prevention of Future Deaths report was issued following the death of Manoel Santos, another suicide at Belmarsh. The 45-year-old Brazilian, who had befriended Julian Assange, suffered from severe mental health issues. An inquest into his suicide at HMP Belmarsh on 2 November 2020 highlighted significant failings.

Santos had lived in the UK since 1997, was serving a two-year sentence and was due for release on 27 October 2020. However, he was informed eight days after his scheduled release that he would be detained under immigration powers pending deportation. This notification was delayed beyond the Home Office's 30-day target, a lapse that occurs in 40 per cent of cases, causing considerable distress to foreign national offenders.

Santos was gay and expressed fears about returning to Brazil, citing concerns related to his sexuality and health. He sought assistance from a charity supporting immigration detainees, but communication breakdowns among prison staff, probation services and immigration authorities led to confusion about his legal status. The jury concluded that this confusion played a part in his decision to take his own life.

Assistant Coroner Jenny Goldring identified several areas of concern in her Prevention of Future Deaths report: including, we spotted, a reference to a persistent misunderstanding among prison staff regarding policies on opening cell doors at night, despite previous guidance.

Julian Assange's partner Stella said that he was 'devastated' by the death. She told the press that 'Julian tells me Manoel was an excellent tenor. He helped Julian read letters in Portuguese and he was a friend. He feared deportation to Brazil after 20 years, because being gay put him at risk where he was from.'

Following a death in custody, it is mandatory to display a notice to staff and a separate notice to prisoners informing them of the incident. Such deaths are always subject to formal investigation, rightly so, as they may need to be treated as potential murder scenes. The police are contacted immediately and proceed to treat the area as a possible crime scene.

A full record must be kept of every individual who has entered or exited the cell, and forensic samples are routinely collected from the scene. Anyone who enters the cell during or after the discovery may be required to provide fingerprint evidence to rule them out of the investigation. The procedures followed are essentially the same as those carried out in the community when a death occurs under suspicious or unexplained circumstances.

One very important way to mitigate against self-harm among the general prison population is to offer some hope for the future, and rehabilitation. This doesn't apply to those serving whole life sentences, but for men who know they are coming out some day, they will need to overcome institutionalisation and stigma and re-enter the workplace.

We were grateful to get the chance to hear Phil Ashford's story, because this is exactly the field that he has been operating in, and has granted him a range of useful insights and learnings.

Phil explained that his organisation, Enterprise Exchange, started as a social enterprise focused on helping people in custody or ex-offenders. Self-employment is a good option for them as they often struggle to get mainstream employment due to disclosure and related issues. He pointed out that research shows people in prison can be quite entrepreneurial. It's all about risk and reward. If they're given legitimate tools, it can help reduce reoffending.

'We started the business around 2010 and designed a self-employment programme specifically for people in custody. A film company then approached us for a Ross Kemp documentary, and we ran a course in Belmarsh. We weren't paid, but it was good for profile. The six-week course included workshops, followed by sales and marketing for beginners. They practised pitching with mentors and presented to a panel including Ross Kemp, the governor and an entrepreneur in the chapel. It was an amazing day.'

The next time he went in was under very different operating conditions, because by then, the global pandemic had hit; by the third time, fortunately, the world had returned to relative sanity.

'The second time at Belmarsh, during Covid, we won an Innovate UK grant to pilot a tech-based, cell-accessible self-employment course. We filmed it in 360 VR on Brighton Beach and made our workbook interactive with augmented reality. We partnered with Coracle Inside to use secure laptops, but despite Belmarsh clearance, the Ministry of Justice blocked it due to Covid. It was frustrating, but we won an award for the programme. Third time, we partnered with Rift Social Enterprise, who do excellent through-the-gate work. We provided in-custody support, including workshops and one-to-ones, and held pitch sessions. It was a very positive experience.

Phil explained that the general population is 90 per cent of whom his organisation have worked with, but they have also run courses for vulnerable prisoners.

'Many have previous offences and aren't likely to get a job, so self-employment is their only option. It's also shown that sex offenders with employment or income are less likely to reoffend. We all know it costs £45,000 to keep someone in jail for a year. If someone can go self-employed and not reoffend, it not only saves money but also changes lives. People usually reoffend due to issues with housing, drugs and alcohol, support and employment.'

These are very persuasive arguments for the work that Phil does, and beyond costs, he explained in more detail the societally transformative thing about it.

'Preventing reoffending is good for everyone. It transforms lives, provides role models for their children, and creates wealth and employment in disadvantaged communities. Research shows people in prison are extremely entrepreneurial, so why not harness those skills? Many already do painting, decorating, bricklaying. All these skills are in demand. Going self-employed in these trades can be lucrative.'

This reminded us of some thoughts that Vanessa Frake-Harris shared with us when we were researching this topic for our previous book *Inside Wakefield*. Fundamentally, she sees the justice system as out of date:

'If you have someone who comes into prison short term, for example, three months, you can't really do much in that time, but that person will probably lose his job, lose his family, lose his relationship and reputation, and once he leaves, he will have gained experience in how to commit crimes from other prisoners, and who does that help? He is then more likely to reoffend.'

Vanessa does not believe taxpayer money should be spent on creating more prison places; she would prefer it to be invested in rehabilitation, crime prevention and education. She views the education of young people, as well as what takes place within prisons, as key preventative measures. With around 80 per cent of prisoners unable to read or write to an expected level, she argues there must be a stronger emphasis on providing education. Many of the problems faced by prisoners, such as addiction and homelessness, are social issues, and it is these underlying causes that she believes need to be addressed.

She was critical of the current state of the prison system and questioned its effectiveness in tackling reoffending. As she put it:

'We have the worst reoffending rates in the rest of Europe, so what does that say to you? Something I get asked all the time is, "Does prison work?" At the moment, no.'

She also highlighted the political reluctance to prioritise reform, pointing out how short-term optics often take precedence over long-term solutions. In her view:

'Prison is not a vote winner. Nobody wants to vote for the party that's going to invest in reducing reoffending, to invest in reoffending programmes for prisoners. Norway completely turned itself on its head and it focused on reducing reoffending and not locking prisoners up, and they've got one of the best rates of non-offending in Europe.'

It's interesting that Colin elsewhere in this book also holds Norway up as a model, and it does seem like sharing best practice from elsewhere is one thing that British prisons could do more of.

Returning to Phil's story, he learned quickly that 'doing anything in prison is incredibly difficult'. His way through it at Belmarsh was to get key staff on his side, and he found them to be very supportive, including in practical ways:

'What we do at Belmarsh is have a "champion": some-one inside who supports the programme and makes it happen. On our first programme, when we did the film, the governor was fully on board, and we had an excellent head of reoffending, who brought in external agencies. The first step is building that relationship – they handle booking rooms, getting participants, and so on – and she was amazing.'

He explained that they set criteria for participants, typically those up for release in the next six to 12 months. 'If they're in for 30 years, there's little point. Especially with RIFT Social Enterprise at Belmarsh, we needed people close to release, with a clear business idea, not just, "I'm thinking of being self-employed".'

With individuals who are often from very educationally impoverished backgrounds, nothing can be taken for granted while setting the criteria.

'They need a certain level of literacy to complete business plans and workbooks. We're not involved in security decisions, but the prison ensures we have the right mix: avoiding conflicts, gang issues and so on. We work closely with the head of reoffending and education.'

He singled Belmarsh out for specific praise in terms of their recognition of the programme's value and their active advocacy.

'Some prisons, education departments aren't keen on external agencies; they feel threatened, although not Belmarsh. We try to say: "You've got the business course, we're the practical bit." Some still see it as a threat. Belmarsh have been great. If tutors are teaching painting, decorating or bricklaying, they can refer people to us.'

Although he would not say so himself, it is clear that Phil has become expert in the appropriate ways to engage prisoners and get results for them.

'We also do taster sessions. I go in with a group who might be interested, and it's about treating them as adults, not showing up in a suit and talking down to them. Usually, 70 to 80 per cent sign up. One of the first things I say is: "We're not part of education," and you can see their faces light up. They don't trust the education system – it feels like school, exams and so on. That's a huge point: they appreciate that we're independent.'

At Belmarsh, Phil and his team have only worked with the general population, but in other prisons, like HMP Lewes, they have worked exclusively with vulnerable prisoners. We knew the meaning of the term of course, but were keen to know what type of individuals he had met that fitted that classification.

'When I say vulnerable, I mean sex offenders, ex-police officers, ex-prison officers, or those with a reputation for informing. They're often on separate wings for safety. The prison always decides who can be in the room. They know the dynamics and we need a focused classroom.'

Phil had described a thorough and inspiring set of inputs to us, but what about the outcomes?

'It's hard to track people after release, but we do have success stories. One man runs a successful kitchen installation business, employing others. Another brought back into prison. That was very difficult to arrange. He has run two or three successful businesses and is married with children. These were habitual offenders. We always get consent and protect identities. Some are really engaged inside, say they'll meet us after, but then disappear. We now understand many want to cut ties with anything related to prison. It's not rudeness: they just want a clean slate. Others get moved around the country, so it's hard to stay in contact.'

Phil was pleased to share that they were just about to run something again at Belmarsh.

'A big insurance company wanted to help but didn't know how. We paired five of their senior managers with mentees on our course. Every two weeks, they'd meet in the prison, one-to-one, and we'd observe and give feedback. It started as CSR, but after three months, the managers reported better listening skills and broader perspectives. We turned it into a management development programme. The biggest impact was on the mentors, breaking preconceptions. They'd be in their staffroom, and someone would say, "They'll nick your wallet," and they'd reply, "Actually, the guy I worked with had a tough life and is trying really hard." We call it "bringing the outside in".'

Once the misconceptions have been broken down, the humanity of not all, but many, prisoners begins to shine through. Phil has heard some real redemption stories since he started Enterprise Exchange.

'I worked with a clever guy from Manchester, in for a violent offence and near the end of his sentence. He had great boxing connections and wanted to start a social enterprise boxing gym in Salford for teenagers at risk. He gave a fantastic presentation. One of the hardest men I've met. But he broke down at one line: "When I look into the eyes of the 14-year-old boys around my area, I can see me." Too emotional. Very interesting.'

We asked him how easy it was for him to connect with people who have gone through so much. His response was grounded in maturity and respect.

'It's hard to quantify, but I treat them as adults and equals from the start: handshake, first names, they call me Phil. The course is all group work, self-expression. It's nothing like a typical prison course. There's always a "tipping point". Some lads arrive sullen, expecting it to be boring. Within half an hour, their body language shifts. They realise I'm there to help.'

These individuals may not have been used to help being offered on the outside, and once inside, their defences go up even higher.

'These are people who've been let down again and again. By education, authority, even in prison. We get very little funding. We were lucky to be in HMP Lewes for 18 months. Usually, prisoners assume the funding will vanish and the course won't continue, and then there is no continuity. Prisoners also get moved a lot. Someone might start with us, then get transferred to Wakefield, where we're not based.'

He pointed out that they now require participants not be moved during the course to mitigate against this disruption. Phil expressed admiration for his business partner, who 'is great at one-to-one work. Within 15 minutes, lads open up – just by asking how they're feeling. Mental health support in prisons is dreadful'.

He opened up about a rookie error that they made, born of idealism and a desire to help more.

'We made a mistake early on, trying to sort housing for 15 lads after release. I'd show up at hostels at 6:00am. A prison officer told me: "You'll burn out. You're not a housing or drugs specialist – focus on what you're good at: teaching business." That was a big lesson. You have to be professional – it's tough.'

The best part of Phil's job is simple.

'Working with the guys. I love every minute. Not everyone will start a business or stop reoffending, but if you can plant a seed or help someone progress, that's a win. We call it enterprise coaching, but it's not just business. It's about being more enterprising. For some, getting up at 9:00am instead of 10:00am is a win. It's about encouraging positive steps.'

They might sound like baby steps, but the impact can be real and swift. They are supported by the staff's in-depth knowledge in terms of the size and structure of the groups that they coach.

'Group size varies. It's usually seven or eight, sometimes up to 15 or 20. It depends on the cohort. Turnout varies too, because of gym clashes, legal visits and so on. We rely on staff. They know the lads best.'

Phil has had 'a lot of induction training', which has been helpful in alerting him to sensitivities.

'You've got to be mindful of language. Something innocent can land badly. Like saying, "Have a good weekend." They're in prison. You've got to be careful.'

If Phil has been trained in how to speak the appropriate language, for Nik, one memorable intervention involved having a language in common. He helped a prisoner from his own country who was deeply traumatised.

'He wouldn't speak for five days, and it took me a long time to get through to him. But I finally did, and he opened up a little and, in the end, we had a good relationship.'

Nik talked about how he could speak to him in his own language, but this also meant he had to translate his psychology sessions, which was traumatic as he 'had to listen to everything, then translate it as well. So, it was like I was telling his story, which just made it even harder.'

Nik saw getting him to speak as an achievement of his time as a prison officer. He also reflected on bending the rules. 'You had to be flexible. If letting a guy take two breakfast packs got me home safe, then so be it.'

Prisoners constantly approached officers with deals: 'They were always trying to make offers, they had nothing to hide.' Nik said that what needed to be remembered was that 'There was a lot of money to be made if you wanted to do stuff like that. You could earn a lot of money.'

Phil highlighted common misconceptions about prison life that he had learned from his visits inside, particularly the idea, in his view often perpetuated by media outlets such as the *Daily Mail*, that prisons are akin to holiday camps, filled with PlayStations and luxuries. In reality, newcomers quickly realise this is not the case. He also noted how diverse the prison population is, with individuals convicted of various crimes from a range of backgrounds. One striking realisation for many was how common factors such as childhood abuse, poverty, poor housing, substance abuse, mental health issues and neurodiversity contributed to criminal behaviour. While not everyone with a troubled background commits crimes, there is very often a link, as we have also seen with every institution we have studied.

For many people from outside the prison system, engaging with prisoners led to a shift in perception. Where they might previously have dismissed offenders as simply 'bad people', often they left with a greater understanding of the circumstances that led to criminality. This transformation was one of the most powerful aspects of Enterprise Exchange's mentoring programme. Many of the corporate professionals who volunteered as mentors came from privileged backgrounds and had never been exposed to such realities.

As we have seen, Phil found that many potential mentors had some personal connection to the justice system: a nephew in prison, or experiences in their youth where they narrowly avoided trouble themselves. This subtle connection often made the experience more meaningful for them.

Phil's vocation, and the psychology sessions that Nik translated for his traumatised fellow countryman, are part of a much wider set of educational and rehabilitative programmes for inmates, which includes job training, drug rehabilitation and psychological support. For more recreational activities rather than training or mental health provision, access is dependent on good behaviour and a risk assessment that goes in the prisoner's favour.

However, in its 2023 to 2024 annual report, the Independent Monitoring Board at HMP Belmarsh highlighted significant concerns regarding the lack of purposeful activities within the prison, which may be contributing to a notable rise in drug use among inmates. It noted that only one-third of the prison population engaged in purposeful activities throughout the year. Many prisoners experienced limited time out of their cells, with some allowed just an hour and a half daily. This restricted regime coincided with a sharp increase in drug use; a recent mandatory drug test revealed that 25 per cent of those tested returned positive results. Dealing with prisoners using drugs is one of many challenges facing staff within prisons.

CHAPTER 15

Staff Training
and Care

'I mean, if I hadn't gone to prison, I'd be dead. The
times I ended up inside, if you asked the people there,
they'd say the same. It's a very vulnerable part of
society, anyway. I've got prison officer friends – some of
them 20 years on the job – and I saw it.'

(COLIN)

Staff joining HMP Belmarsh undergo initial training
that begins with an induction week, followed by a ten-
week residential or non-residential Prison Officer Entry
Level Training (POELT) course. This course includes
practical assessments and takes place at the Prison Service
College (PSC) at Newbold Revel, Rugby. During their
first week at HMP Belmarsh, new staff are introduced
to their mentors and colleagues, learning about the
prison's routine.

The subsequent POELT course is designed to prepare
staff for the complexities of prison life, incorporating
practical learning, project work and day-to-day assessments.

Upon completing the course, staff gain a Level 3 diploma in the management and care of individuals in a custodial environment, a first aid qualification and a certificate in food hygiene.

An event titled 'Prison Officer Foundation Training – An Inside Look' is held at Newbold Revel, providing the public with a view of the end-of-course practical assessments that new prison officers must undertake.

Nik's journey into the prison service began unexpectedly. Originally from outside the UK, he had been rejected from joining the prison service in his home country due to his tattoos. After moving to the UK, while working in a supermarket, he learned of an opportunity in the prison service. 'I was working at Asda, driving a forklift, and one of my colleagues said, "Oh, they are looking for people in prison." Obviously, I looked at it and thought, you know, why not just give it a go?'

After a rigorous application process involving interviews, scenario tests and group assessments, Nik began his training at Newbold Revel. 'You need to do three months of college first to start working in a prison,' he explained. Despite the intense preparation, he insisted, 'You learn as you go, really.'

Caroline went through the standard ten-week training at HMP Newbold Revel, then a week or two of induction.

Her first day? She stood on the landing and thought, *'Fuck, why did I do this?'*

There were more male officers than female on her first day. She remembers a few who still had the old contracts and pension conditions. If you are 18 to 21 years old then the salary sounds amazing, but then you don't have the life experience you need to be effective in the job. On her first day she was 27 years old. It felt intimidating. The first four weeks were a blur.

The youth offenders were 'lairy and in your face, almost like a hazing'.

Ultimately with training, you can't train for time on the landing because in training they cannot be real-life scenarios. In training you can say 'stop'. She felt some feeling of support from other staff, too.

Phil, with a more external perspective, had both praise and concerns.

'One day, something really bad is going to happen. Staff retention is shocking. It's not well paid, and the training is quite minimal. They could see a suicide on their first day or get attacked.'

There are not many, essentially, trainee positions where that is a possibility on the first day. We were disturbed throughout our research into Belmarsh by the number of attacks on staff we heard about, especially given the incredibly tight security protocols. In May 2025, police launched an investigation after Axel Rudakubana, jailed for murdering three young girls in Southport, allegedly attacked a prison officer at Belmarsh by pouring boiling water over him. The officer was taken to hospital as a precaution but discharged the same day.

Rudakubana had been sentenced in January 2025 to a minimum of 52 years for the murders of Alice da Silva

Aguiar, Bebe King, and Elsie Dot Stancombe, as well as the attempted murders of eight other children, a dance instructor, and a businessman during a Taylor Swift-themed workshop in July 2024. He was also found guilty of producing ricin, possessing terrorist material, and carrying a knife. The incident at Belmarsh occurred as overall assaults on staff in adult prisons reached a decade high, with over 10,600 recorded in 2024.

On a more positive note, Phil went on to back the perspective of many others that because of the nature of the offenders they house, Category A prisons are less chronically understaffed than many of the lower categories.

'It's a tough job. But Belmarsh, because of its nature as a Category A prison, has better staffing than most. It's actually easier to work there than in many other places, in terms of cuts.'

Even so, any prison officer role comes with a level of stress that requires the development of coping mechanisms if you plan to survive and thrive in the sector for any length of time. As someone who has done so for 19 years, we wanted to ask Matthew how he did it.

He shared some of his mental and emotional tactics with us to remain professional when he was confronting the challenges of working at Belmarsh. He explained, 'One way I dealt with it was driving home. I lived about a 40-minute drive from Belmarsh, and that gave me space to clear my thoughts. Gave me a bit of time to box off my work personality from my home personality, to decompress.'

In addition to this meditative time, he tried to recalibrate his responses to criminals where he had knowledge of the terrible things that they had done. He reflected, 'I adopted the approach that I would take that person at face value. Yeah, I may hear what they've done, but it wasn't my responsibility to judge them. That was for the courts, the police, the trials. If they were found not guilty, then they were not convicted of that crime. You just have to try and take a step back.'

However, he admitted that some crimes were harder to detach from emotionally, especially 'the most difficult ones to distance myself from were crimes against children or horrendous sexual offences. What's really odd is that you accept horrendous violence and murder at a better personal level than you would do a sexual crime; that's just how it played in your mind sometimes.'

Matthew also enjoyed the special bond that staff members formed in such a unique environment. He noted, 'You spend a lot of time working together. You get to know people and get close to them quickly because you have experienced traumatic events together. As much as you want to try and talk to your friends and family, they don't understand as much as people who have been in that environment, so that type of camaraderie is something that even now I don't have in the jobs that I've done since then: it's that whole bonded with fire type of thing.'

Although Matthew appears to have dealt with it well, we have spoken to so many prison workers, as well as police and close protection officers, whose relationships have broken down because of their job. That's not only because they can't help bringing the strain, and sometimes paranoia, home. It's also because they might have had a working day that is incomprehensible to their loved ones, in terms of violence, cruelty, manipulation or the worst of human nature. A bad day at the office for these brave individuals can involve urine, faeces or, horrifyingly, boiling liquid being thrown in their face. In the event of a serious attack, the pressure usually mounts from partners and children for them to get out and find a new career.

One former officer told us that he knew of 'an ex-staff member who broke his leg during a restraint'.

This serious injury was enough to make that staff member want to leave the service. The same officer also expressed his admiration for trans officers, who can be victimised.

'There have been trans officer assaults. Trans men get assaulted and come back to work. They are very resilient.'

It was distressing to hear of this persecution, and the need for even greater resilience just to get through their working day.

When we asked if he missed working at Belmarsh, Nik responded without hesitation. 'Not really, no. I don't miss it because of what it did to me,' he admitted. The effects of his time in the prison service had been long-lasting, impacting his personal life in ways he hadn't expected. 'It was hard to relate to my wife. That's why so many officers get together. They understand each other.' The job had taken a heavy toll on him, and he didn't shy away from acknowledging it. 'I ended up in rehab. It messed me up.'

Despite the difficulties, he didn't regret his time in the service. 'I don't miss it. But yeah, I mean, I don't regret it.'

This may be in part because, despite this ever-present threat, it also reveals a fascinating, hidden side of society and human nature, as Matthew vividly recalled.

'Talking to the prisoners was a unique experience as well, because some of them had really different backgrounds and different life stories, like some of the decisions they made along the way. That was always quite interesting.'

Typically, Matthew can see the silver lining too. He went into a deeper description of the camaraderie among staff.

'Because it happens all the time: you could have experienced the most vile, horrific event, or someone's tried to take their life, and everyone you can see is visibly shaken or processing. Then you'll have someone go, "Right, who wants a cup of tea? Anyone want a slice of toast?" Just little things, where someone would break down the barriers immediately, and go, "Right? Let's just have a pause; let's have a cup of tea. Let's compose ourselves."'

Even in a diverse team of individuals, he saw this as a unifying factor. 'There's always someone playing that role, providing resolution. Because of that type of environment, you build those bonds, in such extreme ways people look out for each other a little bit more. I don't know if that's the same now. The old saying was, "Sometimes the day's crap, but let's just get on with it together. It's crap, but let's just get it done." It's that type of camaraderie.'

Matthew continued, meditating on his early years. 'I was a young male when I joined the prison service. I was only just 20. It's your formative years. So, it gives you a great deal of confidence in dealing with people and some really, really challenging situations and allows you to – it's a really weird thing to say – you become comfortable in violent situations or how to handle yourself.'

It's true that Matthew exudes a sense of perspective. As a civil servant now, he must be an immense, unflappable asset who never sweats the small stuff after the things he's seen.

'In some situations that people find uncomfortable, it becomes incredibly normal, which is odd to say. So there's a lot of times where, people are talking about "Oh my God, this has happened" and you're like, "OK, that's fine, don't worry about it." A lot of things shaped the fact that I was always calm, but now it's very much a case of, this stuff that I use very much in my life now and even my work life.'

When he witnesses minor panics at work, he will say, 'Just wait, pause this. No one is dying. There's no one about to lose their life. There's no one escaped. Everything's fine. So, you have that level of calmness where it's not world-ending, and it gives you a real sense of perspective in that sense when you used to be dealing with crisis and people's lives. You have been in situations where you must deal with something and it teaches you to make informed decisions on minimal pictures. So, you might have a snapshot of something. "I need to make a decision right now, Let's make it." And then as more information comes on, you make a different decision. It gets you comfortable making decisions really quickly. It's a unique blend and there are not many people in my world now who started their lives in the Prison Service.'

One of our ex-prison staff contacts paints a less rosy picture. Nik suffered from a lack of support after the attack that he suffered. 'None of the governors reached out to me, not one. I spoke to my colleagues and my managers, but from higher up? Nothing.'

Surely the unpredictability and volatility of the environment must have even got to Matthew sometimes, we asked.

'That's the hardest part of the role sometimes. Just the sheer chaotic nature of it. The fact that one minute you could be completely fine, nothing would be happening. It'd be just a normal day and the next day or in the next minute, there could be a descent into violence where people will be trying to attack each other or attack a member of staff or someone would be in crisis trying to kill themselves.'

He was keen to point out that these were not necessarily experienced as isolated incidents, either. There could be a domino effect of violence and unrest at Belmarsh and Isis.

'It was just a pressure cooker of an environment where things were not happening in isolation; there's always something happening. It would be a catalogue of events. Someone would be emotionally unstable because they've just come into prison for the first time or they are withdrawing, they've got a number of psychological issues that they've not really realised and they're now working on, and that's causing them to want to harm themselves.'

Suddenly you could find yourself in a maelstrom of self-harm or murderous intent.

'You've got someone who's trying to potentially end their own life or another person's trying to kill another person. And there's a massive spectrum of psychological influences where one minute, you're OK. Then you have this massive high of dealing with something and then you go back down to normal, where you just try and go, "Right? Everyone, let's do evening meal." There is this real pulling and pushing of psychological events. That was quite hard for everyone because it is a really difficult period.'

As many others have observed to us, times have changed in terms of transparency and mental health provision, but back in the day, things could be swept under the carpet.

'The thing is, back then it wasn't really spoken about, how these influences can have long-term effects on people and what that means for people. So that was always the difficult part of it. Just the sheer unknown. One minute you'll be fine, and the next minute, all hell could be breaking loose.'

Prison officers are trained to be constantly aware of the various psychological tactics prisoners might use to manipulate them. This is a fundamental aspect of their training, designed to ensure that they remain professional and do not inadvertently allow prisoners to gain an upper hand. Multiple sources have confirmed to us that this kind of training is a crucial part of an officer's preparation.

Phil Ashford described a case study that highlighted one such manipulation technique he encountered during his training. He explained, 'We get trained in something called "conditioning" – that's when prisoners might try to manipulate you. A classic one is, you've just finished a course, someone says, "Can you post this birthday card to my niece?" but it's actually a letter to a witness.'

He emphasised the importance of limiting personal information, adding, 'You learn not to give out too much information about yourself – but I think with social media now, that's probably gone out of the window anyway.'

Having worked in the prison service for decades, Matthew was well versed in recognising manipulation attempts. He shared his experience of the constant vigilance required in this line of work: 'One of the biggest challenges in prison is that you have to be constantly aware and constantly on guard. Sometimes these people are not asking you questions because they're nice or because they want to know you; sometimes it's about can they exploit a weakness in you.'

Matthew noted how prisoners, who spend every day of the year in prison, have plenty of time to observe staff and identify vulnerabilities. 'A lot of these guys are in prison every day of the year, 24 hours a day, and they do nothing but study you. They're able to see that if all of a sudden you look different for one day, they're like, "What's up? Why are you not . . ." so they can study you.'

This brought the words of our amazing contributor, former prison governor Vanessa Frake-Harris, sharply back into focus for us. She had put it so eloquently to us during one of our conversations. Vanessa told us that being manipulated can happen to anybody in jail, be they staff or prisoners.

'It usually starts with chatting. You must talk to prisoners as part of your job to build up a rapport and professional relationship with them. A lot of people can't understand it. Many believe we should lock them up and throw away the key, but it will never work like that. At some stage you have to unlock that person and let them out into society.'

Many contributors have told us that manipulation or grooming can start with a cigarette.

For Vanessa, the catalyst for the manipulation could be something as simple as when she used to smoke in the exercise yard. An individual prisoner would start talking to her and ask if they could have a fag. She soon learned how to frame a response to this.

'I would say, "If I give you one, I've got to give 343 cigarettes, because I don't pull you out as anything special." You've got to cut them dead. Some people might give in, and that's how it starts. "Oh, Gov, I've missed the last post. Can you take this out on your way home and post it?" Once you get into a routine where everybody wants a little bit of you to get something, it's a very slippery slope. Myra Hindley manipulated a governor to take her to Regent's Park and get an ice cream. That's how manipulative Myra Hindley was.'

She went on to make a point which chimes closely with our understanding from the prisoners, too, about how manipulation can grow.

'Prisoners have one thing more than we have, and that's time. They have time to sit and watch people and see which ones they think are vulnerable, those of us they think can be exploited, those of us who may stick out.'

This constant awareness becomes a fundamental part of an officer's mindset. Matthew explained the delicate balance officers must maintain, stating, 'You are aware that you have to have this facade on at all times. Come across as friendly, but never friends.'

He further elaborated, 'I always made sure that I was honest to a point. If I said I was going to do something, I would do it. If I couldn't, I'd say why I wouldn't do it.' He added that respect in the prison environment is built on consistency and reliability. 'There's nothing worse in prison than when you say you're going to do something, and you never come back because that just creates an issue for the next person who might have to deal with that prisoner. And it might not be you.'

Initially, this psychological facade can be draining. As Matthew revealed, it was particularly challenging during his early years:

'In the early years, it was a toll on me because you have to keep this facade up all the time, but after a period of time, it just becomes second nature.'

He also reflected on how this way of thinking and behaving became ingrained over time.

'And it's only now, after I've been out for a number of years, that you realise some of those behaviours are not normal life. It's not normal to act like that.'

In his post-prison life, Matthew no longer feels the need to question people's intentions.

'Now, when people ask you something, you don't have to think, "What do they want from me?" It's a real psychological wall that you have to always put up.'

Another thing that Nik remarked on from a staff perspective was the unique atmosphere that Belmarsh carried, one that altered dramatically between night and day. He reflected on the strange contrast that he experienced during his time there.

'It felt weird, but there was something special about it as well,' he explained. 'Walking the grounds in the early hours, just before dawn, was a surreal experience. 'When you're out and about, say 5:00am, you see a lot. It can feel quite eerie, especially in winter when it's cold, and the sun's just setting.'

The prison, usually a place of constant noise and movement, felt strangely peaceful in those quiet moments, especially knowing that 'in a couple of hours, it would be rammed'.

One of the critical night duties that Nik gave an insight into was double-locking the prison. 'You go around the entire perimeter and double-lock every gate and door using a special set of keys,' Nik explained. 'Even if someone had the regular keys, they couldn't get through without these. It's an added layer of security.'

In terms of officer shifts, Nik explained that 'sometimes you have the early shift, sometimes you are there the whole day. And then if you do nights, you do seven nights in a row and then you get a week off afterwards.' In terms of his preference, he said he didn't really mind, 'because overtime was very high'.

'So, sometimes we would do mad shifts, like you would go in in the morning for 6:00am, go home, come back at 6:00pm, do the whole night shift, go back home, and then next day you would start at 12. Which is sort of against the rules, but if needs must . . . They were lenient if they needed you, then you could basically do whatever shifts you wanted to.'

Caroline also gave us her take on what happened at night-time and on night shifts.

'The night shift is from 9:00pm until 6:00am. There are 'alarm checks' and if you're working the night shift, you get an area to check. You do a count and total up. You put the double locks on. All the gates are double-locked and so are all the gates to the house blocks. Typically, you only do nights once or twice a year, although you do them more often in the Seg.'

The check is incredibly thorough, both internally and externally.

'All the windows are completely caged up and secure. You walk around to check if someone threw a line. The windows are secured with something like chicken wire but even stronger.'

As Caroline went on to say, 'Early shifts start from 6:00am or 6:30am, so that's a challenging commute if you live far from the prison.'

Jenny Louis is the current governor of HM Prison

Belmarsh. As Mike noted, 'Governor Louis was the first female black prison governor in the UK.'

She featured in the Ross Kemp TV show filmed inside Belmarsh when she was deputy governor and part of the team pondering what to do with Tommy Robinson on the day of his arrival.

Jenny Louis has been governor since February 2021, having been acting governor since July 2020. The report that followed a surprise prison inspection in 2024 praised the prison's leadership, concluding that Belmarsh was well led.

'The governor, who had been in post since the previous inspection, enjoyed the confidence of the staff at the establishment. The senior team was also well established and had a clear understanding of the key issues facing the prison. The governor had set appropriate priorities in her self-assessment report and, with the notable exception of education and work, had made some improvements since the last inspection.'

One former inmate described some interesting changes in the management of prisons, and their implications.

'Governors. Some years ago, you had a number one governor and a duty governor who basically were in charge of the prison. Custody managers who were once known as a PO (principal officer) would run the wings and various departments. Under the PO you had an SO (senior officer), and below this rank it is the prison officer. A prison officer will have one stripe on his or her shoulder, a senior officer will have two and a CM will have three.'

According to him, more layers and, potentially, more bureaucracy and less accountability had crept in.

'When it was a governor and duty governor who ran a jail, it was more consistent with decision-making. However, over the last ten years, more governor titles have emerged. Grade one, the governing governor. Grade two, the deputy governor. Grade three, the governor of security. There are many governors within HMP Belmarsh. OMU offender management unit, visits, reception, head of residence, the segregation unit, healthcare – all are given the title governor. As a result of this, complaints, adjudications and other important decisions can be inconsistent. You have one governor saying this, the other saying something different. The number one governor would always be seen on the wings, interacting and seeing what is going on within their jail.'

Apparently, this revised hierarchy had made governors less available to prisoners too.

'These days at HMP Belmarsh and other jails, you as an offender will never see the number one governor at all. They hide behind all the other governors. Even if you use the confidential access complaints service, which is supposed to be unique access to the number one governor, the response in every case is a standard opening line. Dear Mr . . ., the number one governor has asked me to look into your complaint. Do you see, this is a standard response and highlights the lack of care by all number ones these days. They simply hide behind the lower-grade governors. The term governor has lost its integrity.'

Perhaps this is what Mike was driving at, too, when he told us that 'Belmarsh is very cliquey.'

Coming back to the 2024 prison inspection, it also noted that 'Belmarsh was fully staffed and had a more stable workforce than many reception prisons.'

It also noticed some churn, however, in key employees, noting the implications that could have.

'The turnover of front-line staff had increased over the two years leading up to the inspection. While this created opportunities, such as increasing the diversity of the staffing group, new staff understandably took time to become fully effective in their roles. The governor had responded well to this challenge and had put support systems in place for new staff. As a result, staff retention levels at Belmarsh were among the best in London. In our staff survey, 75 per cent of respondents reported that the support they received from their line manager was good or very good.'

Nik is, sadly, unlikely to have given that survey response. He left the prison service in 2021, transitioning into a new career. Reflecting on his time as a prison officer, he noted the thankless nature of the job, explaining that 'the system cares more about prisoners than staff.'

He highlighted one of the key issues he had encountered: the influx of young, inexperienced officers. 'I was 25 when I started. You get kids straight out of college at 18. How do you expect a grown man in prison to respect that?'

If someone had asked Nik for advice about joining the prison service, his response was clear. 'I wouldn't recommend it,' he stated firmly. His reasoning went beyond the inherent difficulties of the job – it was about the perception of the role itself. 'It's a very undervalued role in society at the moment, and it's just becoming worse.' He had witnessed a decline in respect for prison officers, noting how the growing disregard for authority had made the job more challenging. 'It's not as highly valued as it used to be, back in the day. You don't get the respect for it.'

According to Nik, rather than feeling like a crucial part of the system, officers were increasingly treated as 'just a number'. A mere cog in a vast, impersonal institution. Despite their sacrifices, prison officers received little recognition or appreciation for their work.

As you can see, staff members, and former inmates, provided a striking and often sobering insight into the staff experience at Belmarsh. It reveals the immense psychological pressure faced by officers who must navigate a daily environment of unpredictability, manipulation and potential violence. It's possible that increased bureaucracy has led to inconsistent decision-making and a greater sense of distance between governors and front-line staff. While the official reports praise the prison's stability and leadership, voices from within suggest a more complicated reality: one where officers often feel overlooked, under-appreciated and left to cope with the emotional toll of a uniquely challenging job. This feeling only intensifies when they are confronted with the extreme situations that can arise in a pressure cooker like Belmarsh.

CHAPTER 16

Rough Justice

*'In prison sometimes you could be doing absolutely
nothing in particular, no sign, and chaos happens.'*
(MATTHEW)

Everyone who was old enough to follow the British press at the time remembers the 'Baby P' case, and everyone wishes that they could forget it. The haunting story of the toddler's torture and murder, and the missed opportunities to save him, is indelibly seared on both of our memories, perhaps in part because we had a child of similar age then.

Difficult as it was to revisit the story, we knew that some of our contributors had many recollections of his killer, Steven Barker. We were also very keen to hear of any repercussions he had suffered for his crimes in prison. Our contacts were happy to oblige. One former inmate recalled him well:

'Steven Barker. Baby P case. He murdered a child and raped a two-year-old baby. However, while he was at extreme risk of harm, he was located on the VP house block 4 spur 3. In his case it was deemed too much of a risk to allow him out of his cell. He was constantly locked up at Belmarsh. He had greasy blond hair; he was very dirty and had poor hygiene and smelt. He is very tall, well over 6ft tall. A Lurch-type character. He had all his meals brought to his door. He never showered, never went out on exercise.'

Barker was evidently kept in an extreme state of enforced solitude. 'Even on the VP spur house block 4 he was isolated and kept behind his door.' Adding an unnerving extra detail, our contributor noted, 'He just sat in his cell watching children's daytime TV.'

This gross hermit existence did not prevent the more resourceful Belmarsh prisoners from getting to him, our interviewee adding that, 'Many inmates would go to his door, shout abuse and squirt urine from a Lynx shower gel bottle under his door. He was detested. Staff at Belmarsh hated him too. Barker and [John] Worboys were transferred to Wakefield on the same van. Worboys and Barker were located on C Wing HMP Wakefield. Worboys, knowing I was there, came to my door. He came with Barker. I said, "Hello, John," but told Barker to fuck off and never speak to me, so he went. Barker was on C Wing for no more than 20 minutes.'

Jo had very clear memories of Barker from the same institution, from a staff rather than an inmate perspective. 'People I remember? Steven Barker, the man convicted in connection with the death of Baby P. I once had a brief conversation with him. I encountered him on the hospital unit where he worked as a cleaner, washing up and doing other basic tasks. I remember walking in and hearing, "Hi, Miss," and I replied, "Hi." When I asked who he was, someone said, "That's the baby killer."'

Jo was taken aback, adding, 'I thought, no wonder he picked on a child, because he certainly wouldn't have dared go after an adult man. They'd have battered him. That was my impression when I first saw him. I didn't expect it to be him. You imagine someone like that to look like a brutish monster, but he was just quietly polite, said "Hi" like anyone else. I'd been working there for a couple of years by then.'

We wondered if her recollection of his appearance aligned with the ex-inmate's 'Lurch' comment.

'What did he look like? He wasn't especially intimidating. You wouldn't look at him and think, "Oh my God, if I were a child, I'd be terrified of him." In some ways, he reminded me of John Worboys: just ordinary-looking. You might even look at him and think he seemed approachable. Barker was the boyfriend, wasn't he? The stepfather. As a child, I wouldn't have liked anyone coming into my life who wasn't my parent, but even so, I could see why some might've thought he looked fairly harmless. He didn't look like a thug. My thought at the time was simply: "Wow. That's the baby killer."'

She also remembered a notorious attack on Barker that she believed happened later, after he was moved to HMP Wakefield, an incident where someone threw boiling sugar water – what they call a 'kettle' – on him during association time. 'We were already locked down at that point. The idea is that the sugar causes the water to stick and peel the skin off. I can't say with 100 per cent certainty, but I believe it happened to him. Someone said, "The baby killer's been kettled," and that's when I realised.'

In a world of rough justice, incidents like this can often be taken very calmly, according to Jo.

'People didn't react with shock. They just wanted to get on with their day. It's the kind of attack that can happen quietly.'

Jo was right. After Barker was moved to Wakefield he suffered three different attacks, and an ex-inmate also recalled his kettling as well as the other assaults.

'A prisoner knocked him out in the dinner line; he had only been there about two hours max. Barker was removed to healthcare and later located on B Wing at Wakefield, where he had hot water thrown in his face by another prisoner, he "hot watered" him. Then a third inmate assaulted him. Staff eventually moved him to the healthcare department, where they gave him a job there.'

We wondered if there were any prisoners that Barker befriended, or if he was universally shunned. Sometimes some very strange alliances can form, after all. Jo didn't think so.

'Did he associate with other notorious prisoners? Not that I ever saw. I mainly saw him when I was covering the hospital wing. I believe he was on B Wing, and I was normally on A Wing as the sitting officer, so my interactions were limited. He likely didn't mix with the more notorious inmates. In prison, people like that – child abusers or killers – are referred to as "nonces" or "beasts". They're at the very bottom of the inmate hierarchy.'

Nobody, it seemed, wanted to say that they were Steven Barker's friend. As Jo concluded, killing kids makes you persona non grata.

'You've got your gangsters and your murderers, but even they have families – children of their own – and they *despise* people who harm kids. So, someone like Barker would most likely have associated only with people of the same category, which is why he was targeted. Even gangsters and serial killers might say, "We might be bad, but we don't kill kids."'

Colin had a breathtaking, and gruesome, story to tell us about an attack that he witnessed.

'As you know, Belmarsh has a "star system" layout, see, with wings running off the star. To go from one wing to another, you've got to go across the centre. And the screws tend to stand on the centre, and they can see the whole jail.'

On this day, though, there was no screw watching, because there was a chair in the centre, and somebody cutting hair.

Colin continued, 'I had gone down to join the queue for the chair they were cutting hair in, standing by the gate, waiting for my turn to get my hair cut. I'm the next person in. Standing with me was a very small Chinese or Vietnamese guy, quite passive. Another guy, a big, big white guy showed up. I didn't like him. He was threatening. An argument broke out between the big guy and the little guy about who was next in the queue. I went and sat in the chair, minding my own business. I was miles away but then my gaze focused back on the gate where I had been standing and where the guy was standing. I saw the little guy come downstairs with a plastic flask full of hot water, and in his right pocket was a PP9 battery in a sock. A PP9 battery is a big fucking battery, the biggest battery you can get. He goes up to the hot water urn which was full of boiling water for tea and he fills up about two litres of hot water.

'I was looking at the big guy, seeing what was going on. The little guy came up behind him and threw the boiling hot water into his left ear. The guy moved rightwards away from the water hitting him, and then the little guy pulled the thing out of his pocket and swung it from the right and clouted him straight round the right earhole with the battery in the sock and his face gashed open.

'I was just sitting in the chair watching, and I swear this is true. Do you know what the barber says? The barber says, "Charlie, don't surf." From that Robert Duvall scene in *Apocalypse Now*. It basically means, we've killed the Vietnamese and now we're taking their waves.

'Here's something mad for you. Guess who broke the fight up? A female prison officer. Really. That's a good example of the ethics of British prisons. A lot of violence is very controlled. The Chinese guy was very controlled. The female officer who ran in, she probably went into 100 similar fights like that in her career and knew exactly what she was doing.'

While fully acknowledging that any assault was one

too many, but keen to make a point about British prisons being relatively well run, Colin observed that statistics on female prison officers being assaulted are 'probably high, but not as high as you'd imagine'.

Returning to his story, 'Everybody else just carries on with their business. I got my haircut finished. The Chinese guy would have got an extra six months, maybe a year on his sentence for that. He could have got an outside court, but the white guy wouldn't go into court against him, so they would probably let it go. He would have lost time too in the prison, though, and he would have been in segregation for a few months. That's why I keep myself to myself!'

The same can't be said of the two inmates who allegedly ambushed Urfan Sharif in a Belmarsh cell on New Year's Day 2025, showing that rough justice is still alive and well in the prison. Urfan has gained notoriety for the torture and murder of his ten-year-old daughter, Sara Sharif, for which he is now serving a life sentence. In August 2023, Sara was found dead at the family home in Woking, Surrey. The post-mortem investigation uncovered that she had been subjected to a 'campaign of torture' over a two-year period, involving beatings, burns and other forms of mistreatment. The day before her body was discovered, Urfan Sharif, along with his wife, Beinash Batool, and brother, Faisal Malik, fled to Pakistan with Sara's five siblings. This set off an international manhunt and the evil trio were brought back to the UK to face justice for what they had done to Sara.

Urfan Sharif and Beinash Batool were convicted at the

Old Bailey for the murder of Sara Sharif in December 2024. The court heard harrowing details of the abuse Sara endured, with the judge describing the acts as 'sadistic' and highlighting the defendants' 'depravity'. Urfan Sharif was sentenced to life imprisonment with a minimum term of 40 years, while Beinash Batool received a minimum term of 33 years. Faisal Malik was sentenced to 16 years for causing or allowing Sara's death. It was off to Belmarsh for Urfan Sharif, and he was in for a gratifyingly unpleasant stay.

On 1 January 2025, just days after arriving at Belmarsh, Sharif was reportedly attacked by two fellow inmates within the prison. The assailants used a makeshift weapon fashioned from a tuna tin lid, slashing his throat and cutting his face. He received medical treatment for his injuries, which were described as non-life-threatening, but the incident prompted an investigation by both the prison authorities and the Metropolitan Police. Even today, just as Jo had said, in prison's 'honour amongst thieves', you are the lowest of the low if you've tortured and murdered children.

Caroline witnessed lots of violence too. Like Jo, she saw a couple of people get kettled. She saw people get slashed. Her good friend left Belmarsh because he was badly assaulted by a prisoner.

'The staff assaults did shake me.' She was not convinced that the resilience was in place with freshly trained officers, either. 'The new staff have no idea about life.'

Perhaps understandably, given that he was a prisoner

and not staff, Mike took a slightly different view of the consistency and effectiveness of any sanctions for these attacks. 'Lots of things don't make sense in Belmarsh. There are lots of extra charges. So, a man is attacked in the dinner queue and he defends himself, but then he gets another 30 days added to his sentence. Even though it was in self-defence.'

Violence was a regular part of life at Belmarsh when Nik was there. He was once assaulted during a night shift. 'We were dealing with a self-harm incident in segregation. A prisoner threw a jumper at my feet, so I told him to pick it up, and he lost it. He punched me in the back of the head,' he recalled.

Other incidents were also disturbing to Nik, and to us, as he recounted them.

'I've seen slashings, boiling water attacks and dirty protests. The aftermath of suicides was another grim reality we faced. One of the worst things was being chained to a prisoner who died during a hospital watch. These experiences stick with you.'

Despite the hardships he endured working in Belmarsh, Nik found moments of connection too. 'I got along with prisoners better than staff most of the time. There was a thin line between us and them. Many officers had done things that could have landed them inside if they had been caught.'

Matthew's account of a defining moment of violence in Belmarsh for him was more shocking because his account of his experiences in general was so measured.

'I can't remember which house blocks I was on, but I remember I was talking to a lady from the board of visitors. The board of visitors are an independent group of volunteers who come in, and they deal with issues on behalf of prisoners, such as a complaint that they've had passed to them. That the prisoners have not been able to identify for themselves or they might be trying to get to the bottom of something where they've heard a report, or something's been raised. They're basically an advocate on behalf of the prisoners. This one lady was asking me a question about something, I can't even remember what it was.

'When you've been in prison long enough just before a general alarm bell there's a sound where the alarm panel, which is on the wall, goes off. It indicates that there's something going on in your house block. I was the custodial manager in charge of that house block, and I remember hearing that sound going off. I came out of my office and asked the office, "Where is it?" They said, "On to this landing," and I've gone up there and there's a group of prisoners fighting. I can't remember what they were fighting over. A member of staff had hold of this prisoner, trying to separate him from the other prisoners.'

What happened next made us wince.

'I went over to assist this guy. I grabbed him and pulled him away. At this point I realised that they'd hit him on the side of the head with something and his artery had been severed, so he was pumping blood all over me, all over my shirt, everywhere. He was trying to fight us because he was obviously really injured, and he thought he was still being attacked. He wasn't. Once we managed to calm him down, it's incredibly difficult to try and grab hold of someone when they're covered in their own blood, and your hands are just slipping off them and you've got this warm fluid over you that smells like red wine, believe it or not. After a while when you calm down and the medical team have turned up, looked at him and gone, "He's in real danger". We need to get an ambulance, so the paramedics arrived and he was taken by ambulance outside into the reception area of the prison. An air ambulance is called and a surgeon had to stitch him before they got into the transport to take him off to hospital.

'It was only then that I paused. I had a white shirt and tie, my trousers stained into a different direction with blood. Mad little things pop into your head, like where am I going to get new clothes from? So, you then have to go out to the store cupboard to get a change of clothes, you go home in a completely different set of clothes while your clothes are seized for forensic evidence and then within half an hour, you're like, right. Let's go back to work. Let's do something different. It's just utter chaos like that and I had to go back and say, to the lady, "I'm terribly sorry." And she said, "Was the young man OK?" I said, "Yeah, he's fine."'

And that was that. With stories like these, it's nothing short of miraculous that it's still possible to recruit staff for prisons at all.

CHAPTER 17

John Worboys

'He would joke about his victims at times. He was
very polite and quite pleasant to talk to, but as I got
to know him very well, I saw another side.'
(FORMER INMATE)

He's changed his name to John Radford, but he was born John Worboys in June 1957 in Enfield, Middlesex. He is a serial sex offender who came to be known in the British tabloid press as the 'Black Cab Rapist'. Between 2000 and 2008, while working as a licensed London taxi driver, he committed numerous sexual assaults, with police estimating over 100 potential victims. His early career included roles as a milkman, security guard and stripper, going by the stage name of 'Terry the Minder'.

He also appeared in porn films and rented out his flat for adult film productions. In 1996, he passed 'The Knowledge', enabling him to operate as a black cab driver in London, and, it turned out, to drug and sexually assault women.

Picking up women late at night, he would claim that

he had won money through gambling or the lottery and offer them champagne laced with sedatives. Once incapacitated, he would sexually assault or rape them. Many victims had little to no memory of the events. Despite reports to the police dating back to 2002, a lack of coordination and seriousness in handling the complaints allowed Worboys to continue his assaults. In 2008, he was arrested after a victim reported her experience, leading to the discovery of incriminating evidence, most notably a 'rape kit' in his vehicle.

Jo could see how he had charmed his way into his awful crimes, with his civil, normal manner.

'Worboys used to say he'd won money at a casino. He had a whole patter. He'd offer women champagne, laced with Rohypnol, I think. They'd pass out, and he'd attack them. Afterwards, he'd make sure they got home safely, as if nothing had happened. He was financially comfortable too. He may have even charged them the taxi fare.'

In 2009, Worboys was convicted of 19 charges related to attacks on 12 women and sentenced to life imprisonment with a minimum term of eight years. A 2018 Parole Board decision to release him was overturned following public outcry and legal challenges. Subsequent investigations led to additional charges, and in 2019, he received two more life sentences after admitting to attacks on four more women.

In 2007, at the age of 19, Carrie Symonds, who would later become the wife of former Prime Minister Boris Johnson, was targeted by Worboys. She recounted that

Worboys approached her while she was waiting at a bus stop, offering her a ride home despite her not necessarily having enough for the fare. He claimed to have won a substantial sum at the races and offered her champagne and vodka to celebrate. As we have seen, this was his standard patter.

After consuming the drinks, Symonds experienced severe disorientation and memory loss. She later described feeling extremely tired and clinging to the side of the cab, with no recollection of events until the following afternoon. Although she believed she had not been assaulted, the uncertainty left her deeply unsettled.

Symonds was among 14 women who testified against Worboys during his 2009 trial at Croydon Crown Court, leading to his conviction for multiple sexual assaults. She waived her anonymity to raise awareness about the case and later campaigned against his early release in 2018, contributing to a successful legal challenge that kept him incarcerated. Symonds has since been an advocate for victims' rights and has spoken publicly about the need for systemic changes to protect vulnerable individuals from predators like Worboys. Worboys' case highlighted significant failures in the criminal justice system, particularly in handling sexual assault allegations and the parole process.

Apparently Worboys made a confession to another very disturbing crime according to the ex-inmate who told us that he confided in him. He claimed to have murdered a boy. With a heavy heart, we asked if he could tell us more about the confession.

'Worboys/Radford. The boy he claimed to have murdered was a young boy from up north who travelled to London. He was 15, had a young face and glasses; I don't remember the name. Worboys was close to Derek Brown, who murdered an Asian DVD seller.'

It's difficult to know if anything is true in this atmosphere of bravado and bragging, and though our contributor is correct about Derek Brown, this was not the only awful crime that he committed. Brown, a newspaper delivery driver from Preston, Lancashire, was convicted at the Old Bailey in October 2008 for the murders of two women: Xiao Mei Guo, 29, a DVD seller, and Bonnie Barrett, 24, a sex worker. Both women were young mothers whom Brown targeted in Whitechapel, East London. The case drew significant attention due to Brown's apparent desire to emulate the world-famous historic serial killer Jack the Ripper.

Damning evidence presented during the trial indicated that Brown had borrowed a book titled *Killers: The Most Barbaric Murderers of Our Time* from his local library. Additionally, he assembled a makeshift 'murder kit' comprising items such as a bow saw, a steam cleaner and waterproof sheeting. A search of his flat in Rotherhithe, South-East London, revealed traces of blood from both victims in the kitchen, corridor and bathroom, suggesting that he may have dismembered the women there. Brown had attempted to eliminate DNA evidence by stripping the walls and removing carpets from his flat.

Despite the absence of the victims' bodies, the jury

found Brown guilty of both murders. Judge Martin Stevens remarked on Brown's 'frightening efficiency' in disposing of the bodies and noted that he had preyed on Guo, an illegal immigrant, and Barrett, a crack addict, because he believed they were vulnerable and unlikely to be missed. Brown was sentenced to life imprisonment, with a minimum term of 30 years.

The victims' families made appeals to Brown to disclose the whereabouts of their loved ones' remains. Guo's husband, Jin Hua, who had come to Britain illegally with his wife, expressed the anguish of their children repeatedly asking about their mother's whereabouts. He lamented his inability to tell them the truth and pleaded for the return of her body so they could say goodbye. Similarly, Barrett's mother, Jackie Summerford, implored Brown to reveal where to find her 'precious little girl'.

Even our hardened prisoner contact was repulsed by the cruelty Brown showed in gloating about this, revelling in the families' pain and lack of closure. He said that both Brown and Worboys had claimed to be 'hide and seek champions'. They were referring to the police never recovering a body in Brown's case.

In this unimaginably ghastly bragging match, it was at this point that the alleged confession came.

'Worboys said he was a hide and seek champion too and referred to the missing boy. Him and his mate in Bournemouth, Dave, did the boy. I left it and thought nothing of it, then it came on TV about the missing boy, a cold case. I saw it. Worboys referred to it again and said that was his case. Brown and Worboys are from the same area and slept with the same prostitutes. They both knew each other, in fact. Brown never said he was involved, but with Worboys, there is a massive dark side to him, huge.'

Jo had professional recollections of Worboys, which seemed aligned with the Belmarsh staff and inmates in preferring Worboys to Barker, but less exposed to the 'dark side' described above.

'John Worboys? Yes, I remember him clearly. He was on C Wing when he first arrived. I said at the time, "If I got into his taxi, I would've felt completely safe." That was the strange part – he had a warm, friendly face.'

His demeanour was obviously very deceptive, as it was just like a typical friendly London cabbie. 'You'd feel comfortable having a chat with him on the way home. He was not at all suspicious. I couldn't believe it was him when I found out.'

Jo was not trying to excuse what he had done in any way. She was, though, struck by the mismatch between his prison persona and what he had done to get in there.

'On the wing, he was always polite. He'd say, "Morning, ma'am," and he wasn't a disciplinary problem. He didn't come across as threatening in any way, though of course, we all knew what he'd done.'

As we have seen so many times, even a rapist like Worboys sat above a child killer in the pecking order. 'As a sex offender and rapist who drugged adult women in his taxi and assaulted them, it was a horrific crime – but very different from harming children. Some officers could tolerate speaking to him in a way they couldn't with the child killers.'

As an ex-Belmarsh inmate remarked, though, that surface charm concealed a monster.

'He would ask me about DNA, all sorts of questions. He attended sex parties. He would joke about his victims at times. He was very polite and quite pleasant to talk to, but as I got to know him very well, I saw another side.'

For Jo, though, 'He never caused problems on the wing. But I heard later that he was attacked – possibly beaten – at Wakefield, though I wasn't there at the time.'

One ex-inmate also had more recent information on his fate, alleging that, 'Since getting another life sentence he is in a bad way, thin and aged and lost it at Wakefield. My friend has just been to Wakefield with John. John openly admits he is bisexual. He has been for years.'

As she often does, Jo was then able to make a fascinating point contrasting men's with women's prisons, having worked for many years in both.

'This sort of violence happens discreetly in men's prisons. They'll go into a cell, carry out the attack, then leave without anyone saying a word. In women's prisons, fights often happen right in front of officers, hoping they'll step in. But in men's prisons, it's done out of sight. In the showers or empty cells. The cameras don't reach everywhere, and no one will "grass" because they know they'd be next. So even if there's an alarm, everyone pretends not to have seen anything.'

How prisoners interact differs between the genders too,

in Jo's experience. She continues: 'I was a senior officer, usually in the office or walking the landings. In women's prisons, inmates associate more openly on the wings. But in men's prisons, they tend to keep to themselves or socialise behind closed doors. It's a very different environment.'

Jo's insights reminded us that what happens on the surface rarely tells the whole story. Beneath the routines and regulations, in both women's and men's prisons, lies an undercurrent of secrecy which extends far beyond violence.

CHAPTER 18

Contraband, Corruption and Love Behind Bars

'There was spice in Belmarsh; there was
everything in Belmarsh!'

(MIKE)

Just as we have seen in a previous chapter, that even in Belmarsh major incidents of violence can kick off at any moment, we also learned from virtually all our contributors that a shadowy world flourishes beneath the surface of discipline and order. Contraband smuggling, institutional corruption and illicit sexual encounters that often defy logic, and can blur the lines between inmate and officer.

Of course, one of the most prized items of contraband in prison is a mobile phone, and Belmarsh, as always, goes the extra mile in terms of security to try to keep them out, or at least render them obsolete. As one former inmate told us:

'Belmarsh has anti-airport style drone detectors and blocking mechanisms and, within the roof space, Wi-Fi and mobile phone blockers. Even if you did manage to get a mobile phone into this prison, and people have, the chances of using it or finding a good reception are slim.'

Vanessa took a different view, describing how they have tried some signal blockers at Wormwood Scrubs to solve the issue of mobiles, but even so, 'young, vulnerable people are targeted by criminals – they can spot a vulnerable prison officer – and that's how you get mobile phones and other contraband in.' She in part blames underfunding for inadequacies here:

'I'm flabbergasted that drones are such an issue. The technology exists to counter it but it's expensive. Every political party wants to be the party of law and order, but people want their taxes spent on the NHS and education, not prisons.'

Even so, prison's use of technology is increasingly sophisticated, but it is still supplemented by formulae that have been in prison for centuries: officers, the night watch and dogs, as the former inmate who told us about drone detectors continued to describe:

'Not content with their technology, at night-time you can hear night staff walking around the prison, past your door with a scanner which detects any mobile phone signals or transmissions. HMP Belmarsh even have specially trained dogs to detect and find hidden mobile phones, drugs, explosives, even hooch – homemade alcohol.'

It's not straightforward, but ingenious prisoners can make homemade hooch by gathering ingredients from their meals. It doesn't have to be grapes to make a (probably revolting) homemade wine – they can use oranges, apples or whatever they can get their hands on, and sugar. If they get hold of bread then the yeast within it aids the fermentation process. If they mash this concoction up with water and shove it in a loosely sealed plastic bag or container, then they just need to find a suitable, warm place for it while it ferments for days and 'keep it down', in other words, keep it hidden.

This is one of many reasons why cells are constantly checked, or 'spun', as the same former inmate recollected.

'Cell searches are regular and random – there is no set time when you are due for a search – but you will be searched on a regular basis, even taken to reception to be placed on the body scanner.'

He went on to begin to make the connection that we had also spotted, that contraband goes hand in hand with corruption. For something to come in from the outside in Belmarsh, it's highly possible that item was brought in by a member of staff.

The staff may be financially motivated, but they may also have been groomed. Prisoners, especially lifers with nothing to do and little to lose, are typically expert manipulators.

'If staff are seen talking to the same offender on a regular basis, it may be innocent, but they can be moved to another location within the prison if this is reported, and it usually is. Staff in high-security prisons actually fear information being given on them, so it is in their best interest to report unusual staff interactions with offenders.'

This brought us the interesting realisation that if they become aware of corruption among their cohort, they must make the rest of the staff feel highly vulnerable and anxious. Have their colleagues got their back, or have they got a prisoner's back? One source who had been in the HSU described the feeling extending even in there, isolated from the rest of the prison and under even stricter security measures.

'The paranoia is high amongst inmates and staff within HMP Belmarsh . . . I would lie in my cell and hear the loud alarm go off and think, someone has just come in, when on that unit you have no contact with the mainstream prison.'

Mike affirmed that it's not easy bringing contraband into Belmarsh, to put it mildly, and the level of difficulty translates into a cash value.

'Screws can charge three times as much for a parcel at Belmarsh as any other prison because of the security.'

Echoing his point, Nik also mentioned the prices of goods, saying that, 'Everything was tenfold what it was on the streets. A little mobile phone could cost you, like, £500 if you brought it in.' In his view, this was not a risk worth taking: 'But was it worth it? I didn't think it was,' stating that it wasn't just your career on the line but also 'your life. If you got thrown into prison, which you probably would because you would get caught sooner or later.'

Also, after the first occasion, the prisoners had something over you and could manipulate you. Nik said that once you did something like that for a prisoner, 'You couldn't get out. Because they had all day to think about stuff, and they could orchestrate stuff from there as well. It wasn't like they just isolated themselves from the world.'

Mike also told us that in terms of surveillance:

'They dispatch undercover officers from other prisons. Undercover officers can be on the wing for months. Belmarsh employ ex-military translators too. They employ lip readers in the crow's nest on visits.'

He elaborated that in addition to undercover officers, translators and lip readers, there were ex-coppers who had lost their jobs for failings or corruption, including, allegedly, a particularly inappropriate example.

'Belmarsh is a stronghold for police who have been kicked out of the force. For example, the Stephen Lawrence policeman who got sacked was the racial equalities officer!'

Mike told us that in Belmarsh they are recording everything, and you are even recorded on a visit.

'You can't get away with anything. In Belmarsh your voice is taken away. Your family could be hearing you dying over the phone and they can't do anything.'

Whether this is objective truth, this is his truth and highlights the extreme sense of vulnerability and paranoia that he experienced while serving his sentence, a feeling only exacerbated at emotional flashpoints like visits from, or conversations with, his family.

Mike also told us that there is a 'spice' epidemic in the prisons, part of a wider issue with illegal drugs and contraband prescription drugs. 'There was spice in Belmarsh; there was everything in Belmarsh.'

Our ex-prisoners, particularly Aitken and one

anonymous contributor, recalled plenty of drugs inside too. The latter saw spice as especially prevalent.

'There is a spice issue within all prisons. Belmarsh was flooded with paper spice. An imam that worked within the prison was suspected of bringing the drugs on paper into the HMP Belmarsh. Security at Belmarsh is very good, and covert listening devices are everywhere. CCTV, even being seen talking to staff too long creates attention. The imam was indeed caught red-handed bringing in pages upon pages of blank white paper which was laced with spice.'

Once we had recovered from the shock allegation that it was an imam doing it, we needed to understand what it was. Until this information was shared with us, we didn't know about 'paper spice'.

It refers to synthetic cannabinoids, man-made substances that imitate THC, the psychoactive component of cannabis, and are applied to paper products. These drugs are often marketed as 'herbal incense' or 'potpourri' and sold in small packages with labels stating 'not for human consumption'.

As described above, a worrying method of smuggling involves soaking paper, such as letters or greeting cards, in a solution of synthetic cannabinoids. Once dried, the paper is mailed, making detection difficult. Nasty side effects of paper spice include severe agitation, hallucinations, seizures and even death.

Jonathan Aitken had some depressing, but lively, recollections of drugs use in Belmarsh, which sounds absolutely rampant back then.

'Belmarsh was an extraordinary place because of the drugs. Everybody was wandering around "clucking", which is Belmarsh slang for making the noise of a hen. Who makes it? Anyone who's had a certain amount of drugs.'

This sounds really weird, and Jonathan too found it foreign and peculiar – 'I thought I was in an Egyptian souk rather than an English jail, with people spinning around.' He was astonished by the level of substance misuse and expressed profound relief to be a distance removed from it now.

'The quantity of drug use was staggering. They were all just off their heads all the time, doing acrobatics, lying on the floor. They were a mess. Now, well, luckily chaplains can stay away from it, but all the drugs have changed since then, in 2000.'

Today, they have changed to spice. Ex-officer Caroline concurred that 'there was definitely spice in Belmarsh', and that wasn't the only thing.

'I never found a phone, but I know it has happened. I haven't found spice, but I have found drug paraphernalia.'

Reports suggest improvement since Aitken's description at the turn of the millennium, but over 20 years on, in the year leading up to March 2021, there were still 198 drug seizures at Belmarsh, the highest number since records began in 2016 to 2017. The most frequently found substances were psychoactive drugs, accounting for 130 of these seizures.

In part to try and combat this issue, Belmarsh

introduced body-scanning technology in 2018, using low-level X-rays to detect inmates concealing contraband. This led to the discovery of mobile phones, weapons and drugs that might have evaded detection during standard strip searches. Interestingly, the initiative received positive feedback from not just staff but prisoners too.

A lover of outlandish tales, Mike also told us that he is a veterinary nurse and that at one time he had the 13th largest private animal collection in the UK. They were kept at three different properties and at one point, his story goes, he had an alligator and a monitor lizard walking around.

On a far less fairy-tale note, he also told the story of how he was electrocuted by a faulty kettle. The cord had become unstable and dangerous, and when he used the kettle, the shock he received was severe enough to land him in hospital. When he came back, he claimed that they had changed his prison number to make sure that the electrocution with the kettle was not reported as an incident.

Though this was an accident, there are many examples in our books of prisoners and patients fashioning lethal weapons out of a plethora of household objects, including 'shanks', which are makeshift stabbing weapons. This may be in part because of their familiarity with knives, guns and other weapons in the outside world.

One ex-inmate described his subject matter expertise on guns in chilling detail.

'I have handled firearms due to my criminality and am

experienced within the field of firearms. Namely shotguns, .410 and 12 bore and handguns 9mm. I could take a standard 9mm handgun apart blindfolded and put it back together.'

As always, exasperated by the many misconceptions and untruths about prison and crime that he's had to listen to over the years, he debunked what he sees as a nonsense misrepresentation about replica firearms.

'Replicas too. A lot is said that these guns are drilled out; this is fantasy. The barrel is simply replaced with a hollow hardened steel barrel to withstand the firing of the bullet. So, I do know my stuff when it comes to guns.'

Prisoners talk to each other and share their knowledge too, as he attested when describing a conversation with another inmate who turned out to be a fellow gun geek.

'I pushed him on the technical aspects of guns, and he knew them well. He even made comments about how to reactivate them, how to change the barrel and replace it with a short length of steel pipe. He talked about making bullets and silencers. He had great knowledge in these areas. Of course, this may have been a result of going through a previous trial and reviewing expert reports, but his knowledge was still impressive.'

Aside from this disturbing vignette of prisoners swapping stories in order to add to their armoury, almost literally as well as figuratively, this account is yet another insight into why the prison deploys the extreme measures that it does. As corroborated by all our other contributors, Caroline describes security at Belmarsh as incredibly tight.

'There is anti-drone technology. The HSU is inescapable. Belmarsh has dogs too. They use Belgian Malinois and German shepherds. As sniffers, they have cocker spaniels and Labradors.'

We asked if the dogs were always disciplined or if it was easy to treat them as pets. Turns out the dogs are as steely and professional as almost everyone else working at Belmarsh.

'The dogs know when they are at work.'

Belmarsh employs these various dog breeds to maintain security and assist in prison operations. They have, as Caroline observed, got distinct functions. German shepherds are mainly used as patrol dogs, providing perimeter security and assisting in controlling prisoner disturbances.

Breeds such as springer spaniels, cocker spaniels and Labradors are trained for detection purposes, including searching for drugs, firearms and other contraband. These breeds are selected for their intelligence, trainability and suitability for specific roles within the prison environment.

The consequences are severe for staff found bringing the wrong things into Belmarsh or sending what are deemed to be the wrong things out, as a former prisoner explained:

'Other staff have been sacked for leaking information to the media about high-profile offenders. I and others were a victim of this one officer. He was convicted for misconduct in a public office and sent to prison. So, corruption is seen at HMP Belmarsh as it is within other prisons.'

We believe he is referring to a case involving Robert

Norman, a former Belmarsh prison officer, who was convicted in 2015 for misconduct in public office, although regarding his personal circumstances, the court acknowledged that Norman was the sole carer for his sick wife, which contributed to a reduced sentence of 20 months' imprisonment. Norman received over £10,000 for providing 40 tips to journalist Stephen Moyes between 2006 and 2011. The information he disclosed included details about staff cuts and incidents within the prison. He claimed his actions were in the public interest, but the court found otherwise, leading to his conviction.

One man's grass is another man's whistleblower, though. The prisoner may not have liked having his details put out there in some way, but Norman was arguably performing a public service. This story is very complicated and rattled those who cherish the anonymity of sources as a cornerstone of a free, democratic society.

The esteemed Chartered Institute of Journalists came out in support for Norman, who was also a trade union representative, jailed as part of what was termed Operation Elveden, the Metropolitan Police operation investigating journalists who paid public official sources. The Chartered Institute of Journalists (CIoJ) is the world's oldest professional association of journalists, operating under a charter granted in 1890 by HM Queen Victoria.

Most of the journalists have been acquitted or told they will not be charged. This was the case with the *Daily Mirror* and *News of the World* reporter Stephen Moyes. The Mirror Group surrendered the confidentiality of his dealings with Mr Norman, who was prosecuted for misconduct in public office and jailed for 20 months. Their statement is a carefully worded and interesting read.

'The institute is the only journalist organisation to campaign for Elveden sources. We are pressing for new laws to give sources greater protection and a legal remedy to sue journalists or publishers who "burn" them to the police or anyone else. Robert Norman is the only Elveden source challenging his conviction and sentence on the grounds that his rights under Article 8 and 10 of the European Convention of Human Rights were violated.'

The article went on to note that the Lord Chief Justice and two other appeal court judges were expected to give their ruling in October. This ruling did not go in Norman's favour.

His barrister Keir Monteith had told the court that Mirror Group Newspapers handed over Norman's details voluntarily to the police without a court-granted production order. He said no newspaper can hand over sources without breaching Article 10 of the European Convention on Human Rights dealing with freedom of expression and information.

The CIoJ article expanded on the reasons why the Norman case could set a dangerous precedent.

'The judge in Norman's original trial should have stayed the prosecution because the police did not go through the proper legal process when obtaining information about a confidential journalistic source from the *Daily Mirror* publisher.'

Given the stories that Norman leaked, many of them were in the public interest, including concerns about staff cuts, a plot to assassinate a governor and claims that a Roman Catholic chaplain was having affairs with inmates. The CIoJ also pushed back on the blanket idea that payment meant bribery and corruption, which 'does not allow for any public interest defence for journalists and the people giving them information'.

The author of the impassioned piece, Tim Crook, was not only concerned for an individual man that he believed had been betrayed, but for the far wider implications for journalists' sources.

'Like the hundreds of public officials I had, and may still have, as protected sources, Mr Norman is a man of courage and conviction. He was on the front line of the acute crisis in our country's prison system. He was a qualified and significant intelligence source serving the public interest to a free media in a democratic society that has a constitutional duty to hold government, and other state bodies, to account in relation to the criminal justice system. He was an agent of democracy. He was not being corrupted. He was being compensated, very modestly, for the appalling consequences of being discovered. This was not even a reward for favours. The £10,000 he received over five years for over 40 stories could not be construed in any way as bribery.'

His argument is persuasive, not least because of the immense suffering that was caused to Norman by being exposed. We can certainly feel the intense paranoia in our own staff contributors, who are extremely careful not to give anything away that could come back to bite them, and we protect them in turn with a thorough legal read. With both our staff and inmates, occasionally we pick up on something that they didn't that we know could unwittingly expose them in some way, and that ends up on the cutting room floor.

While paid whistleblowing might be a grey area, staff having sexual relationships with inmates certainly is not.

Given what we have seen are phenomenally strict security measures, any breaches of conduct involving inappropriate relationships between staff and inmates would be both fairly surprising, and a big cause for concern. Even so, we heard about a few instances, and several more have hit the press.

One such case was told to us by Nik and involved a female prison officer who engaged in a secret relationship with an inmate.

'She was sneaking around, sending him explicit photos marked with "no face, no case",' Nik recalled, expressing both disgust and disbelief.

'One day, she disappeared during her shift. We couldn't find her anywhere, only to discover she was hiding under the inmate's bed! She was caught and later faced court for her actions.'

He emphasised the risks such misconduct posed: 'It wasn't just about her, it jeopardised everyone's safety. You didn't know what else she was smuggling in for him.'

Here, Nik raises the link between sex, contraband and corruption, which so often go hand in hand.

Paris Bregazzi had stuck in Nik's mind too, because, from what he remembered, she tried to use her sexuality inside Belmarsh. Bregazzi, a transgender beautician from London, had been jailed following a series of violent offences, including assaults on police officers and public disturbances. Her criminal history includes 64 prior convictions, reflecting a pattern of aggressive behaviour and mental health challenges.

In July 2017, after consuming four bottles of Prosecco, Bregazzi was involved in an altercation at Hanger Lane station. When off-duty PC Sam Chegwin intervened, she pushed him on to the Tube tracks. Fortunately, he avoided serious injury. In February 2018, she received a six-month suspended sentence for this offence, with the judge citing her 'special vulnerabilities' and mental health issues.

However, in March 2018, Bregazzi committed further offences. She was seen acting aggressively on Stockwell Road, throwing wheelie bins and smashing a car window with a brick. She then assaulted PC Florina Russ by kneeing her in the chest during arrest. While on bail, she sprayed perfume at a security guard at Waterloo Station and caused damage to a police cell. Crystal meth was found in her possession, though no charges were brought for this.

In April 2018, Judge Rebecca Poulet activated her suspended sentence and added additional time, resulting in a total of ten months' imprisonment. In November 2019, Bregazzi was jailed for eight weeks for a racially aggravated assault in Southwark. Earlier that year, she had received a 24-week sentence for assaults against six women. These incidents landed her in Belmarsh while Nik was working there.

According to Nik, Bregazzi 'tried to use her situation to her advantage'.

She would say, 'I'll show you my tits if you get me this or that. Prisoners would take advantage of that too.'

However, not all our former officers witnessed such incidents. Caroline insisted she saw little evidence of either love behind bars or of corruption during her time at Belmarsh. We wanted to know if she'd experienced hassle, though, as a female officer.

'I was propositioned maybe three or four times. I was always very fair with prisoners. You have to learn not to judge. I did experience a disrespectful prisoner, though. He was calling me an unpleasant name. The other prisoners on my block did not like him doing that; they said, "You don't talk to a female like that."'

Those incidents were few and far between for Caroline, we were pleased to hear. She did state that the 'teenagers were disrespectful to everyone' though.

In stark and rather amusing contrast, Mike told us that he 'has been caught' in every prison he has been in with a female!

'One head of an education department even left her husband for me. Said she was in love with me. They will say on your notes that you are a threat to female officers if you have a relationship inside.'

Mike pointed out to us the, in his view, absurdity that he can't be searched by a female officer but a homosexual officer can search him. He also noted a cultural shift within the prison service over the years, observing, 'It has become all zero-hour contracts, and you get 19-year-old girls that flirt with the prisoners. The old ex-military type prison staff are not there any more.'

Perhaps the most high-profile recent case involved Hayley Jones, a 33-year-old prison worker from Kent, who admitted to misconduct in public office after engaging in an inappropriate relationship with Jordan McSweeney, the convicted murderer of Zara Aleena. Jones pleaded guilty in 2023 after her relationship with McSweeney – who was serving a life sentence – came to light at HMP Belmarsh.

A shocking facet of this story is that Hayley Jones was presumably fully aware of the appalling reason that McSweeney was serving a life term at Belmarsh. On 26 June 2022, Zara Aleena, a 35-year-old law graduate, was brutally raped and murdered by McSweeney while walking home in Ilford, East London. He had been released from prison on licence just nine days before. An inquest jury later determined that failures across multiple state agencies – including the Metropolitan Police, HM Prison and Probation Service, and other criminal justice bodies – contributed to her death.

With a staggering 28 previous convictions for 69 offences, including violence and threats against women, he was incorrectly assessed as a medium-risk offender upon his release on 17 June 2022. He failed to attend a probation appointment on the day of his release and missed another on 20 June. Despite these breaches, his recall to prison was not initiated until 22 June, and the police were not informed until 24 June. An attempt to arrest him on 25 June was unsuccessful, and in the early hours of 26 June, he attacked Zara Aleena. The jury concluded that these failures significantly contributed to her death. In December 2022, McSweeney was sentenced to life imprisonment with a minimum term of 38 years, later reduced to 33 years on appeal. Zara Aleena's family has expressed profound grief, emphasising that her death was preventable and calling for systemic reforms to protect others from similar tragedies.

Given his terrible history, it is mind-blowing that Hayley Jones became sexually involved, though she may, of course, have fallen prey to grooming and manipulation by a cold-blooded, violent man with a history of sexual abuse of women and time on his hands.

Even so, from our research, and aside from Mike's evident sexual allure, instances of illicit sex do seem to be rare at Belmarsh, but certainly not unheard of.

His mother certainly wasn't bringing in contraband, but Mike movingly recalled her trauma when visiting him, recounting that she had a panic attack. Sadly, this seemed very plausible, unlike his next story, which was nevertheless highly entertaining.

'Belmarsh has signal blockers so you can't fly a drone. I had a tame eagle that brought me lamb chops. A bateleur eagle. The eagle knew my call. He could carry up to a kilo in weight.'

Mike chuckled at the absurdity of it but in his memory, the ultimate contraband item was the, admittedly moreish and delicious, cereal Cinnamon Grahams.

'They were the hardest thing to get through. They were selling for £80 a box!'

CHAPTER 19

Jonathan Aitken

'I was quite sorry to leave Belmarsh.'

We spent several hours with Jonathan in his stunning West London home, in a book-lined room with a warm period fireplace and walls adorned with art. He started our session by pointing out that he had read our book, *Inside Broadmoor*, much to our delight.

Jonathan Aitken, a former Conservative MP and cabinet minister, was convicted in 1999 for perjury and perverting the course of justice. The case stemmed from his failed libel lawsuit against the *Guardian* newspaper and Granada Television, where he falsely claimed that his wife had paid for his stay at the Paris Ritz hotel. The bill was settled by a Saudi businessman, which was a breach of ministerial rules. He was sentenced to 18 months in prison, serving a part of his sentence at Belmarsh, and the remainder at Standford Hill open prison on the Isle of Sheppey, Kent. He was released in 2000 after serving seven months. Following his release, he pursued theological studies and was ordained in the Church of England in 2018. Since then, he has served as a prison chaplain, dedicating much of his time to helping incarcerated individuals find spiritual guidance. He is philosophical, fiercely intelligent, humble and, unexpectedly, often hilarious about his time in Belmarsh.

'I never shared a cell with anybody in Belmarsh for the simple reason that Belmarsh was scared to put me in a cell with anyone. They were worried that somebody might try something. In actual fact, my memories of Belmarsh, although there were ups and downs, as all prisoners' experiences are, on the whole, are quite positive. It was weird and strange, but I didn't have a bad journey in Belmarsh.'

This stoic stance and good grace appears to have characterised his entire approach to his incarceration and may have helped him to survive it.

'The first thing is, I had no idea I was going to Belmarsh. There was no sinister reason for it, just the usual, dotty prison rules. Everybody that day was sent to Belmarsh.'

He seemed very calm about the unpredictability of the situation, but he had done his best to be prepared, through research and his extraordinary networks.

'The one thing I had done before going to Belmarsh was prepare enormously, thoroughly, for prison. How? I asked anybody I could find – and I found quite a few – who knew about prison. I asked of them, "Just tell me what it's like; tell me how to get ready."'

Jonathan's late wife had been married to Richard Harris, the movie star, 'and he had a lot of acquaintances who had been in prison, including some famous villains. He gave me all kinds of advice before I went inside about needing protection and that sort of thing.'

His fate hanging in the balance at this point, Jonathan emphasised the uncertainty around whether he would end up inside.

'There was a 90 per cent chance I was going to prison. But on the day, I could have received a non-custodial sentence.

My optimistic lawyers thought there was a one-third or more chance I wouldn't go to prison. But I always thought, "You can't take a tall poppy like me and put him on probation."'

Sadly, he turned out to be correct that his high profile may have contributed to his custodial sentence. His experience of the Old Bailey, as he explained, was both strange and familiar at the same time.

'When the sentencing is read out, you stand there, and you go down. I was in Court Number One and, extraordinarily, I was already very familiar with it. I had been there before, in the Official Secrets Act trial, in 1969.'

Before he became a politician, Jonathan had been a journalist, and he was at the Old Bailey in 1969 in that capacity. He continued by describing the imposing physical space and the demeanour of the staff there.

'The dock is enormous – almost the size of this room – because it can accommodate a gang of 20. But in the corner, there's a circular staircase where you go down.

'Everyone was extraordinarily nice to me. Up to that

point, most people had been unpleasant, but now everyone was extremely polite. Even a female journalist was almost sobbing with sorrow for me.

'Having gone down the steps, the next thing was a cup of tea. "You're a prisoner now. Sorry, but we have to do some paperwork."

'That was no small operation. I was then taken somewhere – I've forgotten what the forms were about – but it took about 15 to 20 minutes to fill them in. Not difficult, but extensive.'

Up until this point, boredom appears to have been the most negative emotion that Jonathan Aitken experienced, but all of that was about to change.

'Then, I was put into a holding cell with a lot of other prisoners. The first unpleasant moment came when I was in the Belmarsh waiting cell. "The Cage" was a real eye-opener. A mass holding cell. A big room, five times the size of a normal room. It could take a hundred people, comfortably. It was a very difficult place.

'There was so much noise. I still wake up at night thinking about "the Cage". The shouting, the effings and blindings. The fights. There was one group kicking a man in the testicles, blaming him for their convictions and shouting, "You've got the script wrong, you fucking idiot!" Another prisoner just kept charging into the bars, over and over again, until his head was covered in blood.

'Suddenly, someone said, "I'm terribly sorry, but we have to put you in handcuffs now." It seemed absurd because we were already in an extremely secure area, and we were only going a very short distance from the cells of the Old Bailey to the waiting "sweat box" or prison van.

'They put rather old-fashioned restraints on me: handcuffs on a chain. I think it was some ritual probably invented in the 1920s. But still, suddenly being in chains, in handcuffs – it was a shock. This was a new world, even though I had experience of these things.'

As we have also heard from other contributors, there is an almost balletic or filmic choreography to the prisoner van transportation from the Old Bailey to Belmarsh, although the atmosphere within the van is loud, claustrophobic and intensely stressful.

'Then, you get into the sweat box. It was about the most uncomfortable form of transportation imaginable. I think I called it a "toilet cell" in my book. It was tiny. My 20 fellow passengers were quite noisy. Not about me, but in general. That particular van was exactly what the media wanted: a picture of the "jail minister".

'There was a terrific athleticism around the vans trying to pull out, with the press trying to take pictures through the dark windows, although they hadn't a clue who was in which. It felt like the night of the Oscars. There were so many flashes going off, and so much speculation about who was inside.

'Another thing that struck me was the sheer size of the paparazzi crowd. Enormous. Hundreds, literally hundreds of them. There was no news that day, clearly. I wasn't filled with fear – journalism is full of curiosity – but it was overpowering.

'And, yes, I was still in my suit.

'Then, I think the word had gone around in the van. There was a lot of effing and blinding, and then the van still had, because it was June and daylight, tinted windows you could just about see out of. The route of the van passed endless places where I had had a life in the city of London.

'I thought, "Well, I'll never see these places again."'

Musing on this long, life-changing journey, Jonathan observed that 'Belmarsh is a very strange, difficult place to get to from almost anywhere.' The trip gave him plenty of time to think.

'I was sitting in that tiny little van, and things just went through my head. One of the people I thought about was Richard Nixon, because I had written his biography and knew him well. While I wrestled with leg cramp in my sweat box compartment, I thought about how, when he was flying off in the helicopter on the day of his resignation as president of the United States, he recited a little ballad. I forget who wrote it. It was:

I am hurt, but I am not slain.
So I'll lay me down and bleed awhile
Then I'll rise and fight again.

'That was from Kipling, I think. And I do remember Nixon once saying to me – Nixon was rather given to one-liners – and he said, "You have to remember that failure is not falling down. Failure is falling down and not getting up again to continue with life's race." I thought, "Well, that's good." So, I thought of that.

'It was a very profound journey. Almost like your life flashing before your eyes. Absolutely.'

It may have seemed interminable, but in the end, the journey reached its inevitable destination.

'Then we got to Belmarsh. As we arrived, somebody shouted, "Welcome to Hell!"

'I think that was from the van, and it seemed very appropriate. We swung into these huge fortress-like gates, which are utterly overpowering in their size. We got off the van.'

He recalled massive concrete walls, watchtowers, glinting coils of barbed wire, serried ranks of searchlights, CCTV cameras pointing at you from all angles and the iron bars on every door and window. This, of course, was just the external impressions.

'Once inside, there were a lot of officers, barking dogs on leashes. It really did feel like a sort of Gulag.'

With the term Gulag, Jonathan is referring to the notorious system of Soviet labour camps and accompanying detention and transit camps and prisons that existed for decades in the early to mid-part of the 20th century. Perhaps not quite the comparison you would want to draw with a prison that had only opened its doors in April 1991, in modern Britain. Some of it, he could see, was stage-managed for purposeful effect.

'It was very deliberately intimidating. They put it on.

'I was inside. The number of officers, the dogs, was

overwhelming. We were taken into a building, into a room called "the Cage". This was the reception area.

'The first officer I met was distinctly unpleasant. Not because he did anything particularly cruel, but because of his sharpness, his grip. In Belmarsh, though, in the end I got on well with quite a few officers.

'I felt horribly conspicuous in my suit and tie, trying to fade into the background. One inmate came up and shook my hand. "Sorry, Steven here," he said. "You did my brother a good turn when he was in Ramsgate." Then he asked, "What did the beak give you?" I said, "Eighteen months." "Oh well, that's politics, I suppose."'

Although he had taken advice and tried to think through what he was bringing into Belmarsh carefully, no preparation could be enough.

'Then came the issue of my property. I had brought a small bag, but my notebook wasn't allowed. Its coil binding was a security risk. My radio was confiscated for having a shortwave band.'

His handkerchiefs were disallowed because they were larger than regulation and 'could be used as a noose'. It was unsettling to have what appeared to be anodyne objects confiscated as potential weapons or tools of self-harm.

'Even my belt was taken because the buckle was too large. For a moment I thought my leg was being pulled. Was I going to start on a group of prison officers with my belt buckle?'

After this intensive discussion about his small bag of belongings, there was the question of where to place him.

'I was asked if I wanted to go on the "numbers": the vulnerable prisoners' wing. I didn't understand at first, but a prisoner shouted, "Hey, mate! Whatever you do, don't take the fucking cucumbers!" He meant Rule 43. The wing for sex offenders. I had already decided against it.

'The officers thought I was unwise. "You sure?" they asked. "I'll take my chances," I said. It wasn't courage, just common sense.'

In our view, it was both. The next story he told was one of the highlights of our entire meeting, and a perfect illustration of his ability to relish the absurd even in the most stressful situations, like a psychiatric assessment.

'I was sent to see the psychiatrist. I had no idea why. It was high comedy. My sentencing had been all over the news, but the psychiatrist didn't have a clue who I was. He asked: "Name? Date of birth? Next of kin? Does your next of kin know you're in prison? Does anyone else know?" I smiled. "I think . . . maybe ten million people."

'He didn't react. Instead, he asked, "Do you really mean to tell me that you think ten million people are in prison?" I replied, 'Well . . . I guess.' He put down his pen. "Have you ever suffered from delusions?"

'I thought, "This is fantastic." His note-takers, who understood what was happening, stifled their laughter.'

We weren't able to stifle our laughter. The psychiatrist may not have recognised him, but his reputation spread fast among the general prison population.

'The next day, I met Stokesy, a young black prisoner. He pulled me aside. "Look, I know you're someone who knows the ropes. Could you do me a favour?" He had received a letter but couldn't read it. It was from Lambeth Social Services, informing him of his eviction for unpaid rent. He panicked. "What should I do? My kid's going to be homeless!"

'I explained I'd been an MP and knew eviction law. "If someone pays even a small sum, say, ten shillings a week, you can prevent eviction. A child in the household protects you from immediate removal." His relief was palpable. I suggested he write to the council and a solicitor. His face fell. "Ah, man, I got another problem. I don't do no reading . . . and I don't do no writing either. Could you write it for me?"

'I wrote his appeal in proper, grammatical English. It was a respectful, legally sounding letter that should stop the eviction.

'Stokesy was beyond grateful. Instead of handling it quietly, though, he turned into an 18th-century town crier. "Hey, guys! This MP geezer of ours has got fucking marvellous joined-up writing!"

'Suddenly, a queue formed outside my cell every evening. My status transformed. I was no longer just an 'awful Tory cabinet minister'. I was useful.

'That morning, an officer told me, "Aitken, you're going to Beirut." Another inmate warned, "Oh, don't go to Beirut. That's where the real hard men are. If you get on the wrong side of them, they'll crush your balls, mate." I had no idea what he meant. Eventually, I learned "Beirut" was just B Wing.

'Two jolly officers escorted me down a labyrinth of brick corridors and barred gates. As we passed a staffroom, a group of officers were watching TV. My own picture was on the screen. One of my escorts said, "Oh, look, it's the Channel 4 documentary, *The Real Jonathan Aitken*." My escort chuckled, "Yeah, as soon as we bang you up, we're going back to watch part two."

'I reached my cell. A notice was solemnly read to me: "It is an offence, punishable by 28 days in solitary confinement, to feed the pigeons."'

It was that evening that he first heard an incredibly memorable practice, 'doing a quizzy', that may have died out, as it was not recalled to us in the same terms by any other former prisoners who had done time more recently.

'That night, I heard a ritual called "doing a quizzy". Inmates shouted questions across the wing. Sometimes they were crude: "Who'd like to shag Officer S?" Sometimes they were coded messages: "Remember to tell the court the car was green."

'But that night, it was about me.

"What are we gonna do to him?"

"Let's eat his balls!"

"Let's give him a good kicking!"

'It was nasty. They were high on drugs, but it was still terrifying. The threats felt real, and I took them seriously. I have never felt more lonely, frightened or vulnerable. I knelt and tried to say a prayer, but I was too scared. Then I sat on the edge of the bed and felt the pamphlet *Praying the Psalms* in my pocket. That gave me some solace and reassurance.'

By morning, everything had changed.

'At roll call, the same men greeted me warmly. "Morning, Aitken! Hope you slept well." One added, "Sorry about last night. Nothing personal. Everyone's on the tackle." Suddenly, I was "one of them".

'A huge bruiser leered at me through broken teeth. "All you need to know about Beirut is that it's got new boys, naughty boys and nasty boys. I'm one of the nasty ones."

'"Thank you for telling me," I said.

'I must have passed his test. He stopped leering and started smiling.

'One thing you can do in prison, if you don't like someone, is grass them up. Someone reported I had come in with drugs. What I call "the Ghostbusters" – the drug squad – arrived. They tore the place apart. Eventually, the DST squad leader said, "You are clean. The dogs don't seem to like the smell of an MP."

'After that, my prison nickname, Jonno, stuck.

'I wrote letters. Then came the chaplain, known as "the Pie". I had no idea why. But "Pie and liquor" equals "vicar" in Cockney slang when they don't remember your name.'

It was a long wait, but he managed to get a few more basic supplies to help him through his life inside.

'I was sent an ordinary razor, ordinary writing equipment, but it took days to sort out. The one thing I got quite quickly was because you were allowed to take in a certain amount of money. So, on my private cash and canteen, I could almost immediately buy writing paper. That made everything better. But those first days were difficult, although there were lots of people trying to be helpful too. Some even offered me loans. One man offered me a loan of a million pounds.'

Jonathan recalled the structure and demographic breakdown of the prison and broadly thought that it worked.

'There were terrorists there too. Belmarsh had a unit within the prison – essentially a prison within a prison – part of it Category B, most of it Category A, with a double-A Cat wing for terrorists and habitual escapers . . . On the whole, Belmarsh, in terms of administration and security, was quite well run.'

Even inside, he was aware of media sensationalism and fascination with his story.

'The Sunday papers had nothing to write about except me, publishing the most incredible fictions.

'The reality, though, was that "I was expecting it to be awful, and it wasn't."'

While we appreciated his mental and physical toughness in dealing with it, there must have been things he craved from the outside world, we asked?

'What did I miss? Quiet. And peace, although once the prison settled down at night, it became like a great silent battleship. I've always managed with less sleep than most, so I used to lie awake at night, get up early.'

Many contributors have agreed that the vibe changes

radically at night, to an almost surreal extent, although the noise can continue. Jonathan's profoundly even spiritual nature permitted him to offer gratitude for his experience inside Belmarsh.

'Strangely, I was thankful, because prison wasn't nearly as bad as I'd thought. I never felt dangerously threatened despite all the trialling. I could see at once that this was a community I could live in. Yes, OK, maybe someone was going to hit me for something – and they did occasionally. But if you behaved sensibly, the wing was quite a good community.

'People would say, "Oh, don't get lairy with him – he's a decent bloke." I had chums. "Protection" is too strong a word, but people looked out for me.'

Jonathan was adept at establishing allies, but what about those green-behind-the-ears new arrivals, we wanted to know?

'When an 18-year-old arrives, the older guys take a sort of pride in guiding them. When some accountant who's cooked the books arrives, they see him as a no-hoper. "You don't have a clue," they think. "You know your figures, but you're fucking useless in here. For a start, take your specs off, otherwise, they'll be nicked."

'I was advised to give the gym a miss, which was good advice. I had been a semi-serious club runner for years, did marathons, so I structured my time. I wrote out a routine:

7 – 8:00am: Pray.

8 – 9:00am: Answer letters

9:00am: Read a John le Carré novel.

'Discipline was important. I learned a bit of poetry every day.

'I was taking notes on my book, *Porridge and Passion*, inside Belmarsh. I think I finished the book within a few weeks.'

It's an exceptional book, as we can attest!

Despite this pragmatic establishment of routine, learning and external interaction, Jonathan was in an inappropriate environment which mismatched his crime, as he explained: 'I was kept in Belmarsh longer than I should have been. I was recategorised – unsurprisingly – as Category D, meaning I was not dangerous or likely to escape. But I wasn't allowed to leave.

'That didn't bother me. Within five days, I thought, "I can live here."'

The decision was not simply his, though. The officers in charge of him were concerned about his high categorisation, as he explained:

'The officers tried to move me but couldn't. Prison is chaotic. A governor of any prison can refuse a prisoner, and the Cat D governors all rang each other up and said, "The media coverage is too much. This guy is going to be trouble. Media trouble." So, they all wrote back saying, "I, the governor of *** Prison, object on personal grounds to having Aitken."'

Staff that he had on side despised this behaviour.

'The admissions officer came to me and said, "Look, this is very unfair."

'I said, "What's the terrible injustice? I've been going along fine."'

As he explained, 'That was why I stayed so long. Eventually, the newspapers picked up on it: "It's very unfair that he's been kept in high-security conditions." Jack Straw, who I knew well, asked that I be released from Belmarsh to Cat D.'

He moved into a lower-category prison before being released and continuing his extraordinary life. Colin has vivid and fond memories of Aitken, with whom he struck up a friendship:

'The bottom line is, when Jonathan finally got to the main wing in Wandsworth, we went in together. We were in reception at the same time. I kind of knew who he was, which I think baffled him a bit. There were only two people in the room – he was sitting in a chair facing a desk with a prison officer, and I walked in looking worse for wear, my arm bandaged up from slashing it. At that point, I was looking at seven and a half years in prison. I was withdrawing, sitting next to him.

'I looked him in the eye, and he looked me in the eye. First time. I immediately said, "Oh, Jonathan Aitken, what do you think of the 'trusted sword of British justice' now?"

'He looked slightly wounded, and I immediately felt bad.'

Colin is referring to Jonathan Aitken's challenge to the British press after issuing libel writs, which became notorious once he lost his case.

'If it falls to me to start a fight to cut out the cancer of

bent and twisted journalism in our country with the simple
sword of truth and the trusty shield of fair play, so be it.
I am ready for the fight,' he said.

Colin's opening gambit did not prevent the two men
forming a lasting friendship, as he described:

'Over the next few months, we ended up having a bit
of a crossover. In all my years in prison, I had done an
awful lot of reading. I'm a big reader now. It's a thing of
mine. I read a couple of his books, which really surprised
me. I was impressed. I even went to a couple of book
launches with him. I had quite a lot of time for him.

'We met in Belmarsh, and it was interesting. My
immediate instinct was to be protective of him. On his
first day on the wing, we were in the dinner queue, and
someone behind me shouted, "Kill the MP!" or something
like that. He just ignored it.

'I realised within five seconds that he didn't need any
protection – at all. Just the fact that he was on the main
wing proved that. He could have pulled strings and had
the prison wrapped around his little finger, but he didn't.
And he didn't need me either.

'We were in Belmarsh for maybe two or three months
together. He left before me. He was moved elsewhere. Since
then, when he comes down to the South West, he gives me
a ring, and we spend the day together. Occasionally, I pop
up to see him. He knows my wife and kids.'

Albeit very brief, one of the weirder Belmarsh incarcer-
ations was the seemingly hapless Denis MacShane, a
former Labour MP and Minister for Europe. He had found

himself to be a main character in the UK parliamentary expenses scandal, leading to his resignation and subsequent imprisonment.

Between 2004 and 2008, MacShane submitted 19 false invoices totalling £12,900 for 'research and translation' services purportedly provided by the European Policy Institute (EPI). Investigations revealed that the EPI was a non-existent entity, with no office or staff, and that MacShane controlled its bank account.

It didn't look great that he signed the invoices using a pseudonym, basically authorising payments to himself. The Parliamentary Commissioner for Standards found that these claims bypassed the House's checks and controls, enabling MacShane to spend public funds as he saw fit. Although the total claimed was £12,900, it was determined that at least £7,500 was outside the rules. MacShane repaid the entire amount and acknowledged his misconduct. Sadly, for him it didn't end there.

In November 2012, following a report by the Parliamentary Standards and Privileges Committee, he resigned as MP for Rotherham, which he had been since 1994. From this historic distance somewhat harshly, the committee described his actions as the 'gravest case' of misconduct it had adjudicated. As night follows day, then the Metropolitan Police reopened their investigation, leading to MacShane's arrest and charge for false accounting. In November 2013, he pleaded guilty to the charges at the Old Bailey. The court sentenced him to six months' imprisonment, with the judge emphasising that MPs who abuse their position and public trust must expect custodial sentences.

What they mustn't necessarily expect is to serve that custodial sentence at Belmarsh. He wasn't there for very long – about six weeks before he got out under the home detention curfew scheme, commonly known as tagging – but it still seems absurd. The tagging scheme allows offenders to serve a portion of their sentence under curfew, monitored electronically, to facilitate reintegration into society.

This put us in mind of the criminals who, while still perpetrators of very serious crimes, do not come close to some of the truly ghastly lifers in Belmarsh.

CHAPTER 20

The Securitas Robbers, Ronnie Biggs and the Hatton Garden Gang

'The way the Hatton Garden guys were portrayed on the news was the same as how they came across in person. They were like Dad's Army. Just older gentlemen.'

(MATTHEW)

Belmarsh has a substantial history of robbery gangs as well as terrorists and serial killers. An early celebrity example was the Great Train Robber, Ronnie Biggs. Biggs was a member of the gang that carried out the Great Train Robbery on 8 August 1963, which targeted a Royal Mail train travelling from Glasgow to London. Successfully intercepting the train at Sears Crossing in Buckinghamshire, the robbers grabbed a phenomenal £2.6 million, which is around £30 million in today's money. Part of Biggs's role in the heist was to secure a train driver to operate the hijacked locomotive, and at that point things got messy. The substitute driver could not work the controls out properly, so the original driver of the train, Jack Mills, was forcibly involved and hit with an iron bar.

Biggs was caught soon afterwards and sentenced to 30 years in prison in 1964. However, he had only done 15 months in Wandsworth prison before he escaped in 1965, subsequently spending decades on the run in Brazil and Australia. He didn't have any objection to his celebrity status, collaborating with the Sex Pistols and probably enjoying the Phil Collins, biopic about him. After a very good run, he voluntarily returned to the UK in 2001 aged 71, with his health in tatters after a series of strokes. If not exactly expecting a hero's welcome, he did appear to be hoping for decent medical care and a degree of leniency. However, what he got was an arrest after arrival, and he was banged up in Belmarsh.

Belmarsh doesn't seem to do wonders for many people's health, and it certainly didn't for Ronnie Biggs. He had more strokes, needed a feeding tube, and had to be assisted in walking and talking. The swagger had been knocked out of him entirely, and he became a totemic figure in the ongoing debate about the ethics of imprisoning someone of his age for the type of crime he had committed. His ever-declining health saw him transferred from Belmarsh to Norwich prison on compassionate grounds in July 2007. His first appeals for early release were denied, authorities citing a lack of remorse, but in August 2009 his release came. With his health permanently affected, he died aged 84 in December 2013.

Biggs had made it out of Belmarsh to Norwich, but at the same time, the Securitas robbery gang had shown up there. One prisoner we interviewed was on trial at the same time, in early 2008.

'The Securitas robbers were high risk. I was on trial at the Central Criminal Court at the same time as these; indeed I travelled on their escort with them. A 7½-ton lorry which was bombproof and bulletproof – basically a steel box on wheels. From HMP Belmarsh to the court it was non-stop on blue lights. Quite ironic really because the only suspect that was considered exceptional high risk, and was located on HMP Belmarsh's CSU, was John Fowler and he was the only suspect to be acquitted of all charges after spending months on remand.'

The Securitas depot robbery, one of the largest ever UK cash heists, took place on 21 February 2006 in Tonbridge, Kent. In order to get their hands on an eye-watering £53 million from the high-security cash handling facility, the gang had hatched a very elaborate, ingenious and risky plan. The gang leader was a former mixed martial arts fighter called Lee Murray and there were a number of accomplices. Some of the gang impersonated police officers and intercepted the depot manager, Colin Dixon, on his way home from work. At the same time, other gang members took his wife and young son hostage. Under duress, Dixon was forced to cooperate, allowing the robbers entry into the facility, where staff were restrained while the money was stolen. Kent Police led on investigating this ambitious, grim robbery, and arrests were being made within weeks. They also managed to get quite a bit of the stolen cash back.

Several gang members, including Roger Coutts, Ermir Hysenaj, Stuart Royle and Lea Rusha, were arrested and charged with offences related to the heist, and court proceedings began in 2007 at the Old Bailey. An overwhelming body of evidence from the prosecution included testimonies from depot staff who were held hostage, as well as police investigators, and surveillance footage, phone records and damning forensic evidence. In January 2008, Roger Coutts, Ermir Hysenaj, Stuart Royle and Lea Rusha were all found guilty of charges including conspiracy to commit robbery and kidnapping. They received sentences ranging from 15 to 20 years in prison. The court found that Hysenaj, a former Securitas employee, had played a crucial role in providing inside information that enabled the gang to bypass security measures.

The prisoner who travelled to Belmarsh with them had vivid memories to share of them during their prison stay.

'Roger Coutts was located on house block 4 with me and was very polite. Really nice. A family man, I believe, just mixed up with the others due to childhood loyalties to Rusha. To be honest, they were not very bright at all. For example, given the charges they were facing, (Gangsters) Rusha, a very short, stocky man, would wear a black T-shirt, black suit jacket, black trousers with his hair all greased back; he looked like an Italian Mafia boss. He thought he was a gangster. His walk with a swagger, his attitude, the jury saw this.'

The former inmate had pretty negative recollections of Stuart Royle, too:

'Stuart Royle was a joke, an old man in looks given he was only in his fifties. Very thick, so much so he kept shouting in court and in the end sacked his barrister and decided to defend himself. The questions he was raising in court were causing the others issues and there were arguments in the van, shouting at each other while in their cells.'

He also mentioned Michelle Hogg, someone whose life was turned upside down forever by her chance involvement in the case:

'Royle was just a complete know-it-all, and he refused in the end to attend court. The atmosphere changed when Michelle Hogg turned Queen's evidence on them all for a deal. They were all arguing in the van back, we had a police escort and it was a quick journey back to Belmarsh.'

Michelle Hogg, a make-up artist from Plumstead, South-East London, became a pivotal witness in the investigation of the Securitas depot robbery. Initially charged as a co-conspirator, Hogg had crafted prosthetic disguises for members of the gang, believing they were intended for a martial arts video project. Her involvement came to light when police discovered materials bearing DNA evidence in her rubbish bin.

During the trial, she experienced a nervous breakdown and was permitted to sit apart from other defendants. Four months into proceedings, Hogg agreed to testify against her former associates, leading to the prosecution dropping charges against her. Despite her cooperation, the prosecution acknowledged they still considered her an accomplice. Her testimony, supported by mobile phone and DNA evidence, was instrumental in securing convictions. Following the trial, Hogg entered a witness protection programme, changing her name and relocating. When returning to testify in a subsequent trial, she wore a disguise to conceal her identity. Defence lawyers challenged her credibility, suggesting inconsistencies in her account and questioning her motives. Nevertheless, her evidence was deemed crucial in the successful prosecution of those involved in the robbery. The ex-inmate recalled the officer enjoying the show:

'Michelle Hogg was standing trial with them . . . she turned Queen's evidence on them. The escort officers found this very amusing, Hogg basically put a big nail in all their defence evidence. The only ones who were calm were Coutts and Fowler; Rusha being the wannabe bully, he was shouting abuse about her, basically further hanging himself in front of the prison officers. In the end Royle refused to attend court. It was a circus.'

There was one other individual, John Fowler, who was cleared of all charges, as our ex-inmate mentions above. The ex-inmate had positive memories of Fowler, but also offered us another glimpse into the gang's in-fighting and meltdowns.

'John Fowler was a very successful businessman, medium height, slim with glasses. He was immaculately dressed in a suit, very polite and kept out of the arguments. The foreign lads, Hysenaj and Bucpapa, were involved in the arguments and ended up fighting with Royle. Of course this is a side the media never saw.'

Meanwhile, suspected ringleader Lee Murray had fled to Morocco before he could be arrested. Moroccan authorities caught up with him in June 2006. Due to his Moroccan citizenship, he could not be extradited to the UK but was tried in Morocco, where he was convicted in 2010 and sentenced to 25 years in prison. Despite the best efforts of UK authorities, a big chunk of the missing money has still not been found.

This has echoes of the Hatton Garden heist, including the money still missing. Our prisoner contributor Mike talked to us about the Hatton Garden story because he had seen our book about it:

'It took them just an hour and a half in the vault according to him. Michael Seed is in Belmarsh. He had to go into hospital every day because he had a dodgy heart. There is still stuff buried everywhere. Nobody even knows how many people were in there. The police were asking about three specific box numbers. There was something in there – their sentences were extended because they would not give up those boxes. They kept themselves to themselves. The 50 plus unit isn't just 50 plus; it had lots of boys in there who started fights.'

We discovered when we were writing our first book about the 2015 Hatton Garden heist how shocked and distressed they were to be banged up on remand in the Category A jail HMP Belmarsh with all the murderers when all they had done was steal from a vault.

To cut a long and often contradictory story short, over the Easter bank holiday weekend in April 2015, the Hatton Garden gang executed a sophisticated plan to infiltrate the Hatton Garden Safe Deposit vault. They entered the building, disabled the lift and descended the shaft to the basement. Using an industrial drill, they bore a hole in the 50cm-thick concrete wall of the vault, allowing them access to the safety deposit boxes. Over two nights, they ransacked 73 boxes, stealing cash, gold and precious gems. The meticulously planned heist resulted in the theft of valuables estimated at £14 million, making it the largest burglary in English legal history. Notably, the gang left no forensic evidence at the scene, complicating initial police investigations.

The core members of the gang were all aged in their sixties and seventies apart from Carl Wood, a spring chicken at 58 years of age. Known as the Master, Brian Reader was associated with the 1983 Brink's-Mat gold bullion robbery and had a criminal history going back decades. Danny Jones played a significant role in the planning and execution of the burglary, John 'Kenny' Collins acted as driver and lookout during the heist and Terry Perkins drew on his experience gained in the 1983 Security Express robbery, Perkins during the Hatton Garden heist. William Lincoln and Carl Wood had more minor roles in the burglary and in disposing of the stolen goods.

The gang's downfall began when Collins used his own car during reconnaissance and it was traced through

ANPR cameras. Subsequent surveillance and the use of listening devices captured the gang discussing the heist, leading to their arrests. At Woolwich Crown Court in March 2016, Reader got six years and three months, John Collins, Daniel Jones, William Lincoln and Terry Perkins all got seven years, and Carl Wood got six years.

Then they went into Belmarsh. Reader in particular suffered greatly in there, including a stroke while in custody, which had delayed his sentencing. Appearing via video link at Woolwich Crown Court, Reader was seen using a walking frame, and the judge acknowledged his serious health issues when determining his sentence.

We haven't mentioned the mysterious 'Basil' yet.

Michael Seed, known as 'Basil', was a key figure in the 2015 Hatton Garden burglary. Seed, an electronics expert, was instrumental in disabling the building's alarm system and is believed to have used a set of keys to access the premises. He was one of two individuals who entered the vault.

Despite extensive investigations, Seed evaded capture for three years. In March 2018, police raided his Islington flat, discovering a significant quantity of gold ingots, gems and jewellery. Evidence suggested he had been melting down gold and dismantling jewellery on a workbench in his bedroom.

In March 2019, Seed was convicted at Woolwich Crown Court of conspiracy to burgle and conspiracy to handle criminal property. He received concurrent sentences of ten years and eight years, respectively. The court proceedings revealed that Seed had no recent employment history, did not claim benefits and rarely used a bank account.

In November 2022, Seed's sentence was extended by six and a half years for failing to repay his share of the stolen goods. Authorities estimated his portion at £4.7 million, but he had returned less than £50,000. This extension was part of efforts to recover the outstanding proceeds from the heist.

Currently, Seed is serving his sentence at Belmarsh. Matthew had spent time with the Hatton Garden gang, and found them to be civil and pleasant.

'They were just really polite people where you're just having a conversation. "How are you today?" "I'm good, thanks." "You want a cup of tea, guv?"

'They were very much old-school prisoners in the sense of what I remembered of how prisoners used to be, back in the early days. It may be because they were career criminals, or at least the ringleaders were career criminals and spent periods of time in prison, it was something. I remember being around, in Maidstone, and it's like putting on a comfy old pair of slippers again. You think, "This feels familiar," about how they communicate.'

Matthew continued to say that a lot of the conversations were just general sociable interactions. They were very keen not to give away any kind of information that could be pertained to their ongoing cases. They were friendly, but never to the point of divulging information.

'You got to know them as people over a period of time. Whether how you made your tea, or something like that, or you knew who their family was, because you'd see them visiting, but nothing below surface level in terms of engagement; what they would share was limited. Whereas other prisoners wouldn't even kind of share any information. It was a case of this is what you need to know. I'm not going to talk to you.'

There have been some far less affable gangsters who have passed through the gates of Belmarsh too, Kenny Noye being one of them.

Noye had a long-standing history of criminal activity, but it was the fatal stabbing of Stephen Cameron during a road rage incident that led him to Belmarsh. On 19 May 1996, Noye, aged 53 at the time, became embroiled in a violent altercation with 21-year-old Cameron and his fiancée, Danielle Cable, on the M25. The confrontation began when Noye cut off Cameron's vehicle, triggering a heated dispute. After a brief exchange of words, Noye, armed with a knife, stabbed Cameron in the chest. Cameron was pronounced dead at the scene.

Shortly afterwards, Noye fled the country to Spain to evade arrest. His background as a former gangster with links to organised crime had piqued the authorities' interest, previously playing a role in the 1983 Heathrow bullion robbery, in which £26 million worth of gold was stolen. The murder sparked a national manhunt. After more than two years on the run, Noye was located and arrested in Spain, extradited to the UK, and stood trial for murder in 2000. During the proceedings, Noye's defence claimed he had acted in self-defence, alleging that Cameron had attacked him. However, the jury rejected this version of events and found him guilty of murder. He was sentenced to life imprisonment, with the judge highlighting the grave nature of the offence and the danger posed by his violent disposition. He was initially sent to Belmarsh, where he served time before being moved on to other prisons.

Colin coincided with him at Belmarsh.

'I spent a lot of time in prison but kept to myself. I knew a lot of people but never really got involved. I was on a wing with Kenny Noye, but I'd never have spoken to him in a million years. I always said half the people in prison shouldn't be there, and the other half shouldn't be let out. That was my view. So, I just got on with it and read my books.'

Colin took an identical attitude, not least for his own protection, towards a character that we wrote about extensively in our previous *Inside . . .* series of books.

'Same with Charles Bronson. Yeah, he was a classic character. I'd never, ever talk to him, though. I had friends who were friends with him, and I even have a good friend who's his brother-in-law. His brother-in-law would say, "He's a handful." But I wouldn't go near him.'

Those memories prompted Colin to remember an encounter with arguably one half of the most notorious prisoners the UK has ever known.

'Here's a quick story. This was back in the day, not in Belmarsh, about 40 years ago. I was young, maybe 23 or 24, working as an electrician's assistant in Wormwood Scrubs.

'They took me over to the isolation block, "the Block", to change light bulbs in the corridor. I was standing next to a cell when the door opened. A man was standing there. I was just doing my job, so I said hello. Almost immediately, he told me he'd been in isolation for 11 years.

'I thought, "Jesus, 11 years?"

'When I got back to the wing, one of the civilian electricians told me, "That was Ian Brady."

'This might sound crazy, but I felt compassion for him. He was going to be behind that door forever, feeling whatever he was feeling.'

Despite, or perhaps because of, a life of terrible hardship and tragedy, Colin could even find it in his heart to feel pity for one of the Moors murderers. We would struggle to say the same, nor do we feel a shred of empathy or fellow feeling for what we discovered to be another fiendish double act, Mark Dixie and Steve Wright.

CHAPTER 21

Mark Dixie and
Steve Wright

'Steve Wright was best mates with Dixie at Belmarsh.
Wright is a rude man, he's very overweight now.
Blown up and very ill.'

(FORMER INMATE)

Mark Dixie, a former chef, raped and murdered 18-year-old model Sally Anne Bowman, and is loathed even among the violent characters and fellow murderers in Belmarsh.

On 25 September 2005, Bowman was attacked outside her home in Croydon, South London. She was stabbed multiple times before Dixie raped her as she lay dead or dying. Dixie was arrested in 2006 after a minor altercation led to a routine DNA test, which matched samples found at the crime scene. In 2008, he was convicted of Bowman's murder and sentenced to life imprisonment, with a minimum term of 34 years, and was sent to Belmarsh. Unfortunately for him, as always, the other Belmarsh inmates were well aware of his sickening crimes, and eager to attack him, as one ex-prisoner recounted to us.

'Mark Dixie was located on the VP spur 3 house block 4. He had a cleaner's job, which meant that he was confined to the spur. He has a huge complex and is a very self-centred man; it is all about him. He actually thinks he is better than everyone else. Endeavours to play the gangster in front of other inmates but he is just a sexual beast. When he went to court and his trial started, the details of how he bit Sally Anne's breasts and raped her as she lay dying came out. Upon his return to HMP Belmarsh he was assaulted. No one spoke to him; even the worst sexual offenders were horrified at the depravity of this man.'

If 34 years doesn't seem long enough for a crime of such a horrific nature against a teenage girl, Dixie found a way from within Belmarsh to get his incarceration extended. In 2017, he confessed to two additional violent sexual offences. The first, in 1987, involved the rape of a woman in her car in Croydon. After assaulting her, Dixie tied her up and set the vehicle on fire, though she managed to escape. The second offence occurred in 2002, where he attacked a woman with a chef's steel, which is an object used to sharpen kitchen knives, near a railway bridge, telling her, 'I'm going to kill you,' before molesting her. She escaped when a passer-by intervened. For these crimes, Dixie received two additional life sentences.

Fascinatingly, one ex-prisoner gave us exclusive insight into Dixie's demeanour while the jury was out during his trial, and his disgusting and misplaced display of arrogance.

'Dixie was placed in the same holding cell as me while the jury was out. Belmarsh officers came to the cell door and informed him he was wanted back in court. Such was his arrogant attitude he thought it was just a question from the jury; he thought this because the jury had not been out long, he was smiling and very cocky. He came back down to the cells some 20 minutes later and was in shock.'

It's hard to understand Dixie's train of thought at this time, and his fellow inmate shared that feeling.

'The smile wiped off his face, I asked him what the question was? He said, "It was not a question, it was a verdict, and they found me guilty." It's funny really the jury was back with a verdict, and he got a guilty, and he said, "I've been sentenced (weighed off as we call it) to over 30 years." The judge had sentenced him there and then and gave him over 30 years life.'

It was a busy day at the Old Bailey, with another trial taking place at the same time.

'Another trial was going on which Belmarsh staff were escorting the offenders. The offenders were two brothers from West Drayton, the Atkins brothers – they killed an Asian woman during the course of a robbery. They were shouting abuse at Dixie from the cell next door.'

He's talking about Dean and Michael Atkins, who murdered 65-year-old Chinese restaurant owner Kam Fum Chung in November 2006 at her West London home after she wouldn't tell them the location of her life savings. The following night, they attempted another burglary at the home of Bernard Dwyer in Uxbridge, during which they threatened his family, leading to a violent confrontation where Dwyer was injured but managed to defend his family. These crimes resulted in the Atkins brothers being sentenced to life imprisonment, with a minimum term of 35 years, and sent to Belmarsh.

Shouting abuse is standard stuff in Belmarsh, but what our prisoner alleges happened next is controversial and intriguing if true.

'Belmarsh deliberately walked these brothers past Dixie when the cell door was open and they attacked Dixie. This was clearly deliberate. Staff hated Dixie. When he was carrying out his duties as a cleaner he was not allowed to work if there were just females on the unit.'

Of course, in among prisoners expressing their disgust at the lowest of the low, queasy alliances and friendships form between Category A prisoners too, particularly the sex offenders in our experience.

Revoltingly, Mark Dixie found a kindred spirit in Steve Wright, better known as the 'Suffolk Strangler'.

Serial killer Wright went on a six-week murder spree from October to December 2006, murdering five women in Ipswich, Suffolk. Wright targeted highly vulnerable teenagers and young women working as prostitutes in the town. The victims: Tania Nicol (19), Gemma Adams (25), Anneli Alderton (24), Paula Clennell (24) and Annette Nicholls (29) were all found naked in various locations around Ipswich. The discovery of their bodies over such a short span created fear within the local community and prompted one of the UK's biggest ever police investigations.

Wright lived in the red-light district of Ipswich and was a frequent client of sex workers. Forensic evidence, including DNA and fibre analysis, played a pivotal role in linking him to the murders. There was no getting away from the fact that his DNA was found on three of the victims, and fibres from his clothing, car and home were discovered on all five of the women. A media frenzy erupted around the murders that went on throughout his trial, partly because of the short time span in which he had conducted the five appalling killings.

Wright's trial started in January 2008 at Ipswich Crown Court. He pleaded not guilty, admitting to soliciting the services of the victims but denied any involvement in their deaths. The prosecution's evidence, though, was watertight. It took the jury less than six hours to unanimously find him guilty on five counts of murder. On 22 February 2008, Mr Justice Gross sentenced him to life imprisonment, imposing a rare 'whole life' tariff. This means that Wright is banged up until his death.

After his conviction, Wright ended up in Belmarsh, where we suspect he was placed on suicide watch given the life sentence and his crimes; he would also have had psychiatric assessments.

One of our ex-prisoner contributors remembers him well:

'Steve Wright was housed on house block 4 spur 3 (VP). His trial was in Ipswich. He was a standard escape

Category A offender. HMP Belmarsh staff took him to Ipswich daily. Wright was very quiet; he liked to play pool a lot and was very good. He too claimed he was innocent. He was a very close friend to Dixie.

We were sickened to learn that Wright enjoyed sharing photos of his crimes with his new best friend, Dixie.

'There was an incident where Dixie's crime photos of Sally Anne Bowman were found in Wright's cell. It appears Dixie kept these photos of her naked and battered body. This caused outrage amongst staff and other offenders. It was clear Dixie had given them to him. Disgusting! But this is fact. The random searches discovered them.'

One prisoner who recently left HMP Long Lartin gave an update on both men:

'Dixie is now at HMP Frankland's PIPE UNIT trying to address his offending (well, fool the authorities) to come off the Category A status. Wright is located at HMP Long Lartin and has gained significant weight now. He is huge and over 25 stone. Wright also suffered a heart attack at HMP Long Lartin a few years ago. I believe he is now on another murder charge which has not been exclusively reported on due to the trial pending; he's due to stand trial any moment now.'

The source continued, 'At Belmarsh, best mates with Dixie, rude man, he is overweight. Blown up and very ill. When he stands trial I have no doubt the media will report on him and how fat he is now, I mean really, *really* overweight.'

The institution our source is referring to is HM

Prison Long Lartin. It's a Category A men's prison in South Littleton, Worcestershire. Established in 1971 as a Category C training facility, it was upgraded to a dispersal prison in 1972 and further enhanced to maximum security status between 1995 and 1997. Today, the prison houses around 500 inmates, including some of the UK's most dangerous offenders.

In addition to eight main residential units, the prison features the Perrie Wing, a supermax segregation unit opened in 1999, designed to accommodate the most violent and high-risk prisoners. This unit has faced criticism for the isolation of detainees, particularly those held on terrorism-related charges without conviction.

Long Lartin has been troubled by a number of escape attempts, riots and insurrections over the years. In April 1990, inmates attempted a mass escape, leading to a significant security operation. Subsequent years saw further disturbances, including a 2017 riot involving 81 prisoners attacking staff with pool balls, necessitating intervention by specialist riot teams. In 2018, the prison governor required hospital treatment following an unprovoked attack by an inmate. Another disturbance in September 2019 involved ten prisoners taking over a wing, resulting in injuries to staff.

In addition to Steve Wright and Jordan McSweeney, Long Lartin has hosted many other criminals familiar to us from Wakefield and Belmarsh, including Jeremy Bamber, Abu Hamza, Charlie Kray, John Straffen and Ian Watkins.

CHAPTER 22

Stuart Hazell

*'He has no remorse at all and even years later jokes
about how he pleaded guilty because Belmarsh
broke him with all the escorts to court and having
to get up early.'*
(FORMER INMATE)

Returning to Belmarsh, several other names familiar
from media coverage of their cases were on house
block 4 spur 3 at the same time as Steve Wright.

As our ex-Belmarsh contact states, many of the UK's
most notorious child and youth killers have passed through
Belmarsh's gates. Stuart Hazell, who murdered 12-year-
old Tia Sharp in August 2012, is another one of them.
Tia was reported missing after not coming home as usual
on 3 August 2012. Her sudden disappearance sparked
a massive search operation with, unbelievably, Hazell
among those joining the public appeals for her safe return.
At that point, he was the only one who knew for sure that
she was never coming home safe.

This grotesque display had echoes of Ian Huntley's
behaviour. During the investigation into the disappearance

of Holly Wells and Jessica Chapman, Huntley gave a series of unsettling interactions and press interviews.

Despite barely knowing the girls, Huntley appeared eager to speak to the media. In an interview with PA reporter Brian Farmer, he gave a disturbingly detailed answer to a question that was posed to his partner, Maxine Carr, who had been the girls' teaching assistant. When asked how the girls might react to a stranger, Huntley 'jumped in' and said, 'Holly would probably get in the car and quietly go, but Jessica wouldn't. She'd put up a real fight and a real struggle.'

Farmer recalled that Huntley was visibly agitated and emotional during the conversation. The reporter later told police that Huntley's description seemed eerily accurate, remarking, 'He knew how they'd react because that's how they reacted when he killed them.'

Huntley's alibi quickly began to unravel. Carr had initially claimed in media interviews that they were at home together when the girls vanished. However, she later confessed to police that she had been in North Lincolnshire visiting her mother, leaving Huntley alone in Soham on the day of the disappearance. Huntley's numerous interviews raised suspicions further, prompting members of the public from his former home town of Grimsby to contact authorities. They informed police that he had a troubling history involving inappropriate behaviour around children.

Maxine Carr was later convicted of conspiring to pervert the course of justice for lying to police to support Huntley's alibi.

Sadly, we have seen it is not uncommon for murderers to protract the agony of victims' families with manipulation and lies. As we will reflect on later in this book, this is very powerfully portrayed in the drama about Stephen Port's murder of four young men, and his subsequent dissembling.

Returning to Hazell, he was in a relationship and living with Christine Bicknell, Tia's grandmother, in New Addington, South London. Suspicion soon mounted around Hazell due to inconsistencies in his accounts. A week later, on 10 August, police conducted a search of Bicknell's house and discovered Tia's body wrapped in a sheet and bin bags in the loft. Forensic evidence revealed Hazell's semen on Tia's bed and nightclothes, and her blood on a belt he was wearing at the time of his arrest.

Despite this, the worst imaginable forensic evidence, initially Hazell still tried to maintain his innocence and denied any involvement in Tia's death. With a weight of evidence against him, he caved on the fifth day and changed his plea to guilty, acknowledging the immense suffering inflicted upon Tia's family. However, as we will see below, a former inmate questions whether concern for the family was his true incentive.

The court heard that Hazell had a troubled upbringing, including time in care, early involvement in petty crime, and a history of substance abuse. His criminal record included convictions for drug dealing, burglary, theft, racially aggravated assault and possession of a machete in a public place. Hazell was handed life imprisonment with a minimum term of 38 years on 14 May 2013. Mr Justice Nicol explained why he dodged a whole-life tariff, noting that while there was evidence of sexual activity involving Tia, he could not conclusively determine that the murder was sexually motivated, nor that it was premeditated. Once he got to Belmarsh, we have been told that he went into the VP unit, house block 4 spur 3.

One prisoner whose stint coincided with Hazell recalled:

'He is a tall man with a soft voice. He was polite in his mannerisms. He is over six foot tall, very fat and has an unshaven appearance. He was very quiet. He worked in the workshop in Belmarsh, which is located just off house block 4. He was broken by the brutal regime at HMP Belmarsh. He is a Category A standard escape risk offender.'

We wanted more detail around how he had been broken by the regime and power dynamics at Belmarsh.

'You're in a reception holding cell for hours until 6:00 or 7:00pm. It is all designed to break you. I am convinced it is done on purpose with the intention to destroy you. I have seen offenders simply plead guilty at the last minute because of the stress of it all. One such offender was high-profile Stuart Hazell, who murdered little Tia Sharp. The public were led to believe that the evidence against him was so strong that he did the right thing and pleaded guilty. The facts are, and this was said by him to me, it was simply the aggravation of the journey, the process that made him change his plea to guilty; Belmarsh broke him. Of course, his decision to plead guilty at the last minute was not done out of respect for the victims but done because Belmarsh broke him, and in this case rightly so.'

Hazell is now at HMP Frankland. According to a prisoner who spent time there, he has fallen prey to heavy substance misuse, as so many do.

'He has lost a lot of weight and aged. He gets through his prison sentence, just as he did at Belmarsh, by using medication. He constantly fails mandatory urine drug tests and is punished.'

For decades there has been significant concern among the authorities regarding the harmful effects of drug use in prisons, both for the prisoners themselves and for others.

The National Offender Management Service (NOMS) has implemented a wide-ranging set of measures aimed at preventing drugs from entering prisons and discouraging their use among inmates. One key element of this strategy is the Mandatory Drug Testing (MDT) programme, referred to by our source above, which operates in both prisons and young offender institutions.

Introduced in 1996, the MDT programme serves multiple purposes: to monitor patterns of drug misuse, deter inmates from drug use, identify those who may need treatment, support efforts to reduce drug supply, and enhance overall prison safety, order and control.

Prisoners may be selected for MDT either randomly or on a targeted basis, in other words, based on suspicion or as part of a risk assessment. Once selected, they are required to provide a urine sample, which is then sent to a lab for analysis. Regardless of the reason for testing, inmates who either test positive or refuse to comply are subject to disciplinary action under the prison adjudication system. Those who test positive are also referred to drug treatment services within the prison.

The legal authority for conducting MDT goes way back. It is provided under section 16A of the Prison Act 1952. Importantly, this legislation allows testing only for 'controlled drugs' as defined by the Misuse of Drugs Act 1971.

Whatever his substance misuse issues, we were disgusted to hear that Hazell expresses no regret for his appalling crime.

'He has no remorse at all and even years later jokes about how he pleaded guilty because Belmarsh broke him with all the escorts to court and having to get up early. Hazell was extremely overweight and fat at Belmarsh but ageing and the years of drug abuse has taken its toll on him, and he is now like a tall, skinny old man. He is still polite to his peers and staff and accepts his guilt now, although he still denies it was sexual. Given that he filmed his heinous acts it is quite remarkable he still maintains it was not sexual when it clearly was.'

Even spur 3 couldn't house a more recent Belmarsh arrival, who needed to be kept away from anyone and everyone after what he did.

CHAPTER 23

Wayne Couzens

'He was always in the healthcare wing, under
constant observation because he was a high-risk
target for other inmates, purely because he was
a police officer.'

(NIK)

On 3 March 2021, Wayne Couzens, a serving Metropolitan Police officer, committed a crime that profoundly shocked the UK and far beyond. Sarah Everard, a 33-year-old marketing executive, was walking home in South London after visiting a friend when Couzens, exploiting his position and the authority it conferred, falsely arrested her under the pretext of breaching Covid-19 regulations. He used his Metropolitan Police warrant card and handcuffs to deceive and restrain her before abducting her in a vehicle he had hired specifically for this purpose.

Couzens transported Everard to a secluded area near Dover in Kent, where he subjected her to rape and subsequently murdered her by strangulation using his police belt. To conceal his atrocious actions, he burned her body and disposed of her remains in a pond on land owned by his family near Ashford. The meticulous planning and premeditation involved in the crime were evident, as investigations revealed that Couzens had spent at least a month preparing for the abduction. His internet search history showed a disturbing pattern of activity, including researching methods of abduction and watching violent pornography. He also purchased a roll of self-adhesive carpet protector and booked a hire car days before the murder, all part of his elaborate plan to carry out the crime undetected.

The gravity of Couzens' actions led to his arrest on 9 March 2021 after CCTV and vehicle tracking data linked him to the location where Everard was last seen. He was charged with kidnap, rape and murder, and later pleaded guilty to all charges. During sentencing at the Old Bailey in September 2021, Lord Justice Fulford emphasised the severity of Couzens' betrayal of public trust. He stated that Couzens' abuse of his position as a police officer to detain, rape and murder an innocent woman was of equal seriousness is fine to a murder carried out for a terrorist motive. Couzens was sentenced to a whole-life order, meaning he will spend the rest of his life in prison without the possibility of parole.

The murder of Sarah Everard sparked widespread outrage across the UK and reignited national conversations about violence against women and the conduct of police officers. Public vigils were held in her memory, most notably on Clapham Common, near where she was last seen. The police response to the vigil, which included arrests and the use of force under Covid-19 legislation, drew criticism and intensified public scrutiny of policing practices.

Campaigners, activists and members of the public called for urgent reforms to address systemic misogyny within the police force and to improve safety for women and girls in public spaces. The case prompted inquiries into police vetting procedures and highlighted serious institutional failures, leading to broader demands for cultural and operational changes within UK policing.

Under the terms of Couzens' whole-life order, meaning he would spend the rest of his life in prison without the possibility of parole, he was sent to Belmarsh.

Some high-profile prisoners, like Couzens, were kept on suicide watch while Nik was working at Belmarsh. He remembered him well.

'He barely spoke,' Nik said. 'He was always in the healthcare wing, under constant observation because he was a high-risk target for other inmates, purely because he was a police officer. Nik adds that if the word goes out that you've done this and that to the police officer, you will get street cred for it.'

Another ex-officer recalled:

'Wayne Couzens was there for the trial. He read a Bible for 18 months.'

Caroline was actually on Wayne Couzens' suicide watch.

'He was so quiet. Like a mouse. Wayne Couzens didn't really speak.'

We were curious to know if someone like Couzens would be immediately identified by other inmates.

'They all have TVs. So, someone like Wayne Couzens was recognised instantly.'

In May 2022, Couzens appealed against his whole-life sentence, arguing that while his crimes warranted severe punishment, a whole-life term was excessive. However, in July 2022, the Court of Appeal upheld the original sentence. The Lord Chief Justice, Lord Burnett, stated that the sentencing judge was entitled to impose a whole-life order given the facts of the case, reaffirming the exceptional seriousness of Couzens' offences and the gross abuse of his position as a police officer.

Life should mean life for Wayne Couzens.

CHAPTER 24

Barry George

*'The police investigation into him was a
shambles from the outset.'*

(FORMER INMATE)

Decades, or lifelong, Belmarsh incarceration is necessary and richly deserved for the monsters that live within its walls. However, Belmarsh also housed the victim of one of the greatest and most high-profile miscarriages of justice in recent memory: Barry George, who was wrongfully convicted for the murder of BBC television presenter Jill Dando.

On 26 April 1999, Jill Dando was fatally shot outside her home in Fulham, West London. Despite an extensive investigation, initial leads failed to identify a clear suspect. It was only around a year later that Barry George came under the lens. A local resident with a history of mental health issues and previous convictions, George was known for his eccentric behaviour. He had been observed loitering near Dando's home. A search of his home revealed photographs of women and materials related to firearms, which, combined with his proximity to the crime scene, led to his arrest, and then a 2001 trial at the Old Bailey.

The prosecution's case was mainly circumstantial, with a pivotal piece of evidence being a microscopic particle of gunshot residue found in George's coat pocket. We vividly recall the media frenzy around this case, which shocked the entire country. Jill Dando was a familiar and popular presenter, and her random murder was unsettling and distressing.

Despite the lack of direct evidence linking him to the crime, George was convicted, sentenced to life imprisonment and sent to Belmarsh. This verdict was met with controversy, as many questioned the reliability of the forensic evidence and the strength of the prosecution's case. Over the years, these concerns about the safety of George's conviction and the validity of the forensics only grew.

In 2007, the Court of Appeal quashed his conviction, citing doubts about the reliability of the gunshot residue evidence. A retrial was ordered, and in 2008, after an eight-week trial, George was acquitted of all charges. The jury concluded that the evidence presented was insufficient to prove his guilt beyond a reasonable doubt.

One of our prison contacts spent a lot of time with George at Belmarsh. They were even on the same escort to the Central Criminal Court when his conviction was overturned and set for a retrial.

'He returned to the Central Criminal Court for a bail hearing, which was refused. He was placed in a cell with me.'

With this intimate proximity, our contact took the chance to consider some of the key evidence around the case:

'Before I continue, I would like to say openly that the evidence against George was very weak. The police investigation into him was a shambles from the outset. The public perception of him is that he is a slow individual, a simplistic man with mental health issues, not very articulate and with no academic skills. This view, however, is wrong.'

This former Belmarsh inmate was impressed by George's intellect and recalled that 'his cell was full of law books. Books that are complex to read and understand for the average person.' He also detailed that George was bullied by staff. If this was the case, that is particularly disappointing since in the end his conviction was overturned, so they were goading an innocent man.

'George was a big issue for all staff at HMP Belmarsh. Staff were very hostile towards him. They all called him "Mrs Dando", which was, frankly, a little discourteous. He complained about the food and the conditions.'

Unsurprisingly, George spent time educating himself on legal matters and on his rights, as one way of improving his time within prison and in support of, eventually, being freed for a crime there was insufficient evidence to convict him of.

'He even took out civil claims against the prison service, litigations which, in themselves, are a very complex procedure. To do this, one needs to be aware of laws and procedures. George knew them all. This was not the behaviour of someone with limited intellect or ability.'

George was meticulous and examined even seemingly trivial things with great care, according to our source.

'Such was his legal mind that one day, when he was given a television, he refused to sign the standard common compact required to receive it. The compact was a simple set of rules: you wouldn't lend it out and so on, and 99.9 per cent of offenders would simply sign these without question. But George? He refused to sign until he had read it thoroughly and studied the terms. This infuriated the staff who, as a result, refused to let him have the TV. Naturally, George complained.'

His wrongful conviction, understandably, encouraged George to call out grievances when he experienced them inside Belmarsh, and it did not help that, according to our source, he was bullied by fellow prisoners as well as staff.

'There were media reports about him wearing a gas mask and stalking a woman. Inmates would taunt him, asking where his gas mask was. He hated this, and would shout, "Fuck off."'

Although 'he didn't face violent treatment from other inmates, he was constantly verbally mocked.' His wrongful conviction, understandably, encouraged George to call out grievances when he experienced them inside Belmarsh.

Following his release, George expressed being 'overwhelmed' by the verdict and thanked his family, legal team and supporters for their support during his incarceration. In a statement following his acquittal, he expressed gratitude towards those who supported him during his time in Belmarsh, Whitemoor and Manchester prisons.

George is now living quietly in Ireland with his sister, understandably harbouring anger about his many years inside for the Jill Dando murder. From the source who discussed him with us, 'I wish him well.'

CHAPTER 25

Julian Assange

'Julian Assange was next door to me. He looked like
Father Christmas on crack. He kept himself to himself.'

(MIKE)

J ulian Assange is undoubtedly one of the highest profile
former Belmarsh prisoners, and always one of the
individuals who gets mentioned to us whenever we say we
are writing a book about Belmarsh. How did he come to
be there in the first place?

Assange, the founder of WikiLeaks, was arrested in
April 2019 at the Ecuadorian Embassy in London, where
he had sought asylum since 2012 to avoid extradition
to Sweden over sexual assault allegations. Following his
removal from the embassy, Assange was sentenced to
50 weeks in prison for breaching bail conditions and was
locked up at Belmarsh.

During his time in Belmarsh, the United States unsealed
an indictment against Assange, charging him with 18 counts
related to the unauthorised obtaining and dissemination of
classified information. These charges were linked to his

alleged collaboration with former US Army intelligence analyst Chelsea Manning in 2010. Assange contested extradition to the US, arguing that the case was politically motivated and posed a threat to press freedom.

In January 2021, a UK judge ruled against Assange's extradition to the United States, citing concerns over his mental health and the risk of suicide if he were held under the stringent conditions of US confinement. Despite this decision, Assange remained in Belmarsh as the US government appealed the ruling.

Eventually, after spending five years in Belmarsh, Assange was released in June 2024 following a plea deal in a US federal court. This agreement concluded his prolonged legal battles and allowed him to return to Australia, where he reunited with his family and began adapting to life outside of a British prison.

He made quite an impression on anyone who interacted with him in Belmarsh, including Mike, who had him as a neighbour!

'Julian Assange was next door to me. He looked like Father Christmas on crack. He kept himself to himself. He wore the blue prison tracksuit, prison pumps and he walked around the prison yard. He only came down for his dinner. He never caused a problem. He never spoke.'

One former officer had pretty similar recollections of Assange:

'Julian Assange was a bit of a tramp. He didn't wash as a protest. He was on general population. He was never a problem though.'

Assange left a contrasting image on our contributor Nik, very different to anything else we had heard, which he put to us bluntly:

'He's unhygienic, arrogant and narcissistic. He thought he was above the regime and made life difficult for staff. He refused to conform and thinks of himself like some kind of god.'

Assange did make friends inside, though, and he had to deal with the trauma of one of them, Manoel Santos, committing suicide while in Belmarsh, as we have described.

When we met and spoke with a friend of Assange about his time in Belmarsh, she told us that he had endured a very difficult time; akin to 'torture' for him, noting that he was in constant communication with his legal teams and appeared distracted, preoccupied and under a continuously high level of stress. This no doubt contributed to the perception that he was not the most friendly or companionable of prisoners. However, she did say there were one or two inmates he had hoped to remain in contact with, and although now in Australia, about as far from Belmarsh as one could be, it seems he did form a friendship or two along the way.

Nik added that Assange's reputation didn't earn him much respect inside the prison. Belmarsh's notoriety stems in part from such high-profile residents, which also brings along famous visitors now and then.

We loved Nik's surreal account of *Baywatch* star Pamela Anderson's visit to see Assange at Belmarsh. She was there to 'visit Assange as an advocate for him, his friend', Nik recalled. He remembers the 'havoc this caused among the staff as everyone talk about it' and because people were holding 'protests outside the prison, but they mostly were retired people, so didn't cause much trouble'. He gave a hilarious description of her appearance as she tried to keep it low-key, bundled up in a big puffer coat and Gucci scarf. Nik laughed fondly at this memory, saying, 'It was bizarre seeing someone like her in that environment.'

What would appear to be an equally unexpected visitor was Shaun Wallace, better known as one of the chasers, known as the Dark Destroyer, on the popular UK game show, *The Chase*.

Nik enlightened us that he has another profession too: 'He's a barrister. So, he used to come in for the legal visit with the prisoners. I've never met him, but I know he used to come.'

The next time we spoke to Nik about Assange, his attitude had softened in some respects.

'When it comes to his appearance, obviously he didn't shave or have a haircut at any time when he was there. So basically, he struggled. He looked all scratched up; he was sort of looking basically like a homeless man. He was a little bit erratic and defeated. He was on his own and would go on and do his own thing, but there were days when he just wouldn't interact with anyone, and not all the staff wanted to talk to him as well, so he must have been quite lonely and kind of isolated.'

We imagined that he must have been missing his family terribly, too. Nik agreed.

'Absolutely. I could tell he was missing his family a lot. He spoke a lot about his family and how much he loved them and missed them.'

His wife Stella, who he married in Belmarsh in 2022, has been vocal about the impact of his imprisonment on their family. The couple share two children, and she has frequently highlighted how difficult it was for Assange to maintain contact with them from inside Belmarsh. Family visits were limited, particularly during the pandemic, and, as we have seen, not even permitted on Christmas Day.

That said, in Nik's personal experience, Assange was more reserved and not keen to engage.

'I didn't have any conversation with him, because you just couldn't have a conversation with him. He wasn't friendly because he thought he was better than everyone else, and we were like, "So, we're not on his level?" Arrogant and superior. He was on a main wing, so you wouldn't pay that much attention to him. Most of the time he would just stay away to himself, so you wouldn't really see what he was doing.'

While he was incarcerated in Belmarsh, there was a lot of anxiety expressed about Assange's health and well-being. He has many supporters globally, not just Pamela Anderson but his family, lawyers and human rights organisations.

Groups of supporters used to gather regularly outside the prison, demanding his release and condemning the treatment he had received. We have described the conditions that prisoners like Assange are kept in, essentially solitary confinement for much of his time at the prison, which takes a toll on anyone's physical and mental health. He lost weight, suffered from depression and had serious problems with his teeth. We have also heard that he had some hostility from other inmates, although there were no serious attacks.

The UN Special Rapporteur on Torture, Nils Melzer, visited Assange in November 2019 and expressed deep concern over his treatment in the prison, describing him as showing signs of 'prolonged exposure to psychological torture'.

He was initially held in the prison's healthcare unit, which raised concerns among his legal team and supporters. They feared that the isolation and restricted access to communication were exacerbating his health problems. Although he was later moved out of solitary confinement into a less restrictive regime, his health continued to be a subject of international concern.

He also had issues with access to his legal team, which in fairness weren't helped by the pandemic. His complex extradition hearings took place over several months in 2020 and 2021, but his access to his lawyers was restricted, especially during the early months of his imprisonment. His legal team complained about limited face-to-face contact, exacerbated by Covid-19.

Assange is the other side of his ordeal now, although psychological scars are likely to remain. Another very high-profile former Belmarsh prisoner, however, has suffered

the fate that Assange successfully campaigned against –
extradition to a US high-security penitentiary.

CHAPTER 26

'Sheikh' Abu Hamza

*'Abu Hamza was in HSU. The big Islamic
terrorists are normally in HSU.'*

(CAROLINE)

Abu Hamza al-Masri is the former imam of Finsbury Park Mosque in North London. He gained notoriety for delivering inflammatory sermons that incited violence and promoted racial hatred. His rhetoric included calls for the murder of non-Muslims and support for jihadist activities. In 2006, following a trial at the Old Bailey, Abu Hamza was convicted on several charges, including six counts of soliciting murder and three counts related to stirring up racial hatred. The court found that his sermons and speeches had encouraged his followers to kill non-believers and Jews. As a result, he was sentenced to seven years in prison and was banged up in Belmarsh.

The story didn't end there. Particularly in the wake of 9/11, the US was taking an interest. While he was doing time in the UK, the United States sought his extradition on a number of terrorism-related charges. The roll call included his involvement in a 1998 hostage-taking incident in Yemen, where four hostages were killed during a rescue attempt; attempting to establish a terrorist training camp in Oregon between 1999 and 2000; and providing material support to al-Qaeda by facilitating violent jihad in Afghanistan.

After a protracted legal battle, Abu Hamza was extradited to the US in 2012. In May 2014, a New York federal court found him guilty on 11 terrorism-related charges. Subsequently, in January 2015, he was sentenced to life imprisonment without the possibility of parole. The presiding judge described his actions as 'barbaric' and determined that he was a significant threat to public safety.

Our staff contributor Caroline recollected him as part of a larger group. 'Yes, there were big Islamic terrorist types there. Abu Hamza was in HSU. The big Islamic terrorists are normally in HSU.'

An ex-inmate who coincided with Abu Hamza there recalls him in the following terms:

'When I was first moved to Belmarsh I was placed on the HSU, where I met "the hook", Abu Hamza, a high-profile cleric from the Finsbury Park Mosque. He was in prison on terrorism charges and back then fighting extradition to the USA. He was later extradited to America, where he remains.'

We were curious to know what his demeanour was at this point.

'A man then in his fifties who looked a lot older than

his years. Overweight, diabetic, high blood pressure, not very healthy.'

He also, according to this former inmate, appears to have been a bit of a whinger:

'Hamza was a serious complaints person. His disability allowed him to request a special fitted cell. He had an adapted toilet with holding rails, a new sink with touch taps because of his one hand, even his bed was adapted with an extra mattress to ease his back issue.'

In fairness, these sound like reasonable adjustments to his disability, as do requests for his religious beliefs to be respected.

'He refused to be searched by female staff because of his Muslim faith (it was not allowed for a woman to touch a man), and he would argue with staff at any opportunity.'

In 2012, following an eight-year legal battle, he was extradited to the United States to face terrorism-related charges. In 2015, a US court convicted him on 11 counts, including hostage-taking and plotting to establish a terrorist training camp in Oregon. He was subsequently sentenced to life imprisonment.

These days, Abu Hamza is inside ADX Florence, a super-maximum security prison in Colorado. He has described the conditions there as 'inhuman and degrading', citing his confinement within a cell-sized cage during his limited recreation time. His legal team has argued that these conditions breach assurances given to UK courts during his extradition process.

He's in some grim company. The United States

Penitentiary Administrative Maximum Facility (ADX Florence) houses some of the most notorious criminals in the world. Notable current inmates include Dzhokhar Tsarnaev, who's on Death Row for his role in the 2013 Boston Marathon bombing, and fellow UK citizen Richard Reid, the 'Shoe Bomber', who attempted to detonate explosives on a transatlantic flight in 2001. Unlike Hamza, Reid was not extradited to the US.

Just a couple of months after 9/11, the worst ever terrorist attacks on US soil, on 22 December 2001, Richard Reid boarded American Airlines Flight 63 from Paris to Miami with homemade bombs hidden in his shoes. During the flight, Reid tried to detonate his shoes, but he struggled to light the fuse. Crew members and passengers noticed his failed attempts to blow the plane up and restrained him.

The plane diverted to Logan International Airport in Boston, and State Police officers took Reid into custody. On 4 October 2002, Reid pleaded guilty to eight terrorism-related charges. A judge sentenced him to life in federal prison. The FBI, discussing this case as part of their history, highlights how dangerous the device had the potential to be:

'FBI bomb techs determined that the shoes contained about 10 ounces of explosive material. During a preliminary hearing, an FBI agent revealed how dangerous the homemade bomb was. She said that bomb techs determined that the bomb would have blown a hole in the plane's fuselage and caused the plane to crash if it had detonated.'

The FBI has Richard Reid's black high-top trainers as a piece of American history, and Reid remains in ADX Florence.

Ramzi Yousef is in there too – he's one of the masterminds behind the 1993 World Trade Center bombing. Plus, Terry Nichols, co-conspirator in the 1995 Oklahoma City bombing, Sayfullo Saipov, perpetrator of the 2017 New York City truck attack that killed eight people, and let's not forget El Shafee Elsheikh. He's a member of the Islamic State group dubiously given the nickname 'The Beatles'. He was convicted for involvement in the beheadings of Western hostages.

As we learned from one source, understandably Hamza isn't very happy in Florence and wants to come back to the UK:

'He just complained a lot. He was a very ill man and they took his hook away from him. He tried to preach to me. He was not that tall, had a big, big beard, and wore Islamic clothing all the time. He was just left alone. I never spent a lot of time with him. If you were not interested in his preaching then he would not really chat, and his chat was either moaning or Islamic. I understand he is trying to get back to the UK to serve his time. He wants out of America.'

As one ex-prisoner who met him explained, Hamza was distinct from the norm in another way as well:

'With the exception of Hamza (medical grounds and cell conversion to suit his needs), exceptional high risk offenders are moved from cell to cell on a regular basis.

This is to ensure that over time they cannot damage the walls or weaken the windows. Both are impossible but Belmarsh HSU does not want offenders to be too familiar with one cell so they will just keep moving you from cell to cell.

We were not aware of this prior to him letting us in on it. It sounds rather ingenious as yet another measure to prevent escape.

Belmarsh has an international reputation for housing terrorists, not just 'Captain Hook' Abu Hamza, but the London Bridge mass murderer Usman Khan, and Hashem Abedi, plotter of the Manchester Arena atrocity. This has led to it being described in the media as the UK's 'Guantanamo Bay'.

CHAPTER 27

Terrorism in Belmarsh

'If he was in the kitchen making the prisoners'
food, I'm surprised they would let a high-risk
prisoner work in a kitchen with a lot of different and
dangerous items. He's in for killing people.'

(JO)

Mike was very aware of the terrorist demographic when he was in Belmarsh, saying, 'There are a lot of terrorists around. A lot of beards in Belmarsh! There's a war between the Muslims and others. The Islamic thing is sweeping the jail system. I have heard about the bugging of cells . . .'

Some media accounts have contributed to the impression that Belmarsh functions as a sort of jihadist training camp, bent on radicalising and converting. Jonathan Aitken gave a very different view though, as both a former Belmarsh prisoner and a current prison chaplain.

'People told me about IRA prisoners who were in there when I was. I've always thought the Islamic thing is overdone. I still think so today as a chaplain.'

He had a sense of where the information about it was

coming from. 'There's one particular prison governor, retired, who keeps on writing articles about the number of people trying to convert to Islam. The Islamic people did come and talk to me and asked me if I were interested in reading the Qur'an, giving me a copy. I did learn something about the Qur'an; I was quite interested. They were what Christians used to be quite good at – trying to convert people – but not in a sort of "Come on now, you'll be a mass murderer or bomber." It was totally harmless and very gentle and polite.'

Phil had an interesting experience with a terrorist on his course, telling us that, 'When I worked there, Julian Assange was in the prison, along with some very high-level terrorists. I had one terrorist on my course. He was a young guy in for downloading material and watching terrorist content on social media. He hadn't taken any action, but obviously what he did was wrong. He came on the course, which was really diverse – lads from London, a gangster from Manchester, all sorts. It was a good group and they bonded well, helped each other out. There was a good atmosphere.'

Phil discovered that the young terrorist had an entrepreneurial streak.

'This guy wanted to start an Islamic clothing line. Everyone was helping him, not judging him. Then about the third or fourth day, he said very quietly, "Why am I doing this?" I asked him what he meant, and he said, "Why am I doing this Islamic clothing thing, when everyone here is helping me?"'

The good-humoured, accepting and collaborative environment opened the young man's eyes to his radicalisation and how wrong it was.

'He'd been groomed by older Islamist types who told him everyone was against him. Suddenly he was in a space where people were supporting him. It was a light-bulb moment. It was quite powerful and really emotional.'

It sounded like the sort of redemption story we always love to hear. Phil shared our curiosity about what happened to him.

'He was always very engaged. It was interesting having him on the course. I think he stuck it out for the course, but I'd love to know what happened to him next.'

Some individuals coming into Belmarsh seem less likely to engage with a business training course.

In June 2020, Khairi Saadallah, a 25-year-old Libyan national, perpetrated a brutal attack in Reading's Forbury Gardens, resulting in the deaths of three men: James Furlong, 36; David Wails, 49; and Joe Ritchie-Bennett, 39. On the afternoon of 20 June, as England's first lockdown restrictions were easing, the park was populated with visitors. Saadallah, armed with a large kitchen knife, targeted a group of friends, inflicting fatal stab wounds. Witnesses reported him shouting 'Allahu Akbar' during the assault. The victims had no real chance to react or defend themselves and were pronounced dead at the scene. Saadallah also injured three other individuals before discarding the knife and fleeing. He was apprehended shortly after by police.

Saadallah pleaded guilty to three counts of murder

and three counts of attempted murder. In January 2021, at the Old Bailey, Mr Justice Sweeney sentenced him to a whole-life order, emphasising the substantial degree of premeditation and the ideological motive behind the attack. The judge described the murders as executions carried out as an act of religious jihad.

In October 2021, Saadallah sought to appeal his whole-life sentence, arguing that the degree of premeditation and ideological motivation did not meet the threshold for such a penalty. His legal representation contended that a life sentence with a minimum term would be more appropriate and questioned the classification of the attacks as terror-related. However, the Court of Appeal dismissed these arguments, with Lord Chief Justice Lord Burnett affirming that the sentencing judge's approach was correct and that the whole-life order was neither wrong in principle nor manifestly excessive. The court also rejected claims that Saadallah was suffering from a mental illness at the time of the offences.

We found that there are so many terrorists to write about in Belmarsh, too many to mention certainly. The Usman Khan case stands out because it appears to involve a prisoner 'beating the system' and manipulating his way into release only to kill.

Usman Khan, a British national of Pakistani descent, was born in Stoke-on-Trent in 1991. We all knew who he was after the 2019 Fishmongers' Hall attack in London, but the truth is, his criminal activity kicked off long before that.

In December 2010, Khan and eight associates were arrested for plotting terrorist acts, including plans to bomb the London Stock Exchange and establish a terrorist training camp in Pakistan. In February 2012, Khan pleaded guilty to engaging in conduct in preparation for acts of terrorism. Initially sentenced to an indeterminate imprisonment for public protection, this was later revised in 2013 to a fixed term of 16 years, making him eligible for release after serving half of his sentence. He ended up in Belmarsh.

During his imprisonment, he participated in the 'Healthy Identity Intervention Programme', designed to rehabilitate terrorism offenders. We wonder, given what happened next, if his commitment to deradicalisation was lip service at best, and probably utter deceit. In December 2018, after doing time for about eight years, Khan was released on licence under strict conditions, including electronic monitoring and participation in the Desistance and Disengagement Programme. On 29 November 2019, he attended a prisoner rehabilitation conference at Fishmongers' Hall in London.

While the event was taking place, Khan launched a knife attack, fatally stabbing Jack Merritt and Saskia Jones, and injuring three others. During the event, he had threatened to detonate a fake suicide vest and attacked attendees with two knives taped to his wrists. Several individuals, including a Polish chef armed with a narwhal tusk, confronted him before he fled on to London Bridge, where police fatally shot him. An inquest jury later decided that Khan had been lawfully killed by police.

Jonathan Hall QC completed an Independent Review of Terrorism Legislation for the UK government, which was published in April 2022. His stark noting of a worrying pattern in recent UK domestic terrorism brought the involvement of radicalising in prison to the fore.

'The attack at HMP Whitemoor in January 2020, plus the string of domestic and European cases in which terrorism offences appeared linked to associations formed or ideologies adopted in prison, provided the immediate impetus for this review. The last four completed terrorist attacks in Great Britain have been carried out by prisoners serving their sentences in custody (HMP Whitemoor) or on licence in the community (Fishmongers' Hall, Streatham, Reading). In the course of my annual reviews into the Terrorism Acts, I was alerted to the paradox that individuals subject to strong civil counter-terrorism orders, such as Terrorism Prevention and Investigation Measures in the community, might find it easier to radicalise others if they were imprisoned for breaching their orders, as many of them are.'

One active radicaliser outside prison had been Anjem Choudary, an Islamic preacher from Ilford, East London, who was convicted in 2016 for encouraging support for the Islamic State group, a designated terrorist organisation. A former solicitor and long-time figure in extremist circles, he was sentenced to five and a half years in prison but served less than half before being released from Belmarsh in October 2018 under strict licence conditions.

Choudary co-founded al-Muhajiroun, an extremist

group that was banned in the UK in 2010 due to its links to terrorist activities. Despite the ban, he continued to exert influence over Islamist extremism in Britain. Al-Muhajiroun has been connected to over 100 individuals involved in terrorism-related offences in the UK, including the 7/7 London bombers and Michael Adebolajo, featured in this book, one of the killers of Fusilier Lee Rigby.

Upon his release in 2018, Choudary was placed under strict monitoring, which included electronic tagging, a night-time curfew, internet restrictions and a prohibition on contact with other known extremists. Authorities voiced serious concern about his enduring ideological influence, with the then prisons minister warning that Choudary remained a 'genuinely dangerous' individual capable of radicalising others.

In July 2024, Choudary was once again convicted, this time for directing a terrorist organisation and related offences. He was handed a life sentence with a minimum term of 28 years. Prosecutors presented evidence of his continued leadership role in extremist networks, asserting that he remained an ideological figurehead long after his official release. His activities have been directly linked to several high-profile terrorist attacks and to the radicalisation of individuals such as Usman Khan.

Despite his seemingly proactive approach to terrorist activity in the outside world, his demeanour in Belmarsh seems to have been a little different.

As one ex-prison officer recalled, 'Anjem Choudary just sat there.'

The same cannot be said for Hashem Abedi, who many ex-staff we have interviewed attest is the worst kind of nightmare.

Hashem Abedi is the younger brother of Manchester Arena bomber Salman Abedi.

On 22 May 2017, Salman Abedi detonated a suicide bomb in the foyer of Manchester Arena at the conclusion of an Ariana Grande concert, killing 22 individuals and injuring hundreds more. The victims included children, teenagers and adults, making it one of the deadliest terrorist attacks in the United Kingdom since the 2005 London bombings. The vast majority were young people, many of them teenagers. The youngest victim, the heartbreakingly beautiful and cute Saffie-Rose Roussos, was eight years old. Salman Abedi died at the scene. Public outrage was enormous, and people wanted answers about how this could possibly have happened, and assurance that it would never happen again.

Subsequent investigations revealed that Salman's younger brother, Hashem Abedi, was instrumental in planning the attack. Evidence presented at his trial indicated that Hashem assisted in sourcing, purchasing and stockpiling components for the bomb. His DNA and fingerprints were found at properties in Manchester, where the explosives were assembled. Despite being in Libya at the time of the bombing, Hashem was arrested there shortly after the attack and extradited to the UK in 2019.

In March 2020, he was found guilty on 22 counts

of murder, attempted murder and conspiring to cause explosions. Abedi refused to attend his sentencing at the Old Bailey. Families of the victims expressed their grief and anger, with some calling Abedi a coward for not facing the court. The judge described the crimes as 'atrocious' and noted the profound impact on the victims' families. Because he was under the age of 21 at the time of the murders, the law forbids the imposition of a whole-life order, meaning a life sentence with no minimum term.

However, the judge told Abedi, formerly of Manchester, he would spend at least 55 years in prison before he could even be considered for parole, adding that 'he may never be released'. Family members gasped as the sentence – a record for a determinate prison term and a reflection of his horrifying crime – was handed down.

He was sent to Belmarsh.

During his time there, plenty of shit went down. In May 2020, Abedi, along with other prisoners, including Ahmed Hassan, the Parsons Green bomber, and Muhammed Saeed, attacked a prison officer, Paul Edwards, after their televisions were confiscated. The trio ambushed the officer, who was left with significant injuries, including a head laceration and long-term hearing damage. Pissed off and thirsty for blood, they conducted an attack described as 'animalistic'.

They were later found guilty of assault, with Abedi receiving an extension on his prison sentence.

Abedi was also accused of trying to gain influence within the prison. He apparently tried to take on a leadership role among Muslim prisoners, often referred to as an 'emir'. His actions were noted as part of an effort to stir up conflict within the facility, and this reportedly occurred just before the prison officer attack.

The incident led to Abedi and his fellow prisoners being charged for the assault on the officer. The attack prompted concerns about the level of control and influence that some prisoners were attempting to wield within the institution. The court found Hashem Abedi, Hassan and Saeed guilty of the attack.

In 2021, Abedi was transferred from HMP Belmarsh to HMP Frankland, a high-security prison in County Durham, which houses some of the most infamous offenders in the UK, currently including Levi Bellfield, Wayne Couzens and Ian Huntley.

We had genuinely just written that we wouldn't be surprised to see more stories about him coming out of Frankland when we were alerted to one of the worst incidents of violence against prison staff in recent history.

In April 2025, Abedi launched a violent and premeditated attack on three prison officers at HMP Frankland. The assault took place within the prison's separation centre, a unit specifically designed to house the most dangerous and ideologically extreme inmates. Abedi apparently had access to the kitchen in this tightly controlled environment. Frankland's separation centre is one of only two such centres of their kind currently in use.

According to the Prison Officers' Association (POA), he used boiling oil and improvised weapons crafted from baking trays to ambush the staff, inflicting severe injuries on two male officers and a female officer.

One officer suffered a severed artery after being stabbed in the neck, while another sustained serious stab wounds to the back. The third officer, the woman, was discharged from hospital the same day, but the two men required further treatment. The attack triggered an immediate lockdown and raised urgent questions about the security procedures in place within separation units.

Prime Minister Sir Keir Starmer was 'appalled' by the attack, the prime minister's spokesman said, adding: 'Prison staff work around the clock to keep the country safe, and we will never tolerate the violence that is targeted towards them. It's clear that something went terribly wrong in the management of this offender and the government is committed to carrying out an investigation to urgently get answers.'

The Ministry of Justice has said there will be a full review of the incident, which comes too late for the three injured officers, and access to kitchens in close supervision centres has been suspended.

Abedi had been a long-term inmate at HMP Frankland's separation centre, which holds fewer than ten prisoners and is used to house those considered the most danger-ous and extremist. As we saw, he moved to Frankland after carrying out an attack on prison officers in Belmarsh in 2020.

Mark Fairhurst, the POA's national chair, expressed outrage at the failure to mitigate risk, stating that 'we think that he's made knives out of a baking tray from that kitchen area' and warning that inmates in such units should be for control and containment, because these people are not going to change their ideologies and they are intent on inflicting harm on everyone they come into contact with. He also raised the concern that offenders in these locations were being allowed similar privileges as normal prisoners, which, he argued, should not be the case in separation centres.

Fairhurst's anger was clear and justified, and his protectiveness towards his officers palpable at this grotesque security breach.

Mr Fairhurst had earlier called on the government to 'restrict and remove cooking facilities from separation centres' over worries about 'copycat incidents' following the attack. He said the POA wanted officers to be equipped with stab vests to prevent such incidents but argued that Prison Service leaders 'don't want us all looking too militaristic to the prisoners'.

He said that, during his tenure at Belmarsh, 'we took away metal food trays and we actually designed plastic rounded trays' to avoid them being used as weapons.

The families of five of the Manchester Arena victims wrote a letter to express their outrage, not just at the incident but at the conditions and privileges that Abedi seemed to have enjoyed. The BBC quoted their letter as saying, 'we are writing in absolute disbelief' that, once again, the 'evil Hashem Abedi has been allowed to cause danger to life'.

They continued: 'As the families of Megan Hurley, Eilidh Macleod, Chloe Rutherford, Liam Curry and Kelly Brewster, our beautiful, beloved children who were so tragically murdered along with 16 others in the Manchester Arena terror attack in May 2017, we find this situation beyond comprehension.'

The families said they understood prison to mean 'confinement in a cell for 23 hours a day, meals served through a hatch, and a single hour outside the cell, accompanied by a prison officer . . . the very minimum measure of justice for the devastation he caused'.

They wrote: 'he should not be allowed any privileges whatsoever while serving a sentence for the deaths of 22 innocent lives and the injuring of many more. He should not have access to anything that he can weaponise, such as hot oil or items he can turn into blades'.

Following the April 2025 incident, Abedi was removed from HMP Frankland and transferred to the separation centre at HMP Full Sutton, another high-security facility.

Next thing we heard, he was back in Belmarsh. We asked Jo for her reaction and she was absolutely disgusted, as well as incredulous. She recalled how the kitchens were set up at Wakefield in order to draw comparisons with what had gone so catastrophically wrong at Frankland with Abedi.

'I'm getting the impression that he was working in the kitchen, that it was on the wing. In Wakefield, each wing – there's A, B, C and D – has cooking facilities for cons. So, during evening association, they'll come out of their cell to start cooking their own food. The kitchen utensils, like knives, are kept in a locked tool cabinet in the office down there. They have to give a tally. Then they take the weapon, do the cooking, and bring it back to the staff. The staff put it up and they get the tally back.'

This sounds secure enough but, as Jo continued, she mused on what seemed to be quite a loophole:

'But, and this is really weird, anyone can access that kitchen. The staff are probably doing checks or walking around, so they're not constantly watching the kitchen. So, anyone can go in, and maybe he went in and threw oil over the prison officers. I know they can buy a lot of different stuff from DHL, I think it is, to cook with. The oil. I'm not sure how he's got the oil, but the thing is, they can get access to knives. Cooking knives.'

Was it possible that oil had been mail ordered into the prison? Jo explained that even though risk assessments are carried out, cooking is a sought-after privilege like many others, and that it can be earned.

'I didn't work as an officer on the line, but everything has to be risk assessed, and I'm not sure whether these people are risk assessed to use the kitchen. It's kind of run on goodwill, as it was, because everyone wants to use the kitchens – well, not everyone – but it's a real privilege. You know, you're getting to cook your own food. So, people have always been OK with it.'

Certainly, what happened with Abedi seems to be rare, and the vast majority of prisoners just want to cook a meal they have prepared themselves, out of boredom, taste or just to give a sense of normality. Jo had not seen it go wrong the whole time she was at Wakefield:

'I never had an incident, in the five years I was there, where anyone got assaulted in the prisoners' kitchen when they were cooking their food, because it spoils it for everyone else. And there'll be repercussions. That person would probably get battered, but then he'll be off. He won't even be on the wing now.'

She had focused in on the specifics of the Abedi incident now, and speculated about what might have happened.

'If he was in the kitchen making the prisoners' food, I'm surprised they would let a high-risk prisoner work in a kitchen with a lot of different and dangerous items. He's in for killing people.'

While not making light of the situation in any way, Jo mocked the hypothetical thought process behind letting the Manchester Arena plotter loose with stabbing weapons and boiling oil.

'Let's see how it went. "Oh, did I catch you up in the kitchen?" "Come along now, don't be throwing this hot oil, will you, and these knives?" "Make sure you don't, and don't take any of these trays to make weapons with, will you?" I mean, what's that all about?'

As she re-emphasised, 'It should have been risk assessed. He shouldn't be in it.'

The fact that he was seemed very much out of the norm as far as Jo was concerned:

'I can't think of any high-risk prisoners I remember working in the kitchen. I can't remember that, because

I thought they had to be risk assessed. Something's gone wrong, and somebody should pay: because two prison officers are in hospital with serious wounds and burns. Burns are serious. And scarring. They'll never be able to work again, and all the trauma and stress that comes with it, it's disgusting. I would be suing.'

Jo is protective of other members of her profession, and she knows that every prison officer has to carry the fear of something like this happening to them on the job, and she felt deep anger that this incident had taken place. In Jo's no-nonsense old-school view, there might have been an element of woke tiptoeing around that led to this point.

'Maybe this needs to be the end of letting these parasites cook in the prison. It's just mental, absolutely. It's coming to a point where you can't even say anything. Maybe that's what's happened in the prison. "Oh, you can't stop me from cooking, that's my human right to be able to cook." If you've killed twenty-odd people, do you say, "Well, go on then, but promise you won't do anything bad"? It's mental. Absolutely mental. Something's really wrong with this.'

Vanessa, an expert on prison security and risk assessment after her 27-year career in the service, shared Jo's shock:

'The Ministry of Justice said, "We don't want stab vests, it's too intimidating." The staff had batons and pepper spray, but didn't have time to draw them before Abedi attacked. Who thought it was acceptable for him to cook his own food unsupervised? That person should hang their head in shame. Abedi packed nuts and bolts into a bomb to cause maximum damage at Manchester Arena. A lot of Category C prisoners, trapped in the Category B system waiting to be recategorised, would love to cook for themselves. But murder 22 people – you can have unfettered access to cook your meal! Abedi is not the only highly dangerous prisoner in our system. There are several. He'd done the same at Belmarsh. I spent my last ten years at Scrubs doing risk assessment. This would have been risk assessed!'

Her tone expressed clear disbelief. She had an intelligent suggestion for how security should function for prisoners as dangerous as Abedi: 'The separation units – for people like Abedi – need a tactical unit on standby 24/7, with one issued with a Taser.' Her concern about the more widespread adoption of Tasers by prison officers was twofold. One, that like pepper spray and batons, they would not have time to draw it in time in the face of a cunning, poorly supervised assailant like Abedi. Secondly, especially if staff headcount was low, they could be overpowered and have their Taser grabbed by a prisoner. The fact that security doesn't work this way is partly down to under-resourcing, but also another reason:

'For too long we've appeased prisoners convicted of terrorism: whether Islamic or far right.'

Speaking to BBC Radio 4's *PM* programme after the incident, John Podmore, former governor of HMPs Brixton and Belmarsh, said self-catering facilities should be an incentive for good behaviour instead of a way of persuading prisoners not to be violent or disruptive. He seemed to be making pretty much the same point as Jo, albeit in more measured language.

He said kitchens in separation centres could 'only be there' to serve as a means of appeasing their dangerous inmates, while there were prisoners in low security prisons 'who would dream of having these facilities'.

Mr Podmore stressed that prisoners in separation centres were 'looking to radicalise others and kill staff'. Noting that even a toothbrush could be made into a weapon, he told Radio 4: 'In a kitchen, where you've got not only the hot oil but you've got pans, tins, you've got metal and a whole range of things that can and will be used . . . I've seen serious injuries with a bean tin, with a pool ball, but you try to manage that out.'

In the end, the answer to the mystery of the 'boiling oil' came to us from a Frankland source. According to them, it wasn't oil – prisoners never have access to oil precisely because of this kind of risk. Instead, there was a custom at Frankland: if a prisoner had a bread roll, they could reach into a large plastic bag and pull out one of the small, individually wrapped butters. No one really paid much attention to these butters: they weren't rationed or counted. Apparently Abedi secretly collected dozens of these little wrapped butters over several weeks, hoarding them in his cell. He then melted them all down to create a vat of boiling butter, which he threw over staff.

As a result, all cooking is now banned at Frankland, and the large bag of butters has also been done away with.

Our contributor Matthew didn't coincide with Abedi but he did with others. He told us that as part of his role at Belmarsh he oversaw the Category A prisoners and Category A movement, which was all the high-profile prisoners at the time.

'Michael Adebolajo and Michael Adebowale, I took them to court. Another part of my role was that I was in charge of the security intelligence section, as well as being one of the officers covering general incident response, Crisis management, as well as running one of the house blocks. A lot of responsibility!'

Adebolajo and Adebowale were convicted for the shocking murder of the young soldier Lee Rigby. On 22 May 2013 they carried out a brutal attack near Woolwich Barracks in South-East London. They hit Rigby with a car before stabbing him multiple times. Then they tried to decapitate him with a meat cleaver.

Fusilier Lee Rigby, a 25-year-old soldier in the Royal Regiment of Fusiliers, had served in Afghanistan. He was returning to his barracks at the Royal Artillery Barracks when he was attacked in broad daylight on Artillery Place, just metres from his base.

The attackers, Adebolajo and Adebowale, were British citizens of Nigerian descent who had converted to Islam. Using knives and a meat cleaver, they attempted to behead him and mutilated his body. Witnesses described the attack as frenzied and unrelenting. Several bystanders intervened or attempted to reason with the assailants while others filmed or called the police.

In the aftermath of the killing, Michael Adebolajo, his hands covered in blood, delivered a statement to a bystander filming the scene, saying: 'The only reason we have killed this man today is because Muslims are dying daily by British soldiers.' Both men stayed at the scene and made no attempt to flee. They were shot and wounded by armed officers from the Metropolitan Police's Specialist Firearms Command approximately 14 minutes after the first 999 call was made. They were then arrested and transferred to hospital under armed guard.

The murder, committed in full view of the public and caught on multiple recordings, caused national outrage and was condemned by politicians, religious leaders and community groups across the country. Prime Minister David Cameron described it as an attack on the British way of life and pledged to confront extremism.

Both Adebolajo and Adebowale were known to security services before the attack. Adebolajo had been arrested in Kenya in 2010 on suspicion of attempting to join the Islamist militant group al-Shabaab. Adebowale had previously received mental health treatment. Despite this, neither was under active surveillance at the time of the murder.

During their trial at the Old Bailey in late 2013, both Adebowale and Adebolajo pleaded not guilty to Rigby's murder but did not dispute their involvement. The jury convicted them unanimously. In February 2014,

Adebowale received a life sentence with a minimum term of 45 years before eligibility for parole, while Adebolajo was given a whole-life term, meaning he would spend the rest of his life in prison without the possibility of release.

The murder led to an urgent review of military personnel security in the UK and prompted a broader national conversation about radicalisation and home-grown terrorism. Lee Rigby, who was a father, was honoured at memorial services and vigils across the country. His family later launched the Lee Rigby Foundation to support bereaved military families and to raise awareness of terrorism's long-term impact.

Following this grotesque random murder, both men were apprehended and held at Belmarsh. It seems they didn't have an easy time there. In July 2013, reports emerged that Adebolajo had been injured in an attack. They were both in there during their trial preparations. In December 2015, Adebowale pleaded guilty to punching a healthcare assistant while he was in Broadmoor Hospital. He's been in Broadmoor since 2014.

Caroline made the broader point that in terms of movement between prison and asylums, 'the mental health system is overwhelmed'. Even so, Broadmoor seems like the right place for Adebowale.

As a prison officer, Matthew encountered them too. He was struck by how strange the reality of interacting with them was:

'It was odd because you'd see these people, you'd hear about the crimes that they would commit in the news because high-profile prisoners are in the news all the time, unless there's a really slow media day or really fast media day. You'd see things on the TV where they would be talking about an individual and then the next day, I'd meet them! The police had brought them into custody and sometimes you'd have some very extreme personalities where they didn't want to engage with you or talk to you much at all. They would be minding their own business.'

He had the two Michaels in his sights as specific examples:

'Michael Adebowale and Michael Adebolajo were very much like that. They didn't want to interact with anyone. They had contempt for what we stood for and who we were. It was a very unique experience. Whereas, when we were talking or moving around, say, the Hatton Garden guys, they were a lot more sociable. They would have a chat with you. "How are you today?" It was a really odd blend and then you'd sit in trials with these guys.'

Back in the day, Belmarsh had its fair share of IRA terrorists. In addition to the Islamic terrorists described above, there have been many other domestic terrorists and far-right extremists caged in Belmarsh too, including David Copeland, the 'Nail Bomber'.

At the age of only 23, David Copeland was already full of such racial and ideological hatred that he conducted a series of lethal bombings in London in 1999, which led to his conviction for the murder of three people and the injury of over 100 others. We both have vivid memories of that spring in London and the pall of terror that it cast over the capital.

The first bombing was on 17 April 1999, with an explosion in Brixton, an area with a large Afro-Caribbean population. The bomb, filled with nails, injured 48 people but resulted in no fatalities. Less than a week later, on 24 April, Copeland set off another bomb in Brick Lane, which is known for its large Bangladeshi and Asian community. This second attack injured 13 people.

On 30 April, Copeland carried out his third bombing in Soho, an area popular with the LGBTQ+ community. The attack killed three people and injured 139 others. It was this final bombing that led to his arrest on 2 May 1999. The police had quickly identified Copeland as the bomber. He was charged with three counts of murder and 29 counts of attempted murder.

At his trial, it was revealed that Copeland had been motivated by far-right, racist beliefs. He had chosen his targets based on his hatred of Black, Asian and LGBTQ+ communities. His intent was to instigate fear and violence within these groups. During the trial, Copeland's defence team argued that he had been suffering from mental health issues at the time of the attacks, but this did not stop him being found guilty. He was convicted in 2000 and sentenced to life imprisonment. The judge recommended that he serve a minimum of 50 years before being considered for parole, due to the severity of his crimes, and he was sent to Belmarsh.

He popped up again in 2015, when he was given an

extra three years for attacking another prisoner. The BBC reported the dramatic incident, which appears to indicate more of a security breach than is usual at Belmarsh, in the following terms:

'He had a row or dispute with fellow inmate Thomas McDonagh and entered the exercise yard the next day with a toothbrush, modified to hold two razor blades, hidden in his trousers.

'As he approached McDonagh, another prisoner punched Copeland and there was a chase across the yard. The prisoner ran into the prison laundry, pulled down a noticeboard and said, "I'm going to do him; let me have him."'

However, as a prisoner officer intervened to stop him going after the killer, Copeland turned his attention to McDonagh. Copeland slashed twice at McDonagh, leaving him with parallel scarring from the twin-bladed weapon, one injury running from his ear across his face and the other above his eye. Moments later, Copeland was overpowered by prison officers with a baton strike to his leg. He was placed in solitary confinement for 11 months. If the exercise yard is busy, it's easier to make something kick off, simply because the officers are overstretched.

Copeland, who received six life sentences in 2000, is serving a minimum term of 50 years. He will now serve at least 18 months more and is unlikely to be released before his mid-seventies. The judge, Anuja Dhir QC, later commended the two quick-thinking prison officers, Frank Hughes and Paul Leahy, who intervened in the attack.

Copeland appeared via video from HMP Frankland, where he was by then, and acknowledged the sentence with a wave.

As we have seen so often, these notorious criminals are passed from pillar to post around the Category A prisons. It's also a frequent theme that they can't help themselves from reoffending inside and extending their epic initial sentences even further.

CHAPTER 28

Tommy Robinson

'He was isolated the whole time. He's never
seen another prisoner.'

(NIK)

Tommy Robinson, whose real name is Stephen Yaxley-Lennon, is a far-right activist, who was born in Luton. He co-founded the English Defence League (EDL) in 2009 and led it until 2013. He has been associated with anti-Islam campaigns and has served several prison terms for offences including assault, mortgage fraud and contempt of court.

He first went to Belmarsh in 2019, after he was imprisoned for violating a court order by broadcasting a Facebook Live video of defendants entering court, which was deemed contempt of court. Since October 2024, Robinson has been serving an 18-month prison sentence, again for contempt of court. This time it was for breaching a High Court injunction by airing libellous allegations against Syrian refugee Jamal Hijazi in a documentary. On both occasions he was placed in solitary confinement at Belmarsh.

Robinson was arrested in July 2024 under the Terrorism Act 2000 at the Channel Tunnel in Folkestone, Kent, following his 'Unite the Kingdom' protest at Trafalgar Square, where he allegedly screened the prohibited film. He was released on bail but failed to attend a subsequent High Court hearing, leading to an arrest warrant being issued. In October 2024, Robinson surrendered to authorities and appeared at Woolwich Crown Court, where he admitted to ten breaches of the High Court order. The judge sentenced him to 18 months in prison, citing a lack of remorse as well as ordering him to pay over 80 grand in legal costs. Following his sentencing, Robinson was initially sent to Belmarsh. Due to concerns about his safety, stemming from his high-profile status and the nature of his offences, he was placed in segregation.

Reports came out claiming that Belmarsh received loads of abusive and racist communications, including threats directed at the governor, which necessitated Robinson's isolation. Our contributor Nik confirmed this for us, and shared his own memories:

'He was isolated the whole time. He's never seen another prisoner,' Nik said. His isolation was necessary due to the threats from other inmates, particularly Muslim prisoners.

'There was an article in *The Sun* that said he got beaten up by a pensioner,' Nik laughed. 'I remember that day because I was with him, and we handed him the newspaper. He started reading and said, "What a load of bollocks," because he never saw another prisoner the entire time he was there.'

Despite Robinson's divisive reputation, Nik found him to be more nuanced than his media image.

'We had a great chat about where I'm from. He'd attended an independence rally there and said he loved it. He was just a normal bloke.'

What he particularly liked about it was the show of unity he saw on display of those going into these rallies; he was very fascinated by it.

In November 2024, Robinson was transferred to HMP Woodhill in Milton Keynes, where he continued to be held in segregation for his protection. In March 2025 there were press reports giving details of Tommy Robinson's incarceration, disclosed during a High Court hearing concerning his segregation at HMP Woodhill. He has been isolated from other prisoners due to safety concerns, including intelligence suggesting he 'would be killed by a lifer' if placed among the general population.

Despite his segregation, Robinson's regime is 'substantially more permissive' than standard, granting him access to a laptop and emails, several hours daily in an exercise yard, and four hours of social phone calls each day. He has been authorised over 80 visits, with 120 individuals approved to see him, and has made more than 1,250 social phone calls since 1 November. Additional privileges include daily visits from the prison's chaplaincy team and medical staff, as well as opportunities to work 'painting and decorating' three days a week.

Robinson's legal team argues that his segregation is detrimental to his mental health. The Ministry of Justice maintains that these measures are necessary for his safety, given the credible threats against him. The High Court has dismissed Robinson's bid to challenge his segregation, concluding that the claim was 'not arguable' and that his conditions do not amount to solitary confinement.

Even at Belmarsh, according to Nik, Robinson was receiving visitors:

'If I'm completely frank with you, I don't think he's worse than that Nigel Farage. No, I know – they've got quite similar views, really. I mean, Tommy Robinson has done some controversial things. That's why it brought him so much hatred from people – yeah, from the Muslim community. So I think this is the main thing for him that speaks against it. And obviously I don't condone what he's done. He was kept separate, and that must make for a very lonely, isolated existence for a prisoner like that.

'He would have visitors – definitely, yeah. Obviously, he had some lawyers and barristers. He was kept in the "contingency suite", and it has its own visits room, I'd say. So they'd see him there, so no one else would be aware or see who was visiting him.'

So, while Robinson's time in custody has been marked by strict segregation due to serious threats against his safety, he has also had higher visitor numbers than many other inmates. While he remains a divisive figure, his imprisonment has highlighted the complex balance between ensuring prisoner welfare and maintaining order in high-security environments.

CHAPTER 29

Daniel Khalife

*'Such an escape from HMP Belmarsh by strapping
oneself under a lorry would be impossible.'*
(FORMER INMATE)

Born in London in 2001, Daniel Khalife enlisted in the army in 2018, first working as a network engineer with the Royal Corps of Signals at Beacon Barracks, Stafford. Khalife was arrested in early January 2022 for breaching the Official Secrets Act and was subsequently released on bail. In January 2023, he absconded but was recaptured three weeks later and held on remand. He was discharged from the army in May 2023. On 6 September 2023, he escaped from HM Prison Wandsworth in London, a Category B establishment, triggering a nationwide police search. Concealing himself beneath a food delivery lorry while working in the prison kitchen, and dressed in a cook's uniform, he used bed sheets to strap himself underneath the vehicle. The judge later described him as a 'dangerous fool', driven by a desire to show off.

At the time, Khalife was on remand awaiting trial on

terrorism charges. His escape ignited a media storm and a full-scale police operation. He was spotted three days later, cycling in Northolt, Middlesex, and apprehended by a Metropolitan Police officer.

In November 2024, he was found guilty of spying for Iran and, on 3 February 2025, sentenced to 14 years and three months in custody, which he is currently serving at HMP Belmarsh.

Vanessa believes that the Daniel Khalife escape highlighted issues in the prison system: 'He started everybody's interest in what was going on in our prisons. Society is not bothered until it affects them. There were shortages of staff that day, and they didn't adhere to security procedures.'

We have had it confirmed to us by a contributor that Khalife is still in Belmarsh now.

One former inmate, aware of Khalife's brazen escape like everyone else, told us that:

'Such an escape from HMP Belmarsh by strapping oneself under a lorry would be impossible. Unlike HMP Wandsworth, HMP Belmarsh have provisions in place to stop any escape.'

Of course, we wanted to know what those provisions were.

'Every vehicle that enters the prison to deliver supplies is escorted at all times. You may have seen the escape from HMP Wandsworth in which the offender strapped himself to the underside of the delivery lorry. HMP Wandsworth is a Category B local prison and not part of the high-security estate. The high-security estate prisons are HMP Belmarsh, HMP Long Lartin, HMP Full Sutton, HMP Wakefield, HMP Whitemoor and HMP Manchester. These are the only high-security prisons that can hold Category A offenders within England and Wales, HMP Belmarsh being considered the most secure.'

We wondered what was so unique about Belmarsh's process that it could prevent escapes such as Khalife's. The ex-inmate was happy to explain.

'When a delivery lorry enters HMP Belmarsh it is escorted by four staff at all times. Upon entering the prison and going through vigorous security checks, the lorry/van is restricted to driving slow at walking pace. An OSG (Officer Support Grade) will escort the vehicle. One in front of the vehicle, one either side and one behind. The vehicle is also monitored non-stop by CCTV. No offenders will be in the location.'

Grasping that it would be helpful to give us a specific example to aid our comprehension, he continued:

'If the lorry is delivering to the kitchens or supplying other items such as cleaning products or education materials, there is only one drop-off point. This is called RIDS (Received In Delivery Service). The vehicle is escorted to RIDS and it is unloaded into a holding area where no inmates have access to. Belmarsh staff upon the vehicle leaving the prison will then deliver the goods themselves to the kitchen, stores or the education department. The lorry is watched constantly, no offenders are in the area, and staff deliver the goods on. This makes it impossible for any escape.'

Looks like Khalife won't be repeating his audacious and scintillating escape from Belmarsh. We were intrigued by his escape story when it happened. We had asked our contributor Jo what the consequences of such an escape would be for another institution.

'If the Wandsworth prison break had happened at a Category A prison, they would have lost their Category A status and the governor would have been sacked.'

Though it was not a prison break at Belmarsh, our Wakefield contributor Vanessa has described a prison break from Wormwood Scrubs as the greatest regret of her career. It was an armed escape, and she remains devastated by the effect that the prison break had on the workers involved that were under her care:

'One downgraded jobs, one never worked again and the third killed themselves. I have racked my brains but I can't think of anything I could have done differently.'

Vanessa served 27 years in prisons up until 2013, starting as an officer at HMP Holloway and becoming governor of operations and security at HMP Wormwood Scrubs in 2002. A seasoned officer not easily surprised or rattled, she has worked with some of the most notorious prisoners, male and female, throughout her time at Holloway and Wormwood Scrubs.

A prison escape causes terrible fallout for so many people. No Belmarsh governors or officers have had to go through this process of soul-searching, and with the procedures in place and a 100 per cent record of no prison escapes, it seems unlikely that they ever will. This is just as well in many cases, and not least in the case of Stephen Port.

CHAPTER 30

Stephen Port

*'I have no doubt that the seriousness of the offending
is so exceptionally high that the whole-life order is
justified; indeed it is required.'*
(MR JUSTICE OPENSHAW IN HIS
SENTENCING REMARKS)

Stephen Port is a British serial killer and rapist, convicted of murdering four young men and committing multiple sexual assaults and rapes. He was sentenced to life imprisonment with a whole-life order on 25 November 2016 and he is serving his sentence in Belmarsh.

Port came out as gay in his mid-twenties. He lived with his parents until his early thirties and later moved to a flat in Barking, London, where he worked as a chef at West Ham Bus Garage – he even appeared on *Celebrity MasterChef* when they filmed an episode there. He wore a blond wig to disguise his baldness and boost his confidence when meeting men; there is an unsettling scene in the BBC 2022 drama, *Four Lives*, a dramatisation of his crimes, where he removes it, revealing his baldness, and gazes blankly at his reflection in the mirror. Though he is paunchy and shambling in *Four Lives*, he is still an imposing presence. In real life, he was a gym enthusiast and probably physically intimidating, although he used GHB (gamma-hydroxybutyric acid) rather than brute strength to overpower his victims.

Port met his victims through gay and bisexual social networks and dating apps. Though he became known as the 'Grindr Killer', he also used several other dating apps to contact his victims. In an early indication of his fakery and deceit that would become one of his hallmarks, he used false biographies, including claims of having graduated from Oxford and served in the Royal Navy. Using GHB, a date rape drug, he drugged, raped and murdered the four young men in his flat. GHB was found to be the cause of death in all four victims.

The first victim, 23-year-old Anthony Walgate, a fashion student and part-time escort, was drugged and murdered in June 2014. Port placed Walgate's body outside his flat and called for an ambulance, but evidence linking him to the death was missed at the time. This was the first of many terrible missed opportunities to catch him. Port was later convicted of perverting the course of justice in 2015 after his inconsistent statements about Walgate's death.

In barely over a year, between August 2014 and September 2015, Port killed Gabriel Kovari (22), Daniel Whitworth (21) and Jack Taylor (25). Kovari's and Whitworth's bodies were found in the same graveyard of St Margaret's Church in Barking, and Taylor's body was discovered nearby. Port planted a fake suicide note with Whitworth's body, claiming he had killed Kovari and then taken his own life.

Despite the bodies of the four victims being found near Port's flat within 15 months, the Metropolitan Police failed to link the deaths. Despite the LGBTQ+ advisory group and *PinkNews* believing the crimes were connected, the police did not. A BBC One documentary in 2017 highlighted the police's failures, including not questioning key witnesses, such as Port's neighbour, who reported suspicious behaviour. The neighbour also plays a very important role in *Four Lives* that we discuss below. In one memorable scene, following his sighting of Port's dramatic arrest from his home, the neighbour is turned away from Barking Police Station when he attempts to give crucial evidence within the brief window of time that is available for witnesses to come forward.

The police dismissed the possibility of a serial killer, and crucial evidence, including a bottle of GBL and a bed sheet, was not tested. Whitworth's family was misled into believing his death was an overdose, while Taylor's family struggled to get answers, with police initially dismissing their concerns. It wasn't until two weeks after Taylor's death that the police began to investigate Port, eventually leading to his arrest.

The Independent Police Complaints Commission (IPCC) opened an investigation into 17 officers over potential disciplinary action following Port's conviction. The families of the victims later pursued a civil claim against the Metropolitan Police, which was settled in 2022.

The initial investigation failed to detect Port's actions, with the police making assumptions about the gay community and failing to conduct basic checks. Families of the victims have accused the police of homophobia, and a solicitor representing them stated that the police had 'blood on their hands'.

An inquest in December 2022 identified significant failings in the police's handling of the deaths, including the failure to properly investigate, send evidence for forensic examination, and follow up on leads. The Independent Office for Police Conduct (IOPC) had initially concluded in 2019 that no officers should face misconduct charges, but following new information revealed during the inquest, they have decided to reopen the investigation.

Port was charged with four counts of murder and multiple other sexual offences. At trial in 2016, he was found guilty of murdering Walgate, Kovari, Whitworth and Taylor, as well as raping and assaulting other men. He was sentenced to life imprisonment with a whole-life order.

In 2018, Port's appeal against his convictions was rejected. In 2019, Gerald Matovu, who had supplied Port with GHB, was convicted of the murder of Eric Michels, using similar methods to Port. In 2020, a former partner of Port spoke out, revealing unsettling experiences during their relationship. A fresh inquiry into the police's handling of the cases began in 2021.

As of November 2023, the Independent Office for

Police Conduct (IOPC) was investigating eight former and current officers for gross misconduct over their involvement in the cases.

The Stephen Port case was covered in several documentaries, including the BBC's *How Police Missed the Grindr Killer* (2017). In 2022, the BBC released *Four Lives*, a drama based on the investigation led by the victims' families. The frustrating and possibly lethal failings of the police were a key theme in both of these productions. Channel 4 covered Stephen Port in Series 2, Episode 1 of its *Surviving a Serial Killer* franchise. That programme focused on the story of Ryan Edwards, who had no idea he was inviting a murderer into his life when he welcomed Stephen Port as his new neighbour.

Four Lives first aired from 3 to 5 January 2022 on BBC One.

We caught up with Jeff Pope to ask what had stayed with him most after making *Four Lives*. He reflected carefully before responding:

'What stayed with me most about this piece, which was written by Neil McKay, was what seemed to me to be the police's apparent lack of understanding, or empathy for, the lives of gay men. I believe basic detective work properly carried out would have saved the lives of at least two of Port's victims.'

This sobering reflection on poor policing and the prejudices that can shape investigations is a recurring theme. For Jonathan it brought to mind another example, the case of Lin and Megan Russell, known as the

Chillenden Murders, which he explored in a documentary for Channel 5. Michael Stone, who was convicted of the killings, continues to maintain his innocence. Meanwhile, serial killer Levi Bellfield has claimed responsibility, and Stone's conviction remains under appeal. In that case, the police seemed to focus on securing a perpetrator – Stone, a local wrong'un – rather than pursuing a thorough investigation. In the case of Stephen Port, prejudice about the young men's perceived lifestyle seems to have prohibited a thorough look into how the Barking deaths, including the administration of fatal doses of GHB, were related.

Jeff's words underline a powerful truth, that had the police put aside homophobic bias and concentrated on proper detective work, two, possibly three, of Stephen Port's victims might still be alive.

Port is a complete enigma in Belmarsh. We have not found a single contributor who had one word to say about him, apart from Matthew noting that 'Stephen Port was around' during his tenure. He appears to have disappeared into the shadows. It's remarkable. He's been there since 2016, almost a decade, but he is the invisible man.

The same cannot be said for his presence in popular media.

CHAPTER 31

Belmarsh on Screen

*'I'm stuck in Belmarsh, doing time for a
crime I didn't commit.'*

(PLAN B)

The actor and documentary filmmaker Ross Kemp, who originally gained fame in *EastEnders*, has gained even more widespread recognition for his hard-hitting documentaries, particularly *Ross Kemp on Gangs* (2004). In early 2020, his two-part documentary, *Welcome to HMP Belmarsh*, was aired. The documentary reveals how violence, gang rivalries and a rigid hierarchical structure define life inside the prison. His memorable and well-portrayed night in Belmarsh emphasised how hot, noisy and claustrophobic the cell was. When he visited 'The Box', he noted the absence of a bed, toilet or sink, and said even in contrast to the HSU, there was 'definitely a feeling that you are completely alone. I don't think I could do an hour in here without going round the twist.'

There was also a Channel 5 two-parter, *HMP Belmarsh:*

Evil Behind Bars, that purported to go behind the scenes at the Category A prison, using a cast of excellent contributors, including one of the stars of our last book, Vanessa Frake-Harris.

One former inmate, however, considered it to be riddled with inaccuracies, claiming that it 'does not portray a true reflection of the prison and the regime it operates on'. In addition to being irritated by this, he saw some of the ex-con contributors as big talkers who were taking some poetic licence in describing their own role in prison violence.

'The ex-offenders who appear on these prison-type programmes are not very articulate and seem to stretch the truth, especially when it comes to violence they allege they have done, and particularly their claims to control the prison and its staff. High-security prisons are serious places and staff are in full control. I have spent many years back and forth to Belmarsh and on each occasion, often over a period of years, the regime has not changed.'

When asked to elaborate, he continued, 'What it gets wrong? Basically, all the liars who appear on the programme, sensationalised, knocking out officers, it is brutal, staff are in control; if you attacked an officer you would be dealt with; it was just Channel 5 rubbish. Yammy B was on the programme, AGAIN; that says it all.'

Belmarsh's inclusion in works such as *Four Lives* and *Ross Kemp on Gangs* is testament to the prison's huge role within the public imagination. We can also highly recommend both of Jonathan Aitken's autobiographies, which describe his connection with Belmarsh among many other fascinating things, *Pride and Perjury* (2003) and *Porridge and Passion* (2006).

CHAPTER 32

The Future

'Prison has become a complete joke – let's be real.'
(MIKE)

Understanding the future of Belmarsh, and of the prison system more widely, requires a detailed examination, not just of policy and infrastructure, but of the human experience within these institutions. Through the voices of both prisoners and staff, this book has aimed to walk in their shoes and illuminate realities, both within and outside the walls.

Beyond the physical and procedural aspects of prison life, we hope this book has contributed to challenging misconceptions about the Prison Service. Matthew offered his perspective on this when we spoke with him:

'When the media reports something negative about the Prison Service, you hear them call them wardens. They've not been called wardens in about 30 years. If it's something more positive, you'll hear about prison officers or prison staff. One thing I'd wish for people to be aware of: this is an incredibly difficult job in incredibly challenging circumstances.'

As we know more than most, public curiosity about the realities of prison life remains high, and we were particularly interested in Matthew's view on why prisons remain such closed environments:

'The public are very interested in what goes on inside these walls. It's not deliberately secretive, it's just the nature of the environment. I know people would like to know more . . . But it's a tough world, a tough world. Prisons are communities. They're like towns, except that everyone in your community is a criminal and has committed an offence, except for those on remand, who are allegedly criminals at that moment in time. But the majority of the population have done something wrong.'

Reflecting on his time in the service, Matthew shared his thoughts on how things have changed:

'I look back on the Prison Service with fond memories, and that was purely because of the great people I worked with. If I could go back in time and work with those same people, I'd probably do it again. But the way the Prison Service has changed, and how recruitment is handled now, means that many of those great people have moved on. If I were to go back now, I probably wouldn't recognise it, and I think I would find it quite difficult.'

One reason that he might find it difficult is chronic overcrowding. Overcrowding isn't just a Belmarsh problem, it's a national problem. Not easily fixed. Something more specific that Belmarsh could look at is a review of segregation practices, which, as we have seen, have been singled out for criticism. Maybe limiting the duration of segregation placements and setting up regular reviews to uphold prisoner rights and mental health.

Overcrowding has been identified as a major factor impeding prisoner progression, as it limited opportunities for transfers to more suitable facilities. Additionally, shortages of probation staff often left inmates inadequately prepared for release. One report noted that 17 prisoners were held in segregation for over 100 days during the reporting year, frequently due to the absence of alternative accommodation to meet their needs.

Peter Ward, Chair of the Belmarsh Independent Monitoring Board, acknowledged the challenging environment and commended staff efforts to maintain safety and security. However, he emphasised the limited opportunities for prisoners to engage in education, work or resettlement activities, underscoring the need for improvements in these areas.

It looks like a good idea to implement comprehensive violence reduction plans too. Advances in technology can help here, from crunching data to monitor incidents to ensuring consistent use of body-worn cameras by staff.

A March 2025 court case brought these questions of both staff care and prisoner mental health provision sharply into focus once again. Aklakar Rahman, 38, was accused of attacking staff at both HMP Swaleside in Kent and Belmarsh during September and October 2022. He appeared at the Old Bailey, charged with 20 offences. These included five counts of attempted murder, six of attempted assault on an emergency worker, and possession of sharpened plastic objects. He denied all charges.

Branded 'highly dangerous', the weapons he used as he attempted to kill five prison officers included a sharpened plastic spoon. Rahman was already serving a life sentence for three attempted murders and wounding with intent to cause grievous bodily harm, said prosecutor Alistair Richardson. '[Mr Rahman] wanted to kill prison officers whom he saw as "kuffar", a derogatory term for non-Muslims,' he told the court.

In late September 2022, while housed in the high-security segregation unit at HMP Swaleside due to concerns he was attempting to radicalise fellow inmates to 'extreme versions of Islam', Mr Rahman was being escorted to a shower when he allegedly punched one officer, shouted 'Allahu Akbar', and stabbed another in the forehead with a pen. He was also said to have punched a third officer in the stomach and stamped on another's foot. The following day, during a welfare check, officers found Rahman naked in his cell, holding a three-inch piece of sharpened plastic. As staff tried to disarm him, he allegedly attempted to stab one officer in the neck.

This landed Rahman in Belmarsh, where in October 2022, he allegedly tried to kill three officers while they were trying to escort him to lunch. He allegedly threw a bin and ran at one officer, shouting 'Death to kuffar' while stabbing at her head and neck with what was believed to have been a sharpened plastic spoon. He was also alleged to have slashed two other officers on the neck as they restrained him.

In a note, Rahman wrote that he was angry with the prison, had 'lost it', and attacked officers whom he believed were mocking him. During a police interview, he claimed he had not intended to kill anyone, had been trying to provoke the officers, and said his mental health had been deteriorating. The court heard he suffered from paranoid schizophrenia.

Such cases foreground a need to improve mental health services within the prison system. This could perhaps have included expediting the transfer process for inmates requiring specialist care and expanding mental health support on-site. By focusing on rehabilitation, safety and mental health, the prison could evolve into a more effective institution, balancing security with the humane treatment of prisoners.

Tragically, there will always be fresh criminals ready to contribute to overcrowding at Belmarsh, including those guilty of some of the most shocking crimes of recent years. New arrivals include Kyle Clifford, the crossbow killer. The judge, Mr Justice Bennathan, handed him a whole-life tariff for raping and shooting Louise Hunt, shooting her sister Hannah with a crossbow, and fatally stabbing their mother Carol at the family's home. As we have seen, Urfan Sharif had only been in Belmarsh a few weeks for the horrific torture and murder of his daughter briefly before he was attacked by two inmates.

Writing these books has given us the opportunity to meet and speak with a range of remarkable individuals: prison officers, mental health professionals and ex-prisoners with extraordinary redemption stories. These people should be celebrated; their stories deserve to be heard. We have also come into contact with some of the most notorious – and often deeply unwell – British criminals of recent decades. In such cases, there is a careful balancing act in portraying what life post-incarceration is like for them, while maintaining respect for the families of the victims they committed such utterly appalling acts against.

Through the voices in this book, including staff recalling a service transformed beyond recognition, prisoners reliving violent attacks, to high-profile incidents exposing the cracks in mental health provision, we've seen how systemic pressures, violence, overcrowding, gangs and drugs have left the prison system creaking at the seams. As public interest in prison life remains high, so too must the ongoing will to reform.

Vanessa explained to us the need for systemic change in the prison service: there is not just one thing that will solve it, it's a combination of different areas to be fixed. Starting with vetting: this is conducted by a private firm, and has allowed people who form inappropriate relationships or those who work in organised crime to find their way into prison work. Take the woman filmed having sex in Wandsworth. All you had to do was google her. She is referring to the case of Linda De Sousa Abreu, aged 30, a prison officer at HMP Wandsworth, who was sentenced at Isleworth Crown Court on 6 January 2025 to 15 months' imprisonment after pleading guilty to misconduct in a public office. In June the previous year, she had entered a prisoner's cell during duty hours and engaged in sexual activity, which was filmed by another inmate. The footage, lasting nearly five minutes, was circulated on social media and seen by prison staff, who recognised her.

De Sousa Abreu subsequently informed the prison she would not return to work and that her husband would return her equipment. She was arrested by Metropolitan Police at Heathrow Airport. The prosecution highlighted that she wilfully abused her position, and her conduct was not spontaneous, but calculated. Tetteh Turkson of the Crown Prosecution Service stated she was 'clearly an enthusiastic participant who wrongly thought she would avoid responsibility' and called it a 'shocking breach of the public's trust'.

Vanessa saw both this incident and Daniel Khalife's escape from Wandsworth as reputationally damaging to the institution: 'Women having sex with prisoners is just embarrassing. The female staff at Wandsworth got lots of hassle after that as well.'

Prisoners apparently thought that other officers were fair game in the wake of the scandal. Vanessa concluded, 'We live in a misogynistic society and that is reflected in prison.'

Vanessa also expressed concern that, unlike when she started out and the minimum age was 21, now you can begin training for a job in the prison service on your 18th birthday. In her view that is far too young to put vulnerable young people into training. These days, that training is just five weeks long, which is not long enough to learn vital skills like de-escalation and appropriate communication with prisoners. By contrast, Vanessa recalled that she did three months' training and then probation for a year.

Then there's the physical estate, with what she terms 'a lot of Victoriana prisons, with no investment over the last 20 years. Some prisons have had sewage running down the landings. How are we helping to rehabilitate prisoners living in conditions like that?'

Vanessa cares deeply about these issues and can see all too clearly where they lead. 'We lock up the most people in Western Europe and we have the worst reoffending rates in Western Europe.'

Real change will demand investment in both people and infrastructure, a deeper focus on rehabilitation, and a clear-sighted appraisal of what kind of justice system we want to uphold. The extreme security, secrecy and containment of Belmarsh masks the wider fact that prisons are not isolated from society. They are shaped by it, and they reflect it. The future challenge is whether they can also help to change it.

ACKNOWLEDGEMENTS

Thank you to the inspiring and visionary Ciara Lloyd, publishing director at Bonnier Books UK. It has been a pleasure working together again. Thanks, as always, to our incredible agents on this project, Matt Cole and Diane Banks at Northbank Talent Management.

Heartfelt thanks to our three children, and to the friends who offered encouragement, wisdom and understanding throughout the writing process. That's all of you! Especially Liz Gibbons, Lucy Allen, David Taylor, Eliane Glaser, Heidi Malaure, Mark Winfield, Trevor Griffiths, Kathy Rooney, Simon Brown and Tracy Aristides. Thank you to Roger French for his unswerving support and sharp eye, and to Adrian French and Sarah Field for their love and light relief. Thank you to the bright and brilliant Ruby Paton and to the wonderful, intellectually curious Jaz Thompson.

We have been following the case of the 'little knight' boy who was thrown from the Tate Gallery as he continues his recovery. We have contributed to his GoFundMe and would urge you to do the same. We can only thank God that after this horrifying random attack, the boy has lived and is showing such courage and resilience.

This is the third instalment of our bestselling *Inside* . . . series. We try to read and respond to all the correspondence and feedback we receive from our wonderful readers. They are usually extremely well informed, often with an inside perspective themselves as former staff or prisoners.

At a signing and Q&A at Wakefield Waterstones for our previous book, *Inside Wakefield Prison*, one attendee asked about the purpose behind our *Inside* . . . series. We were delighted to be asked. A significant part of our aim, of course, is to explore vastly different perspectives and life experiences. Over time, we've refined our distinctive blend of exclusive prisoner testimony and staff insight, shaping what we believe to be a gripping, unfiltered portrayal of life inside Belmarsh.

Our goal is to make space for human stories and the breadth of human experience – to listen not passively, but actively. We aim to support our contributors in telling their stories and then step back, free from ego or agenda, to bring those compelling narratives and lived realities to our readers.

Most of all, thank you to all our contributors, both named and anonymous, who made this book so rich in detail, visceral, honest and moving.